HIGHLAND COUNTY PUBLIC LIBRARY
MONTEREY, VA 24465
(540) 468-2373

HARLEY-DAVIDSON BIG TWIN
Performance Handbook

Tom Murphy

Motorbooks International
Publishers & Wholesalers ®

Acknowledgments

If I had to list all the people who helped me write this book, it would be twice as long as it is now. Bar none, everybody from Axtell to Zipper's went out of their way to aid me, either with pictures or information. Everybody learns something from a book; I think I've learned more than most. I've learned there are an awful lot of friendly, intelligent individuals dedicated to the process of building faster Harleys. The old image of Harley people being one-percenters has definitely turned around. Behind the machines and behind the computers are some of the best people I've had the pleasure to meet. I hope they felt the same way about me when I was pestering them for "just one more picture."A note on trademarks: "Harley-Davidson," "Harley," and the abbreviation "H-D" are used for illustration and reference only. All the words copyrighted by Harley-Davidson, including, but not limited to, "Evolution," "Low-Rider," "Super Glide/Low Glide," "Softail," "Heritage Softail Special," and "Screamin' Eagle," are registered trademarks of Harley-Davidson Inc., Milwaukee, Wisconsin.

Any and all model designations used in this book, such as "FXRS," "FXRDG," "FXRC," and "FXE", are used for reference only.
If any information in this book is in error, it's due to my inability to read or listen—everything they gave me was as up-to-date as possible. A list of suppliers will be found at the other end of the book. Thanks to everybody.

See you at the races!
Tom Murphy

First published in 1995 by Motorbooks International Publishers & Wholesalers, PO Box 2, 729 Prospect Avenue, Osceola, WI 54020 USA

© Tom Murphy , 1995

All rights reserved. With the exception of quoting brief passages for the purpose of review no part of this publication may be reproduced without prior written permission from the Publisher

Motorbooks International is a certified trademark, registered with the United States Patent Office

The information in this book is true and complete to the best of our knowledge. All recommendations are made without any guarantee on the part of the author or Publisher, who also disclaim any liability incurred in connection with the use of this data or specific details We recognize that some words, model names and designations, for example, mentioned herein are the property of the trademark holder. We use them for identification purposes only. This is not an official publication

Motorbooks International books are also available at discounts in bulk quantity for industrial or sales-promotional use. For details write to Special Sales Manager at the Publisher's address

Library of Congress Cataloging-in-Publication Data
Murphy, Tom
    Harley-Davidson big twin performance handbook/
    Tom Murphy.
        p.   cm.
    Includes index.
    ISBN 0-7603-0009-7
    1. Harley-Davidson motorcycle--Performance. 1. Title.
TL448.H3M87 1995
629.227'5--dc20

On the front cover: This Evolution-engined Harley-Davidson is tricked out with enough aftermarket goodies to qualify as a catalog-order poster boy. *Jeff Hackett*

On the back cover: Top: Kelly Kerrigan aboard George Matthew's 105ci Redline Oil racer. Bottom: An aftermarket carburetor is often the starting point for Harley-Davidson hop-up projects.

Printed and bound in the United States of America

Contents

Introduction

If it hadn't been for the California Highway Patrol (CHP), I might not be writing this book. No, they didn't stop me for going 110mph in a 65mph zone, racing someone on the freeways of California, or for some other chargeable action. What they did was much worse. They held an auction. In 1969. Of all their pursuit cars and motorcycles. Harley motorcycles. Thus began my downfall. My father-in-law and I decided that it was time for me to learn the wonders of building a custom motorcycle; to him, "Harley-Davidson" and "motorcycle" meant the same thing, with an occasional Indian thrown in now and then for variety.

The CHP handled the disposition of their motorcycles through the "sealed bid" method. Anyone could go look at the motorcycles stored at the Department of Motor Vehicles' vehicle yard in Sacramento, California. A flyer would be mailed out from time to time listing the individual Harleys on the auction block by year and serial number. Most of the bikes were from three to five years old, with 60,000+ miles on the odometer. Some ran. Some just leaned on their side stands in puddles of dark, viscous fluid that may have been oil at one time. All the bikes had been set up with solo seats, saddle bags, and radios. Society hadn't reached the point yet where the CHP felt it necessary to add a Remington 870 shotgun as standard equipment, but other than that, they were fully police-equipped and well used.

The California Department of Transportation, today known as "CALTRANS," took excellent care of the motorcycles. All bikes received regular maintenance at the state's own facilities or through a private contract with a local Harley dealer. We figured that we would enter bids on at least two of the best-looking bikes and two or three of the non-running bikes, with hopes to use the broken ones as parts for the

A much younger author sits astride an ex-CHP bike after restoration. This was my first shot at rejuvenating a Harley.

good Harleys. No one was allowed to fire up any of the sale bikes, so it was a matter of look, hope, and bid $1 higher than the other guy. Most of the inoperable motorcycles had tags listing why they wouldn't run. That was a slight help when it came to figuring bids. A sharp pencil and a real good knowledge of what the bikes were worth were very necessary, as the auction always brought out a large crowd of hopeful future owners all trying to accomplish exactly the same thing.

With all the bikes selling through sealed bids, the biggest challenge was getting the price right the first time. No bidding against one another, just one shot in an envelope. The next biggest problem was

Kelly Kerrigan expertly warms the back tire of his breathed-on Evo. Notice he has both feet firmly planted; the bike didn't move throughout this and the next ten photographs. When it did hook up, he disappeared faster than last week's paycheck.

figuring out how I was going to pay for the three bikes we were successful in buying when the bids were announced two weeks later. As I remember, the top price paid for a three-year-old CHP bike at that auction was $1,300; the two non-runners went for $350 each. Not much today, I agree, but a very large amount for a second-year plumber's apprentice with a grand take-home of $127 per week.

My father-in-law, however, drove airplanes for NASA and was not suffering from a lack of funds, so money was made available, and the bikes were ours. We rented a fairly large U-Haul trailer to bring the Harleys home to San Jose the following weekend. Much hard work later (I think that's why I was along), the bikes reposed in his fully carpeted, well-lit garage, next to a DeTomaso Mangusta that had belonged to the late actor Steve McQueen up till a salesman at the dealership gave it a haircut by trying to fit it under a semi. We acquired that through auction, too.

The first order of the day was to take the bikes apart to be cleaned (me again). Following that, we sat down to work out what all was in front of us.

All the bikes were in some state of disrepair even though two of them ran. I wanted to build a chopper out of one of the bikes; my father-in-law opted for a fully restored stocker.

Back then, not much was available in aftermarket parts. Tom Sifton, and a few others, built cams and engine parts. Long front ends were just coming into vogue. Wild exhaust pipes and what looked like mufflers were available from anyone who owned a wire welder and sheet metal roller. But, all in all, not much was available in the way of aftermarket goodies.

The original method of making a "chopper" was to first get the engine running—then begin unbolting parts off the bike. When the engine quit running, you bolted the last part back on and you were done. All that was left was to learn how to start it.

The 1960s' H-Ds were still somewhat primitive when it came to urging the engine to life. On the right handlebar reposed the throttle, as today. On the left was found the spark retard, a manual method of controlling spark advance. The choke was in its normal place on the left side of the carb. Usual starting procedure was to roll the spark control all the way forward, lift the choke up a certain number of clicks (determined by prior experience, phases of the moon, that sort of thing), roll on

Some of us start from this point. A used '87 for sale on the side of the road. The pipes have been changed and the saddlebags are off, but otherwise it's pretty much stock. I think the owner was looking for $7,200—would you be interested?

about one-eighth inch throttle, then kick it through twice before turning on the ignition and kicking again.

Sometimes this produced the required effect—sometimes not. If the drill was wrong, or if the scooter just wasn't in the mood to light off, sometimes all this produced was a strong KER-CHUG that lifted your foot off the pedal. This is how I learned that it is possible to kick oneself in the kidneys should one's bike backfire.

My 1967 FLH was going to get the chopper treatment. I removed everything not necessary for operation, stuck a twelve inch-longer set of tubes in the front forks, painted the tanks and fenders black, added a decal or two—and I was ready. For what, I don't know, but I was ready. Seems like everything I did to the bike just made it harder to ride. I don't exactly remember what happened to that H-D, but I do remember I didn't own it very long.

Today, you don't have to go through any of the blood, sweat, and tears involved in building the custom Harley of twenty years ago. Aftermarket parts manufacturers can supply you with everything—from frame to paint—necessary to create exactly the bike of your dreams. About all you will need, other than a willing checkbook, is a good idea of what you want your bike to do—oh yes, and a copy of this book, to show you what can be done to a late-model Harley to make it perform better.

We'll spend most of our time talking about the Evo motor, as that's what most of you own now or are planning on buying. Some time will be spent on the Shovelhead, but most of what pertains to the Evo can be carried through to the Shovel.

While pondering purchase of a new bike, consider this: Harley-Davidson posted a record $933 million net sales for 1993, up $110 million over 1992. Profit on 81,696 motorcycles and tons of accessories

Somebody at Custom Chrome spent a lot of time cutting an Evo motor in half just so we could see how the parts work. You can't tell from the picture, but a lot of that engine doesn't have Harley part numbers. Many of Custom Chrome's goodies are visible.

ran $136 million—thirty-three percent over 1992 (info courtesy of the H-D Inc. 1993 Annual Report). They pretty well control the heavyweight motorcycle market. Worldwide demand for Harleys continues to outweigh supply, and will for the foreseeable future. All the dealers in my area have totally bare showrooms—everything coming in the back has a "Sold" tag on it. Owning a new bike will require that you go put a $500 to $1,000 deposit down today, then sit back for a nice few month's wait. Now is the time to make the decision to buy a bike. Go give a deposit and get on the list.

While you wait for your bike to arrive, start figuring out what you want to do to it once it's in your garage. This way you have something to do other than wait, and in the process you'll pick up a lot of useful knowledge about what a H-D is capable of doing with the proper modifications.

While we're covering Big Twin Harleys, might as well cover some of the terms for various models.

For the purpose of this book, the first modern H-D was the Knucklehead, built from 1936 to 1947 as a 61 and 74 cubic inch engine. Seen from the right, the bike's rocker box covers resemble a clenched fist, with the knuckles upward; hence, the name "Knucklehead." This is pretty much collector's territory (no one is pumping up a knuckle anymore), so we won't see much on it.

Next up was the "Panhead," from 1948 to 1965. The rocker covers look like baking pans turned upside down—thus, "Panhead." This bike was the start of the modern Harleys we see today. Hydraulic front forks first appeared in 1949, a vast improvement over the earlier springer forks. The Pan got rear shocks in 1958, giving it modern suspension at both ends. Looking at a 1964 "Duo-Glide" and a 1993 "Heritage Nostalgia," it's easy to see the lineage of today's motorcycles.

Picture the back end of a coal shovel. Now look at the top of a Harley engine from 1966 to 1984. If you work at it a bit, you can see the similarity in the rocker covers and the shovel; hence, the name "Shovelhead." Some of the Shovels went to rubber-mounted motors in 1982, picking up the name "Rubber-Glide" in the process of becoming much smoother bikes. The engine still shook, but the rider was isolated from most of the vibration. Along the way, five-speed transmissions appeared. Belt drives, first used on the V-twins of the early 1900s, reappeared, this time made out of Aramid rubber instead of the leather belts used on the early 1908 models.

The Shovelhead is still with us in great enough numbers that some people are going to want to make theirs run harder, so some of the book will cover what can be done for more go.

A lot of what pertains to Harley's newest engine, the V2 Evolution, will also be useful for the earlier bikes, and will be noted as such.

The V2 Evolution needed some sort of nickname related to the engine configuration, as no self-respecting biker was going to call it by its full name. Thus was born the "Blockhead," or "Evo," motor. I guess the top of the cylinders do look like blocks; therefore, the name.

The Evo is the motor that we will be specifically covering. You will learn how to go from a stock street bike, fresh from the factory, to an all-out 200mph racer. We will start with bolt-on performance—ways to improve some aspect of the bike without having to open up the engine and modify or replace internal parts. Next in line: what can be done without a machine shop's facilities. Costs will be covered along the way as a matter of comparison, as prices can change between the writing and the reading of this book.

It's entirely possible to get so deep into a performance-oriented state of mind that the house will have to have a second mortgage just to cover the work. We'll try to stay away from that type of operation, except on the all-out racing bikes. Do bear in mind the old adage that speed *does* cost money ... how fast do you want to go?

We'll cover what can be done to build a bike that will fly like an F-16, afterburner optional.

Mario Owens' Top Fuel twin-engined Shovelhead waits to go again. It takes a massive aluminum engine plate to handle the output of both engines when the throttle is turned to the stops. If everything isn't tied together securely, the engines will twist enough to throw the drive chains out of alignment and bend parts. *Rich Products*

If all-out performance is your goal—you want to be the fastest man on a bike at Bonneville, surpassing *Easyrider's* streamliner record of 322.150, set July 14, 1990—then we'll help you build the machine to get the job done.

So come along, take a ride through the book with me, and we'll build a Big Twin.

This is what you hope your competitors see of your bike. Leo Hess' dragster sits on the dirt at El Mirage Dry Lakes. The big rear tire gives lots of bite at the start, but it can be a tradeoff in rolling resistance at high speeds. Usually, a smaller tire is run on Land Speed Record bikes, leaving the slick to do its work at the drag strip.

Chapter One

Getting Started

Contrary to popular belief, Harley-Davidson didn't try to race the first motorcycle they built in 1903. But by 1914, they pretty much dominated quarter- and half-mile dirt track racing. Their first serious racer to come from the company was masterminded by Bill Harley and Bill Ottaway, ex-Thor motorcycle racing director and designer. It was a 30.50ci single that had been extensively modified for racing. From their 61ci V-twin, they took the front cylinder, equipped it with a heavy flywheel to smooth out the power pulses, and mounted it on the crankcase of the H-D 5-35 single. The engine had all its moving parts lightened and polished. Bigger valves, worked by heavier springs, let the air-fuel mixture into a custom-honed cylinder fitted with a piston specially made for racing. The carburetor could be adjusted at the track to compensate for temperature and humidity. The frame got the trim treatment, considerably shortening the wheelbase in the process. As there was no suspension, not much was done in that department, except to install lower racing bars on the forks. The bike was started by pedaling until the engine fired, and, as no brakes were fitted, was stopped by killing the spark or shutting off the fuel.

By 1916, H-D dominated the racing scene, winning on dirt and wood tracks alike. One wants to pause for a minute and contemplate the possibility of falling on a board track back in the early 1920s. The race bikes didn't exactly laze around the track. Winning speed at the Chicago 100 miler of 1915 was 89.11mph. Picture the quantity of splinters that you would pick up in a 100mph slide down a quarter mile straightway made of finest pine. Um—yes! Iron men and their motorcycles.

The playful young gentlemen who were the factory riders went by the name "Wrecking Crew," after their rather spirited method of riding. They won every national championship in 1921, and were well on their way to winning everything in 1922 when H-D withdrew its entire factory racing effort.

So you could say that people have been making modifications to their Harleys since the first ones

The Harley-Davidson Flathead has the valves located in the cylinder—the head is simply the top of the combustion chamber, with one hole for the spark plug. The incoming fuel has to make a 180-degree turn into the cylinder so the piston can compress the mixture. After firing, the spent gasses have to make their way back 180 degrees to leave the chamber—this is a less than efficient method of airflow. When the flatheads were raced, only a very few tuners were able to extract maximum power, without reliability being only wishful thinking. At 99%, they'd run OK. At 100%, they'd blow up, unless you really knew how to keep them alive. Harley was able to make one of their KRTT series Flathead racers go over 145mph in the 1960s, so they were heading in the right direction, but overhead valves offered too many benefits.

The valve covers on this Knucklehead clearly show where the name originated.

hit the street. Riders have been looking for ways to make their bikes go a little faster, handle a little better, sometimes even stop quicker than the other guy's. A lot of motivation for improvement came about after watching another bike pull away just after having made a small wager on performance.

Well, the same feeling prevails today. Whether it be a National Hot Rod Association (NHRA)-sanctioned event, a Southern California Timing Association (SCTA) speed run at Bonneville Salt Flats, or the distance from your front tire to the next stoplight, motorcycle racing is big business.

Stock-framed Harleys are going over 170mph at Bonneville with nothing more than the rider's helmet for streamlining. At the drag strip, Top Fuel Harleys, running nitro-methane and alcohol, are covering the quarter mile in the seven-second range at 186mph. People are going fast on their Harleys. The question is: how much performance do you want out of your Harley, and what do you want to do to obtain it?

Perhaps you decide that the next land speed record for stock-frame, under-2000cc motorcycles just has to be yours—how would you go about building a bike to run Bonneville?

Or maybe your idea of a good time is suiting up in a tight-fitting set of leathers and planting yourself on what passes for a seat, bolted to a frame filled with a teeth-loosening, vibrating, loud, expensive engine while mailing yourself down a quarter mile of blue-streaked asphalt in less than ten seconds.

Whichever way you elect to go, the basic engine- and frame-building requirements are the same. The bike has to be safe. All sanctioning groups will subject you, your racing equipment, and your race bike to a rigorous safety inspection before any racing takes place. Whether you set a new record on your first run or have to make a slow 100mph pass through the timing lights to qualify, safety always comes first. When it comes time to spend the money for a helmet or a set of leathers, don't go cheap. I speak from experience when I say that you may never have to call on your helmet to do what it was built for, but if you do, it's nice to know that it's the best money can buy.

One bright afternoon in my early years, I had the dubious pleasure of escorting my motorcycle down the racetrack, using my head as a pivot point. This was before I had firmly fixed in my mind the ratio of lack of traction to distance slid when dropping a bike—a learning experience not to be repeated often. After everything had ground to a halt (literally) and I came back to reality, I found myself lying on the racetrack with 70% of a helmet on my head. The missing 30% was evenly distributed behind me for a distance of 50 yards as a fine white powder overlaying the skid marks of my bike. In between every other racer trying to run over my neck, I remember thinking how grateful I was that I had invested in a new Snell-approved helmet two months before. Not that I was out to buy the safest thing I could find, but the outer surface on my old one was beginning to look like the face of one of the moons of Saturn.

My reasoning behind a new helmet was strictly cosmetic. After all, what hero racing-bike rider wants to be seen in an old trashed-out helmet? My first helmet was approved by no one and probably could have been split by repeated application of a baby's rattle. My new purchase had gone through a severe testing program by the then-new Snell Foun-

This Evo motor, sans everything, has just had the heads bolted down over 91 cubic inches prior to ending up in a street racer. The motor stand is easily fabricated, and makes assembly much easier.

dation, named after a racer, Harry Snell, who—if my mind serves me right—bought the farm due to head injuries in a racing accident. Not to dwell too much on the negative side of the game, but if I had been wearing the old relic, I probably would be just a faint memory at this time. So, if I seem to hammer on safety from time to time, it's just because I've had my chimes rung hard enough to teach me some respect for good equipment.

Back when the earth was flat and all Harley racing bikes were side-valve, the 1938 WRTT Privateer Racer came with a springer front end, foot clutch, and tank shift. Most riders who ran modified street bikes on the flat tracks of the time simply removed whatever lights were on the bike, lost the muffler, disconnected the brakes, and went racing.

The American Motorcycle Association (AMA) had set up rules for Class C racing so that amateurs could afford to go racing on semi-factory-prepped production racers without having to sell the family cow. The formula for Class C set the 750cc bikes of Indian and H-D against the lighter 500cc European overhead valve (ohv) motorcycles, which were faster than the American bikes but had the tendency to leave parts of the "finest English manufacture" sprinkled about the track. The AMA had tried to set up a class in 1934 where the side-valve or Flathead engine could compete fairly with the higher-revving, higher-horsepower 500cc bikes.

The left-side exhaust pipe on this late-model Panhead FLH has to come from the rear cylinder, turn behind the engine, and roll past the starter and down the primary cover to hook up with its muffler. If it were straightened out, it would extend past the bike at least four feet. It looks good, but it's definitely not very efficient.

Strip off the turn signals, remove the seat to lower thy posterior out of the wind, and you're ready to run at El Mirage. 'Course, having 93 cubes, S&S flywheels, Carillo rods, Wiseco pistons, and a set of "bathtub chamber" heads doesn't hurt, either. He was running in the 127mph area .

Now you might think that having 250cc displacement over the competition was an unfair advantage, but remember that Flathead motors were limited by their poor combustion chamber shape and the low rev limits that supposedly kept the horsepower somewhat near the output of the 500cc OVH machines. Bear in mind, too, that the AMA was the AMERICAN motorcycle sanctioning organization. The idea was that we would win and they would watch. This didn't work out quite as planned all the time. The British bikes had an unpleasant habit of going faster and farther at times than the Flatheads, with the 500cc Triumphs and BSAs winning their share of races. Harley and nu-

merous aftermarket tuners of the time finally figured out the secret to keeping the 750cc motor together while it made an indecent amount of power for the design, thus ensuring that the checkered flag fell on American bikes.

Some say the high point of side-valve engines was reached with the Harley XRTT. The bike was easily capable of speeds in the 150mph range, with acceleration to match. However, the motor was at such a high state of tune that it was useless below 3000rpm and would launch a piston into low earth orbit at high rpms if not treated with care. Also, handling was said to be rather interesting at times, requiring a fairly strong set of arms to muscle it around the track.

Early Engines

Harley's large-production V-Twin of the late 1930s was the big Flathead, of 74 or 80ci displacement. The 80ci Flatmotor was introduced in 1936, taking its place in the lineup that included the 45ci side-valve engine, first offered to the public in 1929, and the 74ci motor that came along in 1930.

The Great Depression of the late twenties and early thirties did nothing to help Harley's sales position. By 1932, when every street corner had someone selling apples, and soup kitchens became a familiar sight, the 74 Flathead was being marketed for $320—freight and tax additional. This usually worked out to slightly more than the average worker made in a year, so it's no surprise that H-D only sold 4,000 bikes of all types in 1933. This represented a huge loss for the company, one that couldn't be sustained for long.

From 1930 to 1932, the Big Twin bikes suffered an inordinate amount of problems. Harley probably should have spent another year developing the bike, but Indian was leaving them for dead in sales and Harley needed something to go up against Indian's Chief. The newly issued H-D 74 had a bad habit of swallowing valves if revved too hard, partially due to poor lubrication. Also, parts would depart the bike with discouraging regularity if not wrenched on in a timely basis.

By 1940, the 74 Twin had been updated, with enlarged main bearings, better cooling, and higher quality control, but it still had the springer fork and no rear suspension. The seat was mounted on a sprung shaft, providing some cushioning over the dirt and semi-improved roads of the day. Reliability was finally up to the point where a rider could plan a full day's trip with nothing more than the occasional flat tire to worry about. Things had come a long way from the early Model 30-V, the 74 cubic inch bike produced in 1930.

In 1934, Harley began testing a radically new engine for their Big Twin. The factory learned that more horsepower and greater efficiency could be had by using overhead-valve rather than side-valve engines. The first overhead-valve H-D was a 750cc racer powered by four cams, built in 1930. This engine was used strictly as a racer and for the immensely popular hill climbs of the time. This engine was never developed for the street. Instead, the engineers (yes, H-D had an engineer back then—I think he had started designing horseshoes back in the 1920s and retired just this last year) elected to design a whole new engine, a long-stroke, 45° V-twin with OHV and 74ci of displacement. A low-mounted camshaft drove four unequal-length pushrods, activating overhead valves by means of head-mounted rocker arms. Roller bearings were

used in the bottom end, and a pressurized lubrication system with scavenging pump and oil tank feed was used instead of the old total-loss lubrication system. The old total-loss oiling system guaranteed that your oil was always fresh, the road dust behind the bike was kept down, and the cuffs of your riding pants were always well lubricated. The oil passed from the tank through the engine, then out the bottom or around the case seals or wherever hot oil could find a way out. The new recirculating pressurized system was truly a major improvement, both in motor operation and cleaning bills.

The new bike was introduced in 1936 as the "E series," with a 61ci engine, but quickly came to be called the "Knucklehead" due to its rocker box config-

This photograph of Bianchi's 97-inch dragster shows how low the seat sets in the rigid frame. The pilot flattens out over the tank for less wind resistance during a run. *Rich Products.*

uration, which, as mentioned, resembled a fistful of knuckles when viewed from the side. Harley had a winner in the new bike. Not only was it more reliable than the earlier side-valves, but it also proved to be a good-looking bike that was great fun to ride. In 1941, the 74ci Knucklehead was introduced, only to find itself facing the American entry into WWII, with the Japanese attack on Pearl Harbor creating problems that even Harley-Davidson couldn't handle. Kind of a taste of what was to come with overseas competition in the 1970s and 1980s.

Not too many 1941–42 74ci Knuckleheads were built. Their relative scarcity and high quality

13

Above and next page top: Two shots of Arnold Hardin's ABG 2000 blown gas bike. It runs a turbocharger at 9.5 pounds of boost into a 120ci Harmon motor mounted in a frame by the same company. Originally, it ran a belt final drive, but after breaking a few, Arnold went to a chain. Even the primary chain is a stock two-row roller. The large radiator in the front of the frame acts as an intercooler for the turbo. It reduces the inlet air temp from the turbo to the combustion chamber. On the right side, you can see how the exhaust pipes are wrapped with insulation to keep the temperature (thus the energy) high on the exhaust gasses entering the turbo. The close-up shot of the turbo outlet also shows insulation on the exhaust side. The insulation also serves to keep the rider's right leg from ending up medium-well after a hard run. This bike runs a Halltech Flowmaster Electronic fuel-injection system controlled by the black box sitting above the turbo. The injectors mount on the head just past the hose from the intercooler on the left side.

make them a collector's item, bringing top dollar for a restored, stock model.

During the war years, 1942 to 1945, the factory produced mostly 45ci WLA Flatheads for the US. Army. With a 6:1 compression ratio (4.75 with iron heads), the aluminum-headed engine made a screaming 25hp, but it would run on anything that would flow through a straw and burn.

Panhead

After WWII ended in 1945, Harley-Davidson resumed production of the 61 and 74 Knuckle, continuing until introduction of the Panhead in 1948. The first OHV Panheads were produced in both 61 and 74ci flavors, with the 61 being kept in production up to 1954. The more popular 74ci motor was a better money-maker for Harley, so the demise of the 61 was to their advantage in more ways than one. Rather than having to run two different assembly lines for what was essentially the same engine, Harley was able to slim down the manufacturing process to build just the single-size engine. There really wasn't much difference between the two engines, other than the displacement; building either engine cost the same—better to go with the bigger, more powerful 74.

During the Panhead's life, the rest of the bike received a lot of attention as far as the suspension and starting were concerned. The hydraulic telescoping front fork, introduced in 1949, was a marked improvement over the prior springer front end. Marketing took advantage of the change to re-title the bike the "Hydra-Glide" to point out the new, softer ride controlled by a front suspension dampened with oil. Now the bike could be ridden over rough roads with the reasonable assurance that your fillings would remain in their respective teeth.

With the advent of the FXSTS springer Softail, sporting a set of 1948-style springer forks, suspension engineering in the 1990s seems to be moving in a retrograde manner; however, the new springer actually provides a ride comparable to that with a hydraulic front end. Note I said comparable—the springer is a good way to cruise and be seen, but it is definitely not the way to cover long distances. For those of us who get all warm and silly at the thought of a nostalgic motorcycle, Harley has certainly produced a bike that fits the character while retaining most of the modern conveniences like disc brakes and electric foot. Nostalgia sells today, and sells well.

Along about 1958, the Big Twin gained a new frame, sporting a set of shock absorbers and springs encased in chrome covers. Naturally a name change was in order, and the PR folks at the factory wasted no time in hanging the name "Duo-Glide" on the bike. Now Harley had a bike that actually could cross a steel suspension bridge without the rider's life passing in front of his eyes as expansion strips were encountered. The foot boards still threw up a shower of sparks when the lean angle went more than three degrees past the vertical, but at least the bike was less likely to kick out from under you.

The Panhead was one of the first truly modern engines installed in a Harley. In 1953, the hydraulic lifters were positioned below the pushrods, as in a contemporary automobile engine, instead of being mounted between the pushrods and the rocker arms. The original lifters on the Panhead were such a source of problems that many owners simply welded them shut or replaced them with mechanical lifters.

The Panhead gained an electric starter in 1965, its last year of production. This was hailed as a tremendous advancement by owners who had spent much time jumping up, and occasionally down, on the kick starter. Stories abound of the interesting times had when trying to start a 74 Pan, or any other Big Twin, when the phases of the moon were wrong

Leave it to the racers to find a way to cover the vast distances on the dry lake. I saw many versions of this barstool/cart all over the pits. This one even has a wing mounted on the back to increase downforce above 1.5mph. The cooler behind the engine is probably more useful than the wing. The cart does need the wheelie bars, however; its mid-waist center of gravity makes lifting the front end very easy.

15

White Bros. pipes step up in size just downstream of the head. They look like straights; however, inside the tubes is a metal cone that is purported to be some sort of a sound-deadening system—I found this not to be the case. They are just a tad loud. For larger engines, the bigger pipes will flow more freely. *White Bros.*

or the day was a little too warm or cold, or the bike just plain didn't want to turn over and run.

I personally owned a 1963 ex-San Jose Police bike that taught me a lot about Zen Buddhism before it became the religion of choice of some rock & roll stars. Once upon a time, at 2:30 in the afternoon, I and my trusty steed went out to go to work. I very carefully retarded the spark by turning the left grip away from me. Then I set the choke at two clicks shut, turned on the fuel, and kicked the engine through two times with the throttle open a quarter turn and the ignition off in order to prime the motor. Next it was time to twist the key, give it a little more throttle, and kick smartly with the lever. Sometimes I was rewarded with the sound of 74 cubic inches

turning gas into noise. Sometimes the bike just slid a little on its kickstand, leaving a short drag mark on the driveway.

This was a day that I was semi-late for work, so you have an idea of what happened next. In short order I had removed my helmet, gloves, jacket, shirt, and was seriously considering putting on a pair of shorts. By now the kickstand had inscribed a three-foot mark in the asphalt and I was ready for a home for tired Harley owners. I probably had kicked the engine through enough times to have driven it to Milwaukee from San Jose. I think the bike was trying to teach me something about patience. Finally, between large whooping breaths, I told the bike that if it didn't start this one last time, I was going to turn it into an

A phone call and about $20k to Kosman can net you a frame and transmission (but no engine) identical to H-D of Citrus Height's racer. Look at the picture carefully. The engine has been turned around in the frame; the intake is on the left side of the engine. This way, the motor drives the trans through one side and the rear wheel is driven off the other, making shaft-support easier. The outer end of the transmission final drive shaft is supported in a bearing bolted into the massive trans mount. *Kosman*

agricultural implement and give it to a needy farmer for a water pump. One more kick, one more time. Surprise, surprise, it fired right up and sat there merrily chugging along as if nothing were amiss. I was still late for work, and I'm not too sure the foreman believed my story about a motorcycle smarter than me.

Left: All bikes that run above 125mph on the Lakes or at Bonneville must have a steering damper—one high-speed wobble will show you why. The damper is adjustable from light to hard by turning the knob on the left end of the shaft through fourteen clicks. I prefer to run mine as tight as it will go during a run. After all, if done right, you shouldn't have to move the bars more than a few degrees throughout a pass. Every bike has to go through tech inspection prior to running every event. This bike has its tech sticker on the right front downtube cover.

Mike Geokan gets set to run at El Mirage. His bike carries an R.B. Racing turbo on a 101-inch Evo. Not only will it run 200mph, but Mike says it's docile enough to take to the local bar. Runs gas and even has an electric starter. I don't think Mike would kid us, do you?

The Pan ran its life out in 1965, to be replaced by the refined Shovelhead of 1966. The new engine had the rockers integrated in the rocker box, giving the top of the engine a new appearance. The name stems from the resemblance of the rocker cover to the back end of a coal shovel when the bike is viewed from the carb-side. The first Shovels had the generator mounted in front of the cylinders, similarly to the Panheads. The fuel got to the cylinders through a Linkert carburetor, soon to be replaced by a Tillotson in 1967. It was the company's first motor with automatic spark advance, ending those wonderful times spent trying to pry one's foot out of one's back pocket when the manual ignition was left in full advance and the motor kicked back while trying to start. Prior to the electric foot and auto advance ignition, it was not unusual to see those of slighter build with their left foot on the kick starter, swinging their right foot through an arc, then dropping down with all their weight, trying to light the engine while the bike wobbled around on its kickstand. With the advent of long forks and severely raked frames, this could be quite an entertaining sight, providing no end of amusement for those of us who either weighed

well over 200lbs or had the wherewithal to own an electric-start bike. I never did see anyone high-side the bike while trying to get it to start. Sure was weird to watch, though.

Shovelhead

The 1966 Shovel engine was rated at 60hp—six more than the Panhead. However, the increase in weight of the new FLH made the bike actually slower than the motor it replaced. There was also an FL model with lower compression and 54hp for police departments and G-men. This bike was set up for reliability instead of speed. The only problem with the FL was that 54hp and 800lbs made for a slow motorcycle that wasn't well received by some police departments.

The early Shovelheads suffered from the same lack of brakes as the prior models—some magazines of the time going so far as to say that the front brake

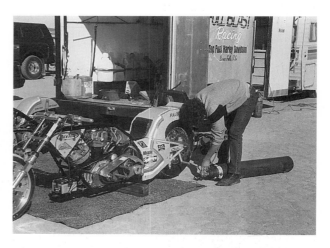

Nitrogen is used to inflate tires on some racing bikes. The rate of expansion is easier to predict, and there's no moisture in N_2. This ensures that the pressure in the tire won't climb when heated during a run.

was good for a hill-holder and not much else. The rear brake did an admirable job of stopping the rear wheel from turning, but this didn't do much towards retarding forward velocity. It was very important to plan all stops well in advance in order not to become someone's hood ornament.

Without a tach, it was pretty hard to tell how high the early Shovels would rev. Usually the limiting factor was the hydraulic lifters going away at about 5500rpm that held down the engine's capability. It was academic anyway, as turning the motor much past 4500rpm was mostly an exercise in vibration. Running the engine to mid-range and grabbing another gear was the best way to use the power band of a stock engine.

The Shovel, like most 74 or 80ci twins, seems happiest running between 2500 and 4000rpm. The modified motors are another thing entirely. I've seen gas-powered 114ci Shovel engines putting out 125 to 145hp at 7000rpm, pushing a 700lb bike down the quarter mile in under eleven seconds. These are engines that could loosely be called "street motors;" however, most of their highway miles are racked up sitting on a trailer.

To build a really fast, big-inch Shovel takes a lot of high-dollar parts and machine work. The cylinders must have a 3 13/16" bore and a full 5" stroke for a total displacement of 114ci. (Stock bore and stroke for an 80in Shovel is 3.5x4.25.) If the bore is held to 3 5/8", the displacement will be just under 103ci. A Sifton 108 Magnum cam, total valve lift of .485in and 279 degrees duration, along with the matching pushrods, tappets, and springs, will help fill the cylinders more efficiently.

The Sifton pushrods are fully adjustable and longer than stock. This, along with shortened tappets, lowers the contact point between pushrod and tappet to reduce the normally severe angle on the front exhaust and, along with the reduced diameter of the pushrods, does away with pushrod "rub." Be sure to include a set of roller rockers on the heads.

Use a carburetor like the S&S Super D gas carb with a 2 1/4" throat into a set of ported heads set up for dual plugs and running a 10 to 1 compression ratio. Pump gas will only allow a 9 to 1 compression ratio with a single plug head. Racing gas will let you get away with higher compression: up to 13.5–14 :1, depending on flame propagation and airflow. Dump the exhaust through a set of 2" headers unless running at a track with a decibel limit, then get a good exhaust system like a Rich Performance "Thunderheader." A well-tuned set of headers will get you off the line faster, enhance throttle response, and boost the top end.

When strokers are installed and the motor treated to a large power massage, a high-quality connecting rod

If you want to go pay and play, a good shop, like Arlen Ness', pictured here, has any number of custom bikes ready to run. Or he will build one to your specs—any specs you can think up.

must be used, as the stock rods won't take the 125hp+ stress. S&S Supreme Big Twin Rods, made from 4140 chrome moly, heat-treated and shot-peened, can be used, but because of their beefier construction, they will necessitate rebalancing the fly wheels.

The ignition will have to be capable of dealing with 5800 to 7000rpm on a sustained basis. High output coils and wires are a necessity.

Transmission, frame, and brakes will be covered in later chapters dealing with the Evolution engine.

Evolution

In 1984, Harley decided it needed to upgrade its product line with newer, more modern engineering and vehicles for the 1990s. One of its biggest new items was the Holiday-Rambler series of motorhomes, purchased in 1986 for $35 million in cash and $120 million in credit. The other new product was the Evolution engine, introduced in 1984.

The Holiday-Rambler series of vehicles are priced in the $15k to $250k range, while a good Evo motor, with a FXLR Low Rider Custom wrapped around it, can be yours for only $12,024 plus the usual gouge for tax, license, and dealer prep. Seeing as how motorhomes don't make very good racers (lots of wind resistance), we will stick to the Evolution motor and bike for the rest of the book.

The new Evolution motors, like most initial products, revealed flaws when subjected to day-to-day riding. In the first year of production, some of the lathes that cut the final dimensions on the cast-iron cylinder liners had defects. Tolerances between the cylinder walls and the pistons were too close. Piston seizures and the resulting warrantee claims continued until the problem was traced to oval cylinders and round pistons.

If the early Evo clutch plates were run in oils other than those particularly specified by H-D, they would stick, slip, and buck. Changing to the proper type of oil didn't cure the problem, as the clutch plates soaked up the wrong oil, retaining it past any reasonable method of removal. The clutch was redesigned with different material, eliminating the problem. Harley-Davidson absorbed most of the cost in replacing the clutch plates and installing the proper fluid.

This was Harley's first shot at an oil bath clutch; earlier Shovelheads ran with a dry-type clutch, as I and a dealer found out when their fresh-out-of-school mechanic serviced my 1982 FXRS, making sure it had the right amount of oil in the clutch. Right amount for an Evo motor, that is; my bike would hardly move away from stoplights. Anything past 1/4 throttle and the clutch made like a roller bearing. The shop tried to dry out the plates

On a show bike, velocity stacks on a twin-throat Solex carb are OK. On your street bike, something like this would simply vacuum up everything in the air from sand to small children. Engine life would be measured in hours.

with alcohol, to no avail. Harley oil does as promised —makes things slippery and won't go away. The bike ended up with a totally new clutch, and all was well. A small point, but one to be watched for those like me who still think the best motor stopped being built in 1984. (Or, in my case, for those who need to sell lots of copies of this book to provide the funds necessary to park a nice new FLHR Electra-Glide in my garage, thank you.)

Also, within the first few thousand miles a metallic rattling sound began to emanate from the upper regions of the Evo engine. Seems as though some of the valve springs were made from a steel that wasn't properly treated, resulting in failure after a short period of operation. This was soon corrected and everybody was happy again.

These few faults made some customers question the worth of the new Evo motor; some people went so far as to lament the passing of the "good old Shovel," expressing a desire to see the old engine return. In reality, the new engine had very few teething problems, most of which could be traced to non-spec lubricants, as in the case of the clutch, or to poor metallurgy in the few cases of valve-spring breakage. Once these few problems were worked out, the Evolution went on to prove itself to be an oil-tight, strong, reliable improvement over what had gone before. Many touring riders have rolled well past the 100,000 mile mark on their FL series Evos without having to open the engine. A few owners expressed the intent to continue to ride towards the 200,000 mile mark, confident that the bike will be running as well then as it did when new.

The Evo motor retains the same bore and stroke dimensions of the Shovelhead, 3 .5"x4.25", as well as the same crankshaft and engine cases. The Evo motor originally put out around 10% more hp than the Shovelhead it replaced, but with emission control rearing its ugly head, power has dropped off a bit, especially in the bikes destined for California.

Variations

Harleys can be found with four- or five-speed transmissions, depending upon model and year. Some engines will be bolted rigidly to the frame, allowing motor vibrations to be transferred directly to the rider and making eyes bounce like ball bearings in a blender above a certain engine speed. Other models have the engine located by means of rubber mounts, letting the engine move around while the frame and rider stay smooth. From personal experience, the rubber mounts begin to show their worth above 2000rpm. Most of the vibration that usually

A tachometer is a necessity on a racing bike. If your bike came with only a speedometer, Drag Specialties offers this 0–8000rpm tach to fit on the triple clamps or bars. *Edge Advertising*

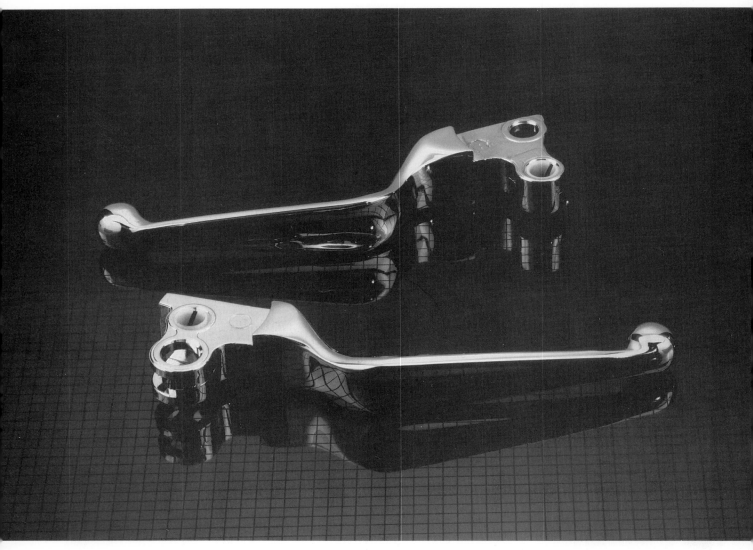

Clutch and brake levers with a step in them make operating an aftermarket clutch or front disc, four-piston calipers a little easier. Drag Specialties also offers these.

Be sure to change, or at least clean and lube, the cables prior to installing new levers. *Edge Advertising*

numbs a rider's arms up to the elbows stays with the engine. No more feeling like your arms have been Novocained after a two-hour ride.

I once owned a Harley of smaller displacement (OK, it was a 1971 XLCH, but I won't do it again, honest!) that had a rather severe vibration at 3400rpm. Below this engine speed the bike rode great. Above this engine speed the vibration transmitted through the back of the step-seat was so nasty that it would create heat from the friction where I contacted the seat. Leather pants worked OK; jeans—no way. It actually created enough heat in that area to be uncomfortable. I sold it rather quickly.

In my opinion—and only my opinion—own-

ing an H-D with the engine clamped straight to the mounts is all right for fifty miles of cruising at speeds under 60mph unless you are into self-flagellation or come from the Marquis de Sade school of motorcycle riding. The rubber mounts on the FXRS and other models, along with belt drive, allow the rider to plan for 400-mile days, knowing that at the end of the ride, he or she will be able to step off the bike without having to seek medical help to have the seat surgically removed.

On the Evo engine, the rocker covers are built out of three pieces for ease of service. All the cam gear and rockers are of a higher quality than the older engines, helping to ensure reliability. Both cylinders are interchangeable, more for commonalty of parts than any other reason. The pistons are double-tapered to reduce cylinder wall contact and wear, adding to longevity. The combustion chamber, while not optimized for power, is redesigned to allow what passes for gasoline these days to burn without pre-ignition. All in all, a large improvement over what went before.

Harley never has felt it must have a 0–60 time less than six seconds, or that a 130mph top end was a necessary design feature for their products. By su-

choked down. Working at low engine speeds, low temperatures, and low compression ratios, the Evo motor should last long enough, with proper mainte-nance, to be handed down to your grandchildren. Given Harley's attitude of "rebuild it, don't throw it away," the heirloom you will to your descendants should run as well as it does while it's in your care.

Harley's continual refinement of what is, admit-tedly, a design with inherent vibration problems, due to its narrow-angle V-twin configuration, shows that

A set of aftermarket mufflers definitely improves looks and sound. Matched with intake and cam changes, you'll think you're riding a different scooter.

perbike standards, the new Harleys at 50–52hp weren't going to rip any big holes in the pavement when the throttle was opened. However, the horse-power that does get through to the rear wheel is dis-tributed over such a wide rpm range that it provides smooth acceleration no matter what gear you've se-lected. So long as you do your part and keep the revs above 1500–1700, the bike doesn't seem to care what gear it's in. It just hunkers down and pulls smoothly throughout the entire rpm range. Actually, as previously mentioned, running the engine much past 4500rpm in stock configuration is largely an ex-ercise in making noise. Between the mild cam timing and restrictive breathing, the Evo engine is pretty

the company is trying to reach a high standard of quali-ty while retaining many of its traditional features. Rub-ber-mounted motors and transmissions, fully isolated from the rest of the bike and rider, allow the bike to reach a higher level of smoothness while retaining all the features that have made a Harley-Davidson unique.

Muffled Rumblings

As we finish up the last five years of this centu-ry, emissions laws and noise standards have made it harder for most vehicle manufacturers to keep their products on the road. Most companies have had to resort to major re-engineering or totally new engine designs to enable them to reduce their noise signa-

Two SU carbs feeding a blown Shovel motor. The blower is driven through a shaft running over to the other side of the engine. This is in a show bike—I bet if it ran, it would provide some interesting moments, trying to run all that drive gear from one side of the engine to the other.

ture in order to comply with Federal regulations.

One of the biggest problems confronting Harley-Davidson as they roll through the nineties is how to lower the sound output of their engines. In order to meet the newest, more stringent laws, Harley has had to resort to methods of control that have choked down horsepower output significantly. Engine noise is a combination of intake airflow, exhaust rumble, gear whine, piston movement, and cooling fin resonance. Harley's engineering department has worked hard to reduce noise while still retaining the traditional look and sound of a big V-twin. Still, keeping up with new regulations is causing Harley, along with all other motorcycle manufacturers, to use computer-produced models to control sound output.

Computers allow much closer tolerances to be held when producing such high-noise items as cam gears. Using closed-loop feedback to monitor real-time operations, along with a much more rigid inspection procedure, has allowed Harley to catch any dimension change during machining due to wear on the tools or other factors, and make running changes to maintain acceptable tolerances on each part.

So far, Harley has been able to keep refining an engine that was initially developed in the early 1900s, back when emissions came from farm animals and noise was what you heard when your mother told you to "get off that dad-ratted motorcycle and come do the chores." Air-cooled engines, by necessity, have to run clearances looser than similar water-cooled designs, due partially to the greater heat expansion inherent in their design. This converts directly to noise.

Various parts in the engine expand at different rates, causing even more rattling and whirring as they come up to operating temperature. In my old Shovelhead, I can hear the pistons sliding up and down in the cylinders before everything gets warmed up enough to take up some of the clearances. Parked next to a 1993 FXDL, my bike makes so much engine gear and exhaust noise, even with its stock 1982 pipes, that I can't hear the new bike run. Anyone who doesn't think Harley has come a long way just has to look at two bikes over an eleven-year time span—no comparison. The new scooters are quieter and smoother all around.

'Course the California bikes are even quieter than the other forty-nine-state bikes—a little slower, too. My old Shovel will leave a new fiftieth state bike for dead in a roll-on from any gear (sure, it's stock!). I have more trouble with the forty-nine-state bikes—after a 1/4 mile run, we are a whole six feet apart. Who's in front depends on who works the throttle and clutch faster. But like I say, 1994 California bikes appear to be a bit lazy on acceleration. Sometimes this comes as a surprise to a twenty-three-year-old rider on his shiny new putt when he sets off to prove that he's faster than that old dude on the relic. That's the price we pay for cleaner air, however, and it's not going to get any better as time goes on.

California is known to have the toughest emissions and noise laws in the US. Most vehicle manufacturers build a specific product strictly for sales in this market. The other 49 states operate with a less rigid set of specifications, but, as the years go by, most of them will probably adopt some semblance of the California regulations.

Power Up

The California-only bikes suffer quite a power loss as compared to the rest of Harley's output. Actual dyno figures show a total of 39hp at the rear wheel of the 80ci Evo motor as compared to 50–52hp for the 49-state bikes. You can see how a California emissions-controlled

This carb is just being set up for the engine. Only one throttle cable is mounted at this time, but you can see where the other one will attach in front of the first. One cable pulls the throttle open and one cable pulls it shut. This way, sticking carbs are avoided.

These Evo valve covers have been ground away on the inside for additional rocker clearance, needed when installing a high-lift cam. Just before bolting them down, turn the engine over and watch to see if the covers lift. If any movement, you need to cut more clearance.

bike could benefit from a serious injection of horsepower.

Most of the material in this book is intended to help you increase the power and performance of your Big Twin Harley through modifications running from the mild—as in installing Custom Chrome's RevTech Kit for an advertised dyno output of close to 92hp—to the wild, like building a monster 140+ cubic inch, 300hp asphalt-ripper that makes the people standing next to it take two steps backwards when it lights off. Be advised, though, that this information on engine modification is intended primarily for off-road operation, due to the Federal restrictions on any part that pertains to emissions control systems on bikes driven on the street.

Many parts mentioned herein have received a CARB (California Air Resources Board) exemption, allowing them to be used on pollution-controlled vehicles in that state and others. Many parts are not intended to be used on the street. Some states have enacted laws that deal with tampering, modifying, or removing any required emissions equipment, and have penalties for their violation. It is up to the individual motorcycle owner to determine the suitability of the product for his or her use, and assume all risk and liability when using them.

Along with all the Federal disclaimers, it is important for the rider to realize that highly modified motorcycles can be more difficult to ride. It behooves the rider of a motorcycle with greatly increased horsepower to use extreme caution when it comes time for the first test ride. Also, an engine modified to produce large quantities of power can have the tendency to reduce itself to small, expensive pieces if not operated properly. This can cause your body to contact the road surface at a high rate of speed, grinding off some fairly important parts in the process—a situation to be avoided at all costs.

Chapter 2

Stage One: Street Performance

Most of us who buy our first new, or fairly new, Harley-Davidson are more than happy with the performance. It takes a few months or a few faster bikes to convince us that maybe we *really* don't own the fastest internal combustion-powered device next to a Ferrari Testarossa 12-cylinder. Usually, getting left in the weeds once is enough to make us think about making sure it doesn't happen again.

So begins the search for speed. The first thing to engrave on your MasterCard is what was mentioned earlier: speed costs money—how fast do you want to go? I've been learning this lesson since I stripped down my first Harley, a 1963 Duo-Glide 1200cc Panhead. With the wisdom of the young, I first sawed off half the mufflers to acquire that "throaty" sound. Next, I used the time-honored method of stripping all the useless (to my 21-year-old way of thinking) parts on the bike by the expedient method of firing up the engine and unbolting parts until it quit. Then I proceeded to bolt that part back on. I figure that I probably cut about 75lbs and fifteen percent of the performance off the bike.

I found that the Linkert carburetor had all kinds of levers and screws that I could play with while I "tuned" the bike. Sometimes I "tuned" the bike so well it wouldn't run! Luckily for me I had a friend with a pickup who helped me load the bike into the bed for the ten-mile drive down to the H-D dealer. I will pass over in silence what the mechanics said to me about my "speed modifications." Wiser and poorer, I picked up the bike a week later with the stern admonition by the mechanic who had to straighten out my mess to keep my "@#&$®¥ hands" off the engine. So ended my first attempt at speed.

Today, the average Harley owner doesn't have to resort to trial and error (mostly error in my case) when looking to improve performance. There are more than 150 different companies dedicated to im-

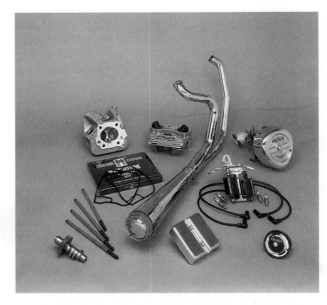

Custom Chrome, Inc. (CCI) includes everything in its RevTech kit to really wake up your Evo. Some machining of the piston tops is necessary to clear the valves, and the intake manifold might have to be cut a tad, but it's still one of the easiest ways to add a lot of horsepower. *Custom Chrome*

proving or modifying the Harley-Davidson motorcycle. Nowadays, the hardest part is trying to figure out which way to go and what components to use.

In this chapter we will try to cover some methods to improve your bike's performance without opening up the engine or buying shares in a machine shop. In the next chapter we will go into detail on what can be done to an engine by replacing cylinders, heads, and the like. Chapter four will cover all-out modifications to the engine for maximum horsepower.

Here's CCI's kit mounted with a set of staggered duals instead of the SuperTrapp system normally found in the kit. You pays your money and you takes your choice. *Custom Chrome*

Package Power Production

There are many ways to go about building more horsepower into an engine. The variety of cams, carbs, pipes, heads, pistons, and other parts is staggering. There are numerous aftermarket parts manufacturers and performance shops ready to help you lighten your wallet and pump up your engine—usually not in that order. What you need to do first is decide which combination of parts will work best for you and what you want to accomplish with the modifications.

It does no good to go buy an S&S Super D gas carburetor with a 2 1/4 throat normally used on Big Twins of large displacement (not 1200 or 1340cc engines) and bolt it on to a stock displacement motorcycle. It's intended for engines where some performance modifications, such as head porting, a cam change, big bore cylinders, stroker flywheels, etc., have been done or will be done. On a stock bike, the performance would actually be hurt by this installation without other modifications. The engine would-n't be able to flow enough air to make use of the big carb. You'd be much better off to use a Super B carb, with a 1 7/8 throat, from the same manufacturer, as this carb is intended for use on any Big Twin with any degree of modification—both stock and performance engines.

The best way to gain an increase in performance from a Big Twin is to figure your budget available for engine modifications, what performance gain you want, and what steps you plan on taking to get to that point. The stage one engine will consist of bolt-on parts such as exhaust systems and air cleaners. We will see the best way to deal with the modifications to the engine is to treat it as a complete assembly, as opposed to looking at one modification at a time. This idea of a total performance engine is the best approach to more power, and we will work with this in mind. Any changes made at the intake side of the engine will have to be balanced by similar improvements on the exhaust side to produce a reliable, fast, finished product.

27

CCI supports their products with this rig. It can be found at most of the shows and races throughout the country. Their tech people are always on hand to answer any questions. CCI's business must be relatively good; that's a whole lot of truck and trailer.

Look at the engine as an air pump. The more air that can be pumped, the more power that can be made. Just opening up the inlet side of the pump, without giving the increased incoming airflow a way to exit the engine, will result in a slight—if any—improvement in performance. Using the "suck, bang, and blow" theory of engine operation, changing any one of the operations, such as "suck" or intake, without changing the two others will not result in maximum gain for dollar spent. It's better to wait until you have enough money to make a complete change of all the performance components than to go at it piecemeal, changing just a carb or just the pipes. Yes, some performance gains will be seen with just one change but in order to make the most of any improvements you should cover all motor modifications as a package.

Stage One Engine

Before changing any parts on your H-D, you must first decide what you want to do with the finished product. Do you want to run with the big dogs, or will you be happy to spend most of your time sitting on the porch, only going out for an occasional growl on Friday nights? Are you willing to accept a shorter engine life in return for increased power? What kind of performance tradeoff can you handle? Or will you be happy with simply improving the overall performance and rideability of the bike up to the point of greater wear rates? Bumping the power and using all of it will increase your maintenance bills.

I know, I know, you just want to have the ability to smoke the competition at any time; you don't plan on really using all the improvements, so gas mileage and reliability aren't a concern—or are they? If you intend on pumping 30% or more power out of your engine, be prepared to accept more wear and tear on moving parts.

This stage of the modification game we will only deal with changes that you, or a relatively skilled mechanic, can make without having to deal with any major engine modifications. We will stay with stock displacement and heads. Most of these changes can be done in a few hours with a fairly complete set of hand tools. You will need a good set of standard and deep sockets. Buy a full set of combination wrenches from 1/4in to 3/4in, and a good set of hex wrenches—5/64ths to 1/4in. You will have to acquire a range of screwdrivers, both flat and Phillips, capable of fitting all the screws on the bike without marring the screw heads as leverage is applied.

The old adage about a hammer being the primary Harley tool won't work here. H-D Inc. manufactures a precision product built to very close tolerances. Working on their products requires equally precise equipment if you want to do a professional job.

Tools are not a place to economize. Buy everything from wrenches to screwdrivers from a quality supplier such as Snap-On or Sears Craftsman Series. Good tools are easier to work with than cheap tools and won't break under hard usage. Nothing, but nothing, hurts more than nailing a knuckle when a socket cracks while trying to free up a tight bolt. I carry a vivid memory of snapping an end wrench while trying to loosen a cylinder case nut on my early Panhead. The memory of cylinder fins slicing my knuckles still sends shivers down my back.

The Stock Engine

The stock 49-state Evo motor is good for about 50–52hp, depending on manufacturing tolerances on each individual bike. Torque peaks at 65–67lb-ft. Torque is a measure of the force pushing down on an object, say a piston, around a given axis, so it's properly expressed as "pounds per foot," or "lb-ft," as opposed to the incorrect term of "foot-pounds" or "ft-lbs" that's been in use for a number of years. We'll stick with "lb-ft" during this discussion.

Torque and horsepower are sometimes confused, although one won't exist in an engine without the other being present and working. The only real way to measure horsepower output is to measure torque and then, taking into consideration air density and barometric pressure, convert it into horsepower. Horsepower = torque x rpm divided by time. Or, for those of us who operate a dynamometer, horsepower is usually equal to whatever the computer says it is.

Using the analogy of an air pump, the factors that limit power output, other than ignition, are the ability of the engine to pump air into the cylinder and get it out when combustion is complete. The cam, carb, and exhaust system all play a part in determining when and where this limit is reached. The Big Twin's torque falls off above a certain rpm because of the cylinder's inability to fill on the intake stroke. Percentage of cylinder fill is known as "volumetric efficiency" (VE) of the engine. Torque peak is

Jim McClure's beautiful single-engined racer gets worked on between heats. *Rich Products*

reached at the point where the cylinder reaches maximum capacity. When an engine's torque drops faster than its horsepower rises, VE drops off.

However, many other factors, including spark plug location and combustion chamber shape, will also affect the ability of the engine to make power up to a certain rpm.

The stock Big Twin, due to its poor breathing and choked exhaust, hits its torque peak of 67lb-ft at somewhere near 3000rpm and drops off from there to 60lb-ft at 5000rpm. This peak occurs at 55% of the engine's redline, whereas a tuner usually aims his high-performance engine to peak past 70% of redline.

CCI's 30,000 volt coil for single-fire, dual-plug engines has to be mounted with another one to fire all four plugs. *Custom Chrome*

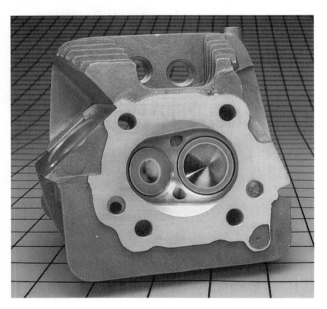

The working side of a RevTech head. The polished surfaces and holes for the dual-plug setup can easily be seen. To run one plug, a socket head bolt is included in the kit to fill the second spark plug hole. I recommend, though, that you set the engine up to run twin plugs. *Custom Chrome*

The key to modifying a Big Twin engine to fit your needs is to figure out what type of riding you will be doing and what rpm range you will be operating within. If you are going to be pulling a sidecar or a trailer with a heavy load, it makes no sense to build an engine that reaches peak torque at 4000rpm when most of your riding will be at 2500–3000rpm. Conversely, if you are planning on running your bike a 1/4 mile at a time while trying to blow the handlebars off the guy in the next lane, then you will be willing to live with an engine that won't pull the skin off a chocolate pudding below 3000rpm but takes both hands and a sincere wish to stay aboard when the tach climbs above 4500rpm. In each case, different requirements will result in entirely different engines.

So, what can you do to your stock engine when you're tired of having the Cadillacs suck the tassels off your saddlebags, or when you decide to try your hand (and both feet, perspiration, intestinal fortitude, and wallet) at drag racing?

If you're happy with a modest increase in overall performance and don't want to open the engine every 10,000 miles, 80hp won't have you leaping tall buildings at a single bound, but it will see off the average car and make passing those Peterbuilts more an exercise in the throttle rather than the "punch it and pray" method that sometimes happens with a stock bike.

For the stage one engine we will limit the engine displacement to the stock 80 cubic inches, considering this will be a bolt-on-improvement motor. Increasing horsepower is not limited to any one particular method. A lot of different suppliers offer the same type of part for the Big Twin, and there are many ways to reach the same goal. We will discuss a few different ways to go, but there will be other, just as good, methods of improving performance using different parts from other suppliers.

Initial modifications should be made to the induction and exhaust system. To improve over the smog motor's 50–52hp (39 in sunny California), the engine will have to breathe better, burn the fuel at a higher rpm, and get the burnt gasses out the exhaust in the most efficient manner.

Using 6200rpm as a limit will keep the piston speed below 4,500 feet per minute, a reasonable number to use if you want the engine to last longer than an inside straight in a draw poker game. Seventy horsepower will not put any undue strain on stock chassis equipment, and it will still be enough power to make full throttle runs fairly interesting.

Out of the Box

Custom Chrome (CCI; 800–729–3332 for the nearest dealer) produces, imports, or sources a complete performance package set up for the owner to install. This consists of a set of parts, marketed under the CCI "RevTech" banner, advertised as producing 92 bolt-on horsepower for a stock displacement Evo.

Opening all the boxes yields new, dual-plug, increased compression heads, a RevTech 40 cam and kit, adjustable aluminum pushrods, a new ignition system—coil wires and 30,0000-volt coil included with mounting kit—, an Accelerator Two carburetor and shorty manifold, and a SuperTrapp two-into-one exhaust system.

The cam has 0.560in lift and 266 degrees duration, designed to operate in the 2800–6500rpm range. The valve springs have to be set at a minimum travel of 0.590in. Late 1984 to early 1986 Evos have to have their pistons notched for clearance. The pushrods are 7/16in diameter tubing. Your hydraulic lifters can be set up to run as solids by the use of hydraulic lifter deactivators that will keep the lifters from pumping up at high revs, or you can opt out for a new set of solid lifters.

The carb is pre-jetted for the kit and ready to bolt on. The manifold is 7/8in shorter than stock, ex-trude-honed for smoother flow. The carb sports a longer enrichment lever, making operation a little bit easier during cold starts.

Where most of the power increase originates is in the dual-plug heads. If you only want to run single plugs in the heads, a 12mm socket head plug will have to be installed in the second hole. There's no real reason not to run dual plugs, considering all the benefits they provide.

The intake ports have been reshaped to "D" configuration and raised 0.100in. All ports and bath-tub-shaped combustion chambers have been treated to the extrude-honed process for smoothness. Compression is 10:1, requiring a good brand of fuel to prevent any chance of detonation. Intake valves (1.940in) have nitrided stems, hardened tips to decrease wear, and swirl-polished faces. Both the intake and 1.610in diameter exhaust valves sit on heat-treated nickel seats. Three-piece valve springs include a flat-wound damper spring that works to hold down

Drag Specialties has a good-looking air cleaner with no name stamped on it for those who don't want to run with someone else's name on the bike. *Edge Advertising*

CCI built up this bike to show how its RevTech kit looks installed. The only part I don't like is the phony fitting on the braided fuel line running from under the fuel tank. If you want to run braided lines with A&N fittings, do it right. The biggest reason racers run braided lines is for

safety. Stainless steel doesn't even burn anything, like rubber, and the connections, if done properly, are very strong. You really don't want a line coming adrift and spraying nice flammable fuel all over your new leathers should you—God forbid—drop it.

surge. The heads can also be ordered with a wider 77cc combustion chamber to match larger bores with stock head-bolt pattern.

The ignition system uses a Hall-effect transducer to trigger the spark. It's unaffected by dirt or oil that might seep into the timing housing. Timing never shifts, nor does anything have to be adjusted, ever. It's a single-fire system giving increased fuel mileage (slight) over the stock system. Any improvement in economy is usually lost in the first couple of hundred miles of operation due to the throttle always seeming to be in the wide-open position. To steal a saying: "Power corrupts. Absolute power corrupts absolutely." Or, It's a whole pile of fun to put all the new horses found in the engine to work on a regular basis.

Starting will improve and the engine will be smoother when the ignition is changed over to the

single-fire system. The single-fire system only fires the plug that's on the compression stroke, as opposed to the factory system's lighting both plugs every time either piston is up.

The coils in the kit are CCI's American-made, 30,000-volt dual-primary winding type, with both coils built into a single housing. The stock coil cover won't fit over the new coils, so CCI includes a mount and cover in the kit.

As far as real-life performance, *Cycle World (CW)*, in its September 1993 issue, installed the kit on a 1990 Sturgis. CCI said that only basic tools and average ability were needed to install the kit, but *CW* found that the average tools had better include the equipment to machine notches in the piston for valve clearance. This means the pistons have to come out and go to a machine shop for work, unless you're real good and can cut the clearances on the piston tops while still in the cylinders. A very good cleanup afterwards will keep the grindings out of the bearings. Flush the engine with solvent and change oil after the first fifty miles. I personally would pull the engine down to do the work.

Probably, if the bike has many miles on it, this would be a good time to look into a cleanup pass with a boring bar and installing a new set of rings. You can go for an increase in displacement by way of a bigger cut with the bar or install different cylinders entirely. As the heads can be ordered to fit Axtell 3 13/16in, 97ci cylinders, you could come away with a major stump-puller motor. However, new cylinders or bigger pistons are modifications that will be covered on the stage two engine, as they are beyond stage one parameters.

With the RevTech kit, some of the case material around the cam lobes had to be removed with an air grinder to clear the new 0.560 lift cam. This is a fairly normal procedure for any big cam installation. Also, the intake manifold had to have .040 knocked off both ends in order to fit between the cylinders.

CW wasn't too happy with the instructions in the kit. They felt that too much was left up to guesswork instead of being clearly spelled out. I talked to Frank Keisler at CCI, and he said that the instructions were to be updated with more complete informa-

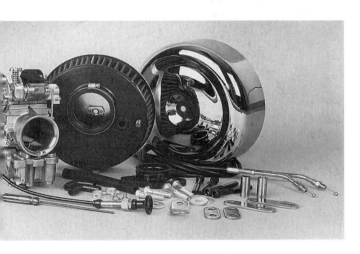

Here's the complete kit necessary to mount a Mikuni HS 40 carb on an Evo or Shovel. A manifold change is sometimes necessary on Shovels. Everything necessary, even the dual push-pull throttle cables, is included. *Mikuni*

tion. They should be part of the kit by the time you read this.

As far as performance, *CW*'s test bike only generated 77hp at stock 35 degrees BTDC timing set-tings—80hp with the timing changed to 31 degrees BTDC. Not a bad jump from the California bike's 39 lazy ponies, but a ways from the claimed 92.

I saw slightly more power on one of CCI's bikes they had strapped to their rear wheel dyno. They were working on a staggered dual exhaust system, changing header pipe length to see where the power would peak with each 2 inch change in length. What looked like mufflers probably were hollow, or close to it, judging by the noise output. Winding the engine to 6000rpm on the street would require ear plugs and very tolerant neighbors. I saw a high of 84hp during one of the runs, so it's possible to make a lot more go than stock, but it had better be at a drag strip with loose noise regulations.

This much increase from stock, be it 77 or 80hp gained with lots of time and tuning, represents a 38–41hp bump from the stock 39 quivering California horsepower motor. Even taking into consideration all the extra work involved in the installation, this represents a tremendous power increase for the retail price of $2,700, plus whatever machine work you need to contract out. When you get really tired of being last, this is the way to go.

Carburetors

Starting with the intake, the first thing to do is lose the carburetor and air cleaner. The stock 40mm Keihin does an adequate job of keeping nasty ol' pollutants from being formed in the engine, but, as a performance device, it leaves a lot to be desired. The air cleaner does the job for which it was intended, which is to clean and quiet the air entering the carb; however, it extracts a penalty in cubic feet per minute (CFM) of air flow. It's a lot like trying to run a lion through a mouse's nose .

There's a few ways to go in the carb replacement department. S&S Cycle (Box 215, Rt. 2 County G, Viola, WI 54664) makes a number of direct replacement carbs for the Big Twin. Two of their more popular models are the S&S Super B gas carb and the S&S Two Throat gas carb. Both are designed for the stock displacement engine. The twin throat carb will require a manifold change to a twin plenum manifold to allow each cylinder to be fed separately. The two throat is not available for the Evo motor, but will fit the Shovel.

When installing a S&S carb, it's important to note a couple of items.

First, all the replacement carbs require the use of a two-cable, pull-open/pull-closed-type throttle. Single braided-wire cable throttle mechanisms cannot mechanically close the throttle. If the throttle sticks in the wide-open position, you will have to rely on an ignition kill switch, great brakes, and perhaps a healthy helping of luck to shut down. S&S offers a high-quality, two-cable assembly to replace your existing setup.

Second, because of the possibility of getting buffing compound in fuel passages or feed holes, S&S does not recommend polishing or chrome-plating the carb. Once the crud inhabits the feed holes, it's as hard to remove as a speeding ticket on your driving record.

The S&S Super B carb is a butterfly-type carb with a fully adjustable idle mixture screw and changeable mid-range and high-speed jets. This carb doesn't have an accelerator pump or a conventional choke system, but uses a mixture enrichment device for starting. When you buy the carb as a kit, you receive, along with the Super B carb: an intake manifold; teardrop air cleaner; two extra main jets; fuel line and mounting hardware; plus a comprehensive

Zipper's Cycle sells a Thunder kit for stock or aftermarket carbs. This is nothing more than a way of injecting more fuel into the venturi. I've seen it used to good effect on some racing bikes when set up to dump more fuel at wide-open throttle. *Zipper's*

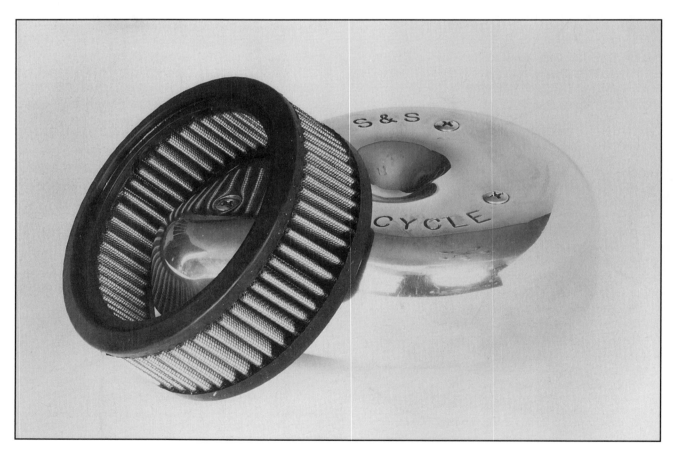

K&N has a new air filter to fit under the S&S teardrop air cleaner. Tests show the same airflow with or without the filter installed. The element can be washed and reused for the life of the bike. One's going on my old Shovel real soon. *K&N*

instruction manual that even I could follow. Just make sure the gas is drained from the carb and your cigar is out when beginning the installation. Disconnecting the battery to keep down the possibility of sparks is a real good idea, too.

Speaking of disconnecting batteries: I have a friend who had an intermittent starter solenoid problem with his 1976 Shovelhead. He pulled the primary cover and reached in over the primary chain to see why the starter wasn't engaging the ring gear. As you might guess, the battery was left hooked up, so when he manually pulled the solenoid forward to where its contacts closed, the starter did what it was built to do: engaged the ring gear and turned the motor through about 1/2 revolution before he could let go. He had to use a screwdriver to turn the primary chain backwards enough to release his index finger from where it had gotten caught between the chain and ring gear on the clutch. Well, he managed

to have the finger reattached and it sorta works, but he now disconnects the battery if he just changes the oil. Be careful!

Tuning the Super B for the street is a fairly simple five-step operation:
1. Warm the engine to normal operating temperature (make sure the oil has a chance to get above 150 degrees before running the engine hard);
2. Accelerate rapidly through the gears, noting how quickly and smoothly the engine reaches rpm level where power begins to fade and you shift up;
3. If any backfiring or sputtering is noticed, or if the engine breaks up or dies during acceleration, increase the size of the main jet by .004 and try again;
4. If the engine runs flat or sluggish, or will not take throttle, lean out the main jet .004 and try again;
5. Continue changing main jets until one is found that makes the engine run the smoothest through the gears.

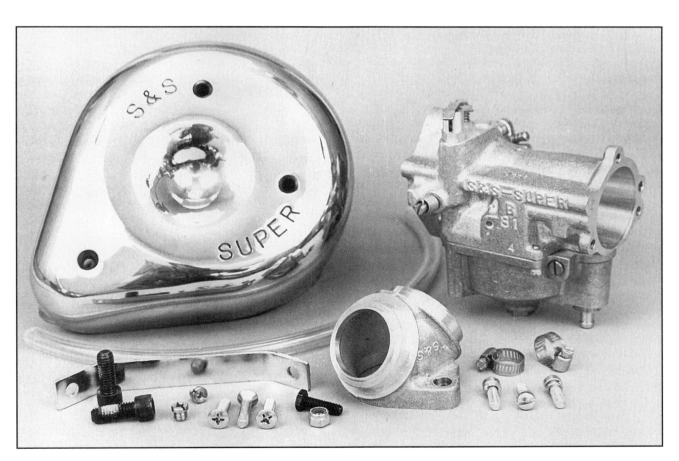

Nothing else has product identification quite like S&S' air cleaner—even if not mounted on the S&S Super B carb shown. The first thing I'd do to my new California ragging-39-horsepower bike is lose the factory fuel mixer and install one of these or another aftermarket carb, like RevTech or Mikuni. *S&S*

Once the proper size jet has been installed, any change more than .006 in either direction will cause poor running conditions. Further info on fine-tuning and troubleshooting can be found in the eight-page direction sheet enclosed with the kit.

S&S also recommends that their air cleaner be used with all S&S carb installations. This is the teardrop cleaner that has become the signature of S&S products. The air cleaner back plate has been designed with an air horn-style radiused entryway and a dimpled cover with an air-directing cone on the inside to smooth out the airflow as it enters the carb. Both features help maximize airflow by giving the intake air an efficient, easy path to follow. The S&S air cleaner also fits the stock carb on all Big Twins with the same bolt-mounting pattern on the inlet side of the carb.

One of the non-performance advantages gained by the air cleaner installation is the substitution of a much smaller cover in place of the stock H-D coffee-can-sized air scrubber. For those of us whose leg just won't fit around the stock equipment without a few extra joints, the S&S cleaner gives the space needed for comfort.

Mikuni (8910 Mikuni Avenue, Northridge, CA 91324) builds a 40mm (1 7/8") flat-side carb called the "HS 40," which will flow a larger volume of air into the engine than the stocker. Most of its advantage over the stock 40mm Keihin is concentrated in the low and mid ranges, where throttle response is greatly enhanced over the stock carb. The Mikuni is equipped with an accelerator pump capable of being adjusted over a wide range to enable each application to be set for best engine response. Usually, the Mikuni will improve gas mileage, providing you can keep the throttle from banging against the stops too often. The problem with a better-running, faster, more powerful motorcycle is that you and I tend to like to use what's there—gas mileage being rather low on our list of priorities. Let's face it, you aren't going through all this time, money, and effort just to make the ride to the 7-11 smoother.

When I was actively racing, my mechanic would tell me to take it easy for the first few laps or so, as he wanted the new engine to have a little time to get used to itself before I tried to drive the pistons through the bottom of the cases. My response was always: "OK, no problem , I'll cool it for the first practice session. Then we'll make it go next time out." I'd go line up on the practice grid with my mechanic alongside the bike, checking final adjustments. We were racing sidehacks at the time, powered by large displacement Shovelheads. In sidecar racing, usually it helped to have about a room temperature IQ to be

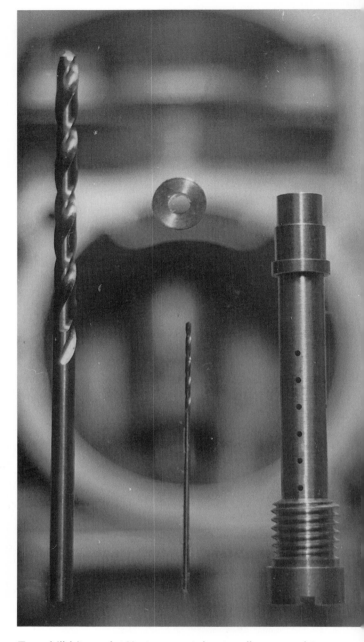

Two drill bits and a Yost power tube are all you need to make the stock carb, Mikuni Flatsider, or S&S Super B, E, or G run better. The tube helps atomize incoming fuel for better distribution. For a small investment, you pick up a bit more power and smoother engine. *Yost*

a driver or the guy who rode on the hack, the "monkey." Normal procedure was to hang off the bike in every corner, trying to keep the weight inside the turn. The monkey would either crawl across the bike from the hack and hang over the rear fender, or hang off the hack with his shoulder dragging the as-

With a big-inch bike, increased fuel delivery becomes very important. Pingel makes petcocks in many different flavors to cover everything from mountain motors to turbo bikes. Any major engine modification will require one of these, to keep the engine from starving at high revs, and a fuel filter. They can be ordered to fit regular fuel line as well as A&N fittings. *Pingel*

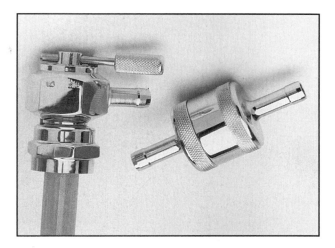

When you change the petcock and filter, be sure to note the date and mileage. The screen on the petcock needs to be cleaned at regular intervals and the fuel filter replaced at the same time. *Pingel*

phalt at 100+. Should you come adrift from the bike, most of the riders would as soon run over your neck as drive around you. We all thought it was great fun at the time!

Last I heard from my wrench as I fired up to pull on the track for the first practice session was, "Remember, take it easy." Usually I held onto this thought all the way out of the pits, then it was racing as usual: 6500rpm, full throttle, and slide it sideways to slow down. Out of desperation, my mechanic finally set the engine up fairly loose and made sure he was able to run it around the shop parking lot enough times to let the parts get to work in a bit. We

even used to take the rig down to a nearby store once in a while, just to watch people watch us.

The Mikuni can be ordered as a complete kit: choke and throttle cables; adapters; clamps; a K&N filter assembly with a chrome cover and a detailed instruction/tuning manual. If you're trying to maintain the stock look to your bike, the original air cleaner will fit.

Numerous aftermarket suppliers offer a manifold kit for the 40mm Mikuni to mount on the Evo and Shovel motors. CCI has a kit to adapt a Mikuni Smoothbore to any Evo Big Twin or Sportster. It replaces the stock manifold with one that has improved flow characteristics as well as a lower installed height, giving additional clearance for the installation of larger gas tanks. While it's designed primarily for models from 1990 and up, it can be fitted to earlier motorcycles.

When installing a Mikuni on an Evo motor, a crankcase breather kit must be installed to allow the engine crankcase to vent. Custom Chrome just happens to sell the required parts to hook up the breather.

Another way to go in the fuel mixing business is to modify the stock constant velocity (CV)-type Keihin carb that comes on all Big Twin Harleys after 1988. One hour's work and a Power Tube Kit from Yost Performance Products (PO Box 33408, Coon Rapids, MN 55433) will transform the stock carb into a high-performance item through better fuel atomization and flow regulation. The kit was installed on a stock engine and the carb was rejetted for lower restriction mufflers at the same time. The bike was then run on a Dynojet Model 100 Dyno under various operating conditions. With the Power Tube installed, the engine showed an uncorrected horsepower gain of two to four horsepower over the stock engine. What didn't show on the dyno chart was the increase in smoothness during day-to-day operation. The kit comes with a new emulsion tube, flat washer, and two drill bits for installation. This kit can also be installed on the S&S carb, although Yost doesn't recommend running the Power Tube on any carb with a 0.100 or larger main jet.

An increased flow petcock is sometimes necessary to move enough fuel to the carb under high-speed operations. Pingel Enterprises Inc. (2076 C 11th Ave., Adams, WI 53910) manufactures high-flow petcocks specially designed for use with S&S and other aftermarket carbs. They also manufacture inline fuel filters, both 1-1/2in and 3in long, to fit most every application. Given what passes for gasoline today, I would make the installation of a fuel filter a high priority. After four to five thousand miles of riding with the filter installed, open it up and see what interesting and mysterious crud has collected on the element. You sure don't want that gunk running through all those small bleed holes in your fine new carb!

Air Filtration

Some more thoughts on air filters:

No matter what type of induction system you use on your engine, it must have a supply of clean air, unless you want to take it apart every few thousand miles to replace rings and other worn parts. The guys you see running velocity stacks on their dragsters open up the engine or wear out their parts so fast that airborne contaminants just aren't a problem. Some of the top fuel guys get to take their engines apart almost every run and replace just about everything that moves. So dirty air is way down their list of worries.

The dragracers are looking for every .0009hp available; that's why you see velocity stacks on their engines instead of air filters. But I don't think too many street/bracket racers could tell the difference between the performance with a velocity stack or an air filter. The stack sure makes the bike look fast, but looks don't get you to the timing lights first. Most of your miles will be spent on the street, and you want the engine to live as long as possible.

Besides, most new air cleaners, like the S&S, help direct the airflow to the carb mouth for a performance increase. Also, very few air cleaners will suck in your Levi's pants leg while shifting from third to no power at all, like a velocity stack can.

I sure felt funny when it happened to me in front of a large crowd at the old Baylands Racetrack in Fremont, CA. Lost the race, too! This sure cured me from velocity stacks in a hurry. Plus it was fitted to an old SU carb that had more flat spots than a parking lot, and it stuck out far enough to hang a camera bag on it.

SU carbs (for those of you who *must* know, SU = "Skinners Union") look real good, and when you can find someone who knows how to oil the dashpot and set needle jet height properly, they work fairly good. One big problem: they do tend to stick out a ways past your knee. With a velocity stack

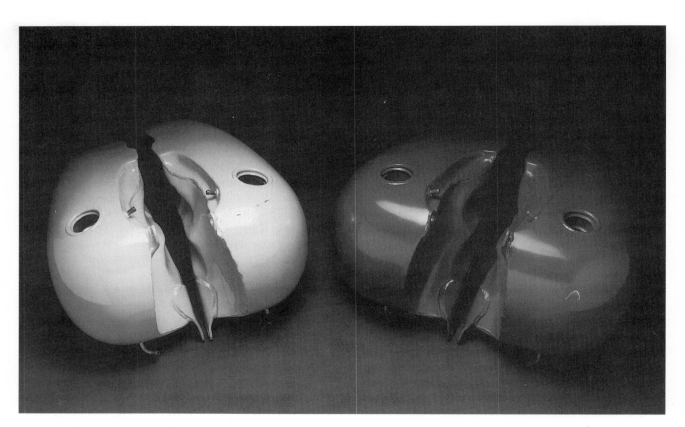

More gas flow uses up what's in the tank faster. Bigger, five-gallon tanks and mounting equipment are available from CCI. There are places in this country where an extra gallon or two will give a secure feeling when touring on a big-inch bike. *Custom Chrome*

on the end, if the bike falls over, the engine won't touch the pavement (how *do* you think I know?). But there are better ways to mix air today, so I don't recommend using a SU on anything except an old Jaguar.

Selecting a carb for street work is sometimes much harder than coming up with one strictly for racing. Usually, under racing conditions, the carb is all the way open or real close to it (well, maybe I back off a little bit now and then, but it's not 'cause of nerves or anything—oh no!). When a carb is wide open and the engine is turning over 4000rpm, maximum airflow is the primary consideration. A large carb will give better high-speed mixing under high rpm conditions, while if the revs drop off below 3000rpm, it may sputter and talk back to you until the airflow increases. This hurts low-speed throttle response.

A carb too small for a given displacement will give good response down low, but will limit power at max revs. For a motor that primarily lives on the street, the power band usually has to extend from 2000 to 6000rpm. Flat spots need to be eliminated and response has to be rapid. The higher the airflow through the carb, the quicker the throttle response, other factors not being considered at this time. Cylinder head design, cam, and exhaust back-pressure can influence airflow and response. Trick heads and wild cams are out of the province of a stage one engine, so we will just stick to the basic improvements for a stock displacement engine, with a small digression into mild camshafts.

Camshaft

One area where a large performance gain is possible is in cam modifications on a fairly stock, pollution-controlled engine. Because of that state's emissions laws, the newer California Big Twins come with a cam whose lift, overlap, and duration are so mild that it might as well have roller bearing lobes for all the affect they have on the valves.

In order to comply with the more stringent California emissions regulations, Harley had to design a different Big Twin intake system and camshaft for that state alone. The California-only cam has very mild lift and almost no overlap. This makes for a smog-legal engine, but a *slow* smog-legal engine. Don't be surprised if the California standards creep into the rest of the forty-nine states fairly soon. Emissions laws aren't going to get any looser in the near future, as far as I know.

Airflow into the cylinder is directly controlled by the distance the valve lifts off its seat. Theoretically, the higher a valve lifts, the greater the airflow. Other factors aside, higher valve lift, the rate at which the valve lifts and the time the valve is open, all con-

Here's a good reason to run an air cleaner. The gunk on the inside of the cover is a result of backfiring and carb spit-back. A little breather oil is thrown in for good measure. This air cleaner has been on the bike less than 2,000 miles.

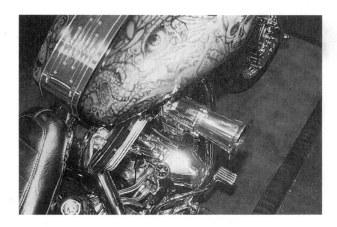

Not much knee-room with a straight stack. This one's where it belongs—on a show bike, not on the street.

tribute to horsepower. The stock lift for an Evo motor is 0.495 for a 1988–1991 model and 0.472 for other years. For an example of an aftermarket cam with increased lift, Sifton Motorcycle Products (800-227-1962) offers a replacement cam, the 143-EV Interstate, with a total valve lift of 0.500. This cam gives a major improvement in the low and mid range while offering adequate performance on the top end. For those of you who like to twist the throttle and taste the torque at the low end of the rpm range, this cam

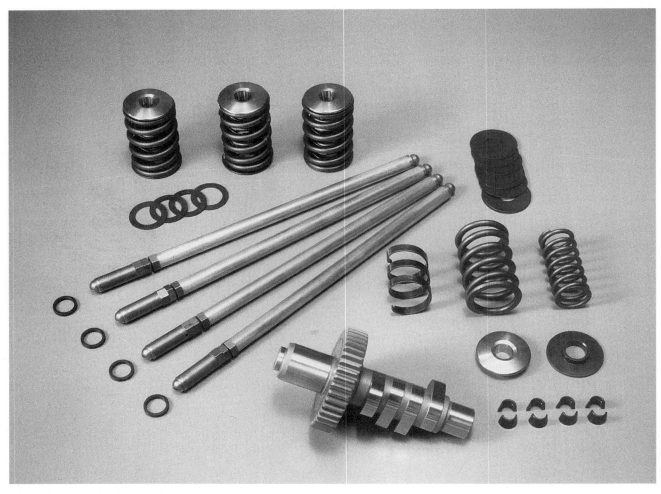

A typical Evo cam kit from S&S showing titanium spring collars, shims, and the HL2T adapters to convert hydraulic lifters to semi-solids. This clearly shows the third, flat-wire valve spring used to control harmonics. One cam pretty much looks like another, so you must read the spec sheet to see which way to go when contemplating a cam change. *S&S*

will greatly outperform the stock cam. Stock springs can be used along with stock lifters and pushrods. The cam works through 2000 to 5700rpm, so it would be a good choice for a stage one engine.

Valve Timing

Overlap is the time, measured in degrees of crankshaft rotation, that the intake and exhaust valves are open at the same time. This occurs as the piston approaches top dead center (TDC). The intake valve is just being lifted off its seat and the exhaust valve is on its way to being closed. The amount of overlap is a major factor in how much power the engine produces. When the last of the exhaust flows out the cylinder after combustion, the moving gasses can help suck in fresh fuel-air mixture if the intake valve is partially open at the same time. If the bike is fitted with an exhaust system that matches the cam, the flow of exhaust from the cylinder head through the pipe and out the muffler will create a partial low-pressure area behind it that will help pull in the fresh mixture, which will, in turn, increase the amount of fuel-air mixture in the cylinder, raising volumetric efficiency over a similar engine equipped with a cam of shorter (fewer degrees of rotation) duration.

If your cam has a lot of overlap, low rpm performance can be degraded. Exhaust reversion back into the cylinder can cause a loss of fresh fuel charge by pulsing back into the intake manifold and carb. You can actually see and feel the intake charge spitting back out of the carb when the rpm is down. An unfiltered carburetor will allow the back spit to leave the engine and gather on the first available object—your pants leg, for instance. Besides producing a very cold feeling as the gas evaporates, this can be a big fire hazard if allowed to accumulate. Here's another reason to have a good air cleaner installed. As the rpms rise, the airflow increases to the point where all the charge flows into the engine. The benefits of overlap can only be maximized with a tuned exhaust system, so a well-tuned exhaust system should always accompany a cam change.

The amount of crankshaft rotation degrees that an intake or exhaust valve is off its seat, either opening or closing, is the duration. The greater number of degrees of duration, the longer the valve is open. Increased duration can increase engine power

The cam goes in behind the points cover. Looking down through the lifter galley, you can clearly see the lobes. At this point, a dial indicator should be mounted on the engine and the cam lift checked.

only if the engine's carburetion can get the mixture in the cylinder and the exhaust can move it out. Opening up cam duration will move the power peak to a higher rpm, with the low end dropping off. As in all phases of engine modification, gaining on one end usually results in losing on the other. Again, think about what you want to do before buying a cam.

Evo engines sold in California have about 178 degrees of duration on both intake and exhaust. 49-state engines have between 208 to 222 degrees on the intake and 202 to 236 on the exhaust side. What and where depends on year of engine. Shovels have split duration on the intakes, with the front cam lobe at 220 degrees and the rear lobe at 232 degrees. Both exhaust cam lobs have the same duration—244 degrees.

When speaking of Evo motors, any duration in the 240 degree area is considered mild. Up to 265 degrees is moderate; anything higher is extreme. A Shovel needs about 10 more degrees duration than an Evo for the same category of cam because the ports on a Shovel flow at a lower velocity.

Rather than trying to explain the entire theory of cam dynamics—a subject for another book—we'll just cover a few cams that would work on a stage one engine.

Already mentioned is the Sifton 143-EV cam for Evos. This cam has 34 degrees of overlap, 235 degrees duration on the intake, and 240 degrees on the exhaust. The 144-EV cam has 0.480" valve lift with 49 degrees of overlap. Duration is 253 degrees intake and 258 degrees exhaust. You can see by the specs that the 144-EV is working into the "moderate" range as far as duration. The 141-EV cam gives a power boost throughout the range, with most of the increase being in the higher revs. This cam isn't really for a stage one engine because it needs higher valve spring pressure, free exhaust, performance carb and different, nonrestrictive, ignition module to let the engine turn to 6250rpm and beyond (how far beyond is up to you, but without the rest of the engine go-fast parts installed, I'd keep it below 6500rpm, or be prepared to own a lot of broken parts). The single biggest problem with installing this cam on a stage one engine is the need to notch the tops of the pistons to ensure that the valves have the proper clearance. This goes beyond the scope of the basic stage one premise of minor or bolt-on work, even though it's required for the RevTech installation.

The reason we get into the additional work of installing different cams at this point is that the right cam can really wake up an engine and the California engine might as well have sleeping sickness for all the performance the stock cam produces.

S&S has a #502 cam that's a bolt-on for the Evo. It has 248 degrees intake, 254 exhaust, and 0.500 lift. Spring-bind isn't a problem, and the cam will run with factory hydraulic lifters or a set of solids. High-performance Evos with juice lifters can benefit from using an S&S HL2T Hydraulic Lifter Limited Travel Kit. This kit enables the owner to rev his engine higher without the fear of lifter collapse and the resulting poor performance and possible valvetrain damage. If a hydraulic lifter pumps down (i.e.: oil flows out of it) during a run, you may find yourself with a very loud Harley putting out about the same power as a Maytag washer. Only in this case you *will* need a repairman.

One frequently made mistake in selecting a cam for the street is the "Why use a .357, when a .44

Magnum is available?" method of picking out a cam. Too radical of a cam on a street motor will give you real nice power from 4000 to 7000rpm—say between 80 and 120mph on your FXRS in fifth gear. Might be a smidgen much for riding around town, what with all the spitting and lurching below 65, but it certainly would add a new dimension to the Sunday ride with the guys. They could either watch you blow and snort while you try to run at freeway speeds, or come see you in the slammer for running 90 in a 55 zone!

Sparks

Unless you change your ignition system to something like an MSD (1490 Henry Brennan Dr., El Paso, Texas 79936) MC1 High Performance Ignition, you'll be stuck with the stock redline of 5250rpm: not a lot of use with a cam that doesn't come on until 4000 and fades at 7500. The MC1 comes with a rev control feature that's adjustable to any limit up to 12000rpm. If you think you need more than that for your Evo, drop me a line and let me know how it runs between oh, say 8000 and 11500—OK?

While we are belaboring the ignition point, remember, your engine is only as good as the ignition that fires it. If your equipment can't make sparks up where the power happens, then you won't be getting anywhere near the full potential out of the motor. Along with MSD's box of sparks, consider changing the coil and plug wires. Their new coil will produce a spark that could jump-start the Bride of Frankenstein. Coupled with a set of MSD's 8mm plug wires, the ignition can fire just about anything that will pour faster than 90-weight and burn. You can buy pre-cut wiring assemblies for any H-D from 1982 on from the same source as the rest of the ignition parts, and the wires come with a five-year warranty against end terminal pull-off. In my fumble-fingers case, that sounds like a great idea. I'm not saying that my mechanical skills are in any way lacking, but it's been said by others that I could break an anvil in a sandbox and lose two of the pieces. I have pulled my share of terminals off spark plug wires in the past—usually five minutes before the first practice session. The idea of terminals that won't depart when the wires are removed works for me.

When making any cam change, or any internal engine parts change for that matter, you must check all clearances very carefully prior to putting the spurs to the engine. After installing the new parts, turn the engine through slowly, watching for any interference anywhere. Pull the plugs to make it easier to rotate the engine. If you have no other way to spin it over, put the transmission in third gear and slowly walk the bike for-

Shovelheads and Panheads use a slightly different spring than an Evo. Overall height is different. *S&S*

ward while listening and watching for anything out of the ordinary. Also, when it comes to fitting aftermarket parts from a reputable supplier, remember Murphy's first law of assembly: "If it's right, it's easy." Nothing should need a heavy blunt object to "help" assemble it. Companies like S&S, Sifton, Drag Specialties, and others have very concise instruction packets with their parts. Read the instructions before you pick up a tool. I know you have better mechanical skills than an Indy crew chief, but read the paperwork first. You'll be surprised what you might learn.

Exhaust System

Now that the mixture is in the engine, and the ignition system has a way to ignite it, it's time to figure out how to get it out of the engine in the most efficient manner. Exhaust pipes are one of the first things a proud new owner changes on his or her H-D. Usually the factory shorty duals find a new home in the circular storage can within the initial 1,000 miles of operation. Next, a pair of aftermarket pipes, claimed to increase HP by 15% and look good while doing it are bolted to the engine without any other modification. Sometimes the motor only drops about 5hp while the noise level jumps 150%. Just installing good-looking pipes isn't the performance answer.

Moving the exhaust gasses out of the cylinder in the most efficient manner takes more than bolting on a set of pipes that show well. They have to perform well, too. Due to noise regulations, Harley-Davidson has had to design a very restrictive exhaust system to ensure quiet operation on all its new street bikes. The famous Harley sound is still there; however, it's a real *quiet* famous Harley sound. They don't do much for top-end power either, and a change to a set of free-flow pipes should be included in the planned refit.

Mufflers control noise, measured in decibels (dBa), by absorbing sound waves with a sound-deadening material. Fiberglass or a similar substance is used to hold the noise down to an acceptable level. This works well until the fiberglass burns out and the dBa climbs back up . Modern systems use a material similar to fiberglass, but one that has a much higher resistance to heat and lasts much longer.

Another method of noise control is to run the exhaust through a tube with its center blocked and a series of small holes around its exterior or with an insert that has an opening smaller than the pipe's inside diameter to restrict the flow. One of the methods used in the early 1960s to (slightly) control exhaust noise on straight-pipe, four-stroke dirt bikes

was to install a device called a "Snuff-or-Not." This was nothing more than a thick washer, slightly smaller in diameter than the inside of the pipe, attached to a spring-loaded shaft that was installed through the pipe. The washer could be turned parallel to the pipe for maximum noise or swung perpendicular, for a quieting effect. Although this sounds like a crude approach to silencing, it worked fairly well. There was a considerable noise drop when the washer was turned so that the exhaust had to flow through the small hole or around the edge of the washer. This method, without the swivel capabilities, is used in the same manner on the steel baffles installed in some aftermarket pipes.

A third method of reducing sound is by reflecting the sound waves back towards the muffler inlet. Mufflers are usually made of sheet metal rolled to shape. Most modern ones use a combination of noise reduction methods to not only cut down noise but also to give it a more pleasing quality while keeping back pressure to acceptable limits.

We're in the process of fabricating a top engine mount. The dual coils are mounted in a custom bracket. We helped pay the polisher's son's way through college with this engine. It won't go any faster, but it sure looks purdy sitting still.

In a two-into-one system where both pipes meet in a single muffler, such as a SuperTrapp (916-372-5000) or a Rich Products' (510-234-7547) Thunderheader, the diameter of the muffler should equal the diameter of the two entering pipes to keep the restriction in the system to a minimum.

Don Rich of Rich Products states that his Thunderheader exhaust system will enable the bike to get off the line a little faster, perform better through the mid range, and add more top-end power. Sounds good; how does it work?

Well, according to Rich, when an exhaust valve opens, the gasses head down the pipe at high velocity, creating a pressure wave that expands after exiting the muffler. This sets up an opposite wave heading back up from the end of the muffler towards the engine. When the reverse wave hits the open exhaust valve, it will slow down the flow of gas, causing some burnt gas to flow back into the cylinder. The wave can even move up through the open intake valve during overlap all the way to the carburetor, causing poor throttle response and a loss in power. This "reversion" can cause a mist of fuel vapor at the mouth of a carb while running at low rpm with a cam that has a large amount of overlap. This is one good reason to have an air cleaner instead of your pants leg in front of the carb. Helps keep insurance claims for fire damage down to a reasonable level.

A reverse cone muffler will dampen the negative wave, increasing horsepower (the idea being to have a lower-pressure area right at the exhaust valve when it begins to open). This will help scavenge the exhaust gasses and aid the intake charge in filling the cylinder. If both pipes are run into a collector, one pipe will help the other flow by reducing the pressure as the gas exits the first pipe. This will improve the scavenging effect of both pipes.

The length of the header pipes will determine at what rpm the scavenging effect will work for maximum power. In general, a long pipe will work better at low rpm, due to the slower power pulses, while a shorter pipe works better at high rpm, when the pulses are closer together. It's rather hard to change pipe lengths as rpm changes, so most systems are tuned for a particular power range. Usually, on a street bike, the headers are tuned for the middle 2000rpm of the power band. When setting up a bike to run at El Mirage Dry lakes, where weight isn't a penalty and the engine can make use of a long, tapered pipe with a reverse cone megaphone at the end, the pipe will be tuned to make maximum power above 3800rpm. At the drags, short, lightweight pipes will make good power above 4000rpm, where

the engine spends most of its time, while cutting it down low where it doesn't matter.

Rich Products has designed an exhaust system that minimizes and redirects the negative wave effect. They have run over 1,500 dyno tests on many different designs of pipes and mufflers, coming up with their Thunderheader exhaust system.

The exhaust system is comprised of an internal flow director (similar to a baffle) moving the exhaust gasses into a diffuser—a second reverse cone welded into place over an inner, similar, reverse taper cone. The diffuser traps the negative, reverse wave, venting it to the atmosphere. This creates a low-pressure area in the ex-

Behind this riveted-on cover is the ignition pickup. To change any timing, the rivets have to be drilled out to remove the cover, then riveted back on when the timing's set and it's replaced.

haust that works something like a two-stroke's expansion chamber, cutting about 25% of the reverse wave.

An anti-reversion tube can help reduce the wave traveling back to the exhaust valve. This is a smaller-diameter tube, usually one to three inches long, installed at the flange, next to the head. It's inserted inside the header pipe and acts as a check valve, stopping the reverse wave before it can get back inside the head. This allows the use of a larger-diameter head pipe for high-end performance, while negating some of the torque loss at lower rpm.

Sometimes the reversion tube is built into a chamber located on the header pipe. It can be set up anywhere on the header to allow for outside clearance where the flange bolts to the head. Custom Chrome has their AR II 1 3/4" Tapered Staggered Duals for modified Shovels and Evo motors with this feature. These pipes use the anti-reversion chamber on a set of

40-inch-long pipes with tapered or "bologna" style muffler bodies. They retain good mid-range power by using the chambers but still have lots of top-end available for modified motors.

These pipes won't reach their maximum potential on a stock Evo motor, especially a California special. According to a dyno test done by *American Rider* in their Winter 1994 issue, simply changing the pipes on a stock California bike is good only for a one or two horsepower gain at 4100 to 4500rpm. In some cases, the actual power recorded is less than the stock system's. *American Rider* only saw 42.6hp from the stock motor on their chassis dyno, so any performance loss isn't welcome. When mounted on a 49-state bike, you might see a four

to five horsepower gain, but some of the systems tested were good for a lot of noise with no significant power gain. The SuperTrapp two-into-one was the only system that made more power than the stock pipes. This system is constructed along the above-mentioned collector/common plenum type of design and works well, even though it's rather hard to get a collector to work with an unevenly firing V-twin, as opposed to a multiple-cylinder engine, where the firing pulses are more evenly spaced.

Ignition System

Intake modifications, cam changes, and hot pipes won't do much for an Evo motor if the spark

Rich Products makes a two-into-one set of pipes called "Thunderheaders." This set is pulling gasses out of a four-valve head mounted on a 96-inch motor. Looks almost stock, doesn't it? *Rich Products*

Here's a Thunderheader on a sport tourer—my choice for a long way to go and hours to spend. *Rich Products*

won't ignite the mixture. The stock Big Twin ignition system uses the inductive method to produce sparks. After 1979, all engines used an electronic sensor in place of the points for firing the coil and a PROM (programmable read only memory) chip that controls the ignition timing. This factory ignition has a few performance-related drawbacks, as it is set for emissions control more than maximum power. It also has a built-in rev limiter that shuts everything down at 5250rpm for reliability. The stock bike doesn't make much power above 5000rpm anyway, so higher revs are mostly an exercise in futility.

A modified Evo motor can take advantage of an aftermarket ignition system containing a higher rev limiter and better spark curve. All OEM ignitions on Big Twins are set up to fire both plugs at the same time, mainly because such a system is cheaper to manufacture. This doesn't make for the smoothest-running engine at low rpm, but H-D has made it work for many years. Having both plugs fire at the same time can cause the incoming mixture on the rear cylinder to partially ignite before it's due to fire. This contributes to the Harley's characteristically lumpy idle, backfiring if the engine is too cold or running lean. The sooner the rear intake valve opens, like when a radical cam with a lot of duration and overlap is installed, the more likely the engine is to spit back.

Single-fire ignition systems that fire one plug at a time make for easier starting and a hotter spark over the entire rpm range. Carb backfires tend to go away and the engine will pull better below 2500rpm. Most of the time, my engine is running between 2000 and 3500rpm, and some of the roughness I thought was related to lean running went away when a single-fire system was installed. Now I can run the engine smoothly below 1800rpm, whereas before it didn't want to do much below 2200—a nice 400rpm gain in useful range.

A single-fire ignition requires two separate coils to operate instead of one. Custom Chrome and others offer a mounting bracket that allows the coils to be mounted easily in place of the stock setup. They also market their RevTech dual-lead coil for single-fire systems. This eliminates the need for two coils and the mounting problems that you sometimes run into when looking for a place on a frame to hang parts.

The stock Harley V-Fire electronic ignition's coil produces about 24,000 volts—sufficient to run a stock motor, but not really enough zap for anything with large horsepower. Most of the time, if an ignition system doesn't match the performance of the rest of the motor, nothing catastrophic happens—the motor just flattens out and quits making power.

If you're going to turn the engine much above 4500rpm with a reasonable expectation of power production, the stock ignition has to be modified or replaced. The stock coil can be replaced with a high output, 30,000+ volt coil giving more spark within the stock rev range while using the rest of the factory components. Economical, yes, although not necessarily the way to go on an engine built for racing. I personally vote for pulling the stock stuff and replacing it with something that makes a hotter spark farther up the rpm range.

Modern electronic ignitions use sensors and chips to fire the plugs at the most optimum time. The stock factory system uses a Hall-effect sensor mounted in place of the old breaker points to sense the position of the cam and crank. It consists of a permanent magnet that sits opposite a transistor extra-sensitive to magnetic fields. A cup with two windows on the rotor cuts the magnetic field, causing a signal to be sent to the microprocessor which switches the magnetic field on and off. The black box also determines when the spark should fire, depending on rpm and advance curve. As the engine revs rise, the spark must be delivered earlier before the piston reaches TDC to obtain maximum combustion efficiency.

The electronic processor also serves as a preset, non-adjustable rev limiter and a source for the tachometer signal. Harley also makes use of a vacuum operated electric switch (VOES) to retard ignition advance under high load conditions, helping to prevent detonation and possible mechanical damage. The switch is mounted near the top engine mount, with a vacuum hose and two wires running from it to the ignition module. Disconnecting this switch can make for smoother running, provided detonation doesn't become a problem. With a heavy touring bike and what passes for gasoline today , bypassing any control that keeps the engine from pinging probably isn't a good idea on a bike used principally on the road. However, if the fuel used has a high enough octane rating (100 or better) the switch can be eliminated. Should the familiar rattling return, the switch will have to be reconnected or you will have to learn how to drive around the detonation.

The H-D electronic ignition sensor is factory-set and -sealed under a pop-riveted cover on the engine's right side in the cam gear case. All the electronics provide much more accurate timing and, unlike a points and condenser ignition, should never need adjustment.

In the past, some riders opted to change their systems over to the older "points" style, feeling that they could then set their own timing. Chevrolet six-cylinder breaker points would bolt right into the engine, providing better performance than the stock H-D parts. But going back to points for performance today is like switching to coal for heat. Sure it will work, but the disadvantages of mechanical spark control far outweigh any imagined gains. All you get with points is more moving parts, less reliability, and the possibility of adjusting them so that the engine hardly runs.

MSD Ignition (1490 Henry Brennan Dr., El Paso, TX 79936) builds a multiple-spark-discharge motorcycle ignition that provides easier starting, less plug fouling, and quicker engine response. Where the stock ignition only provides one spark during every firing of the plug, MSD's system will produce a shower of sparks over the same time-frame. This will ensure complete ignition of the air-fuel mixture in the cylinder.

There is more to ignition systems than just having a high-output coil voltage. Spark duration and the amperage driving that spark are the primary, important factors. Having a coil capable of putting out 60,000 volts under a no-load situation in a controlled environment does no good if, under compression, it lacks the energy to fire the mixture. High-output voltage figures are popular to use in reference to ignition systems mostly because of the old theory: "If some's good, more's gotta be better."

From this angle, you can see the reverse cone, diffuser, and vent used to keep reversion to a minimum. The vent helps channel incoming air back to the atmosphere to limit its effect on flow. *Rich Products*

MSD's MC1 motorcycle ignition will operate reliably up to 12000rpm in some applications—a figure that is slightly beyond the capability of Harley's V-Twin, no matter how long you hold the throttle open. When used in conjunction with the company's MC-Blaster 40KV (40,000 volt) coil, it will provide smooth, reliable ignition even with ultra-high-compression engines. The MC1 incorporates a "Soft Touch" rev control to keep the engine from launching itself if a shift is missed. There is an air-shifter ignition kill feature built into it that allows the sparks to be cut off momentarily to unload the transmission, allowing air pressure to pick up the next gear. It also comes with a tach terminal to facilitate the use of an electric tach.

Custom Chrome has a rev limiter designed to operate with all types of inductive electronic ignitions as found on H-Ds. It can be set to any rpm range that an Evo motor can reach, but it can't be used with aftermarket capacitive discharge (CD) spark boxes.

Custom Chrome also makes a two-stage limiter for racing. It uses a clutch lever with an internal switch to set one limit when the clutch is engaged and another when it's disengaged, so that adrenaline doesn't overpower the engine at the starting line.

Accel (PO Box 142, Branford, CT 06405) makes a limit control module incorporating a signal shunt to control engine speed between 1900 and 8100rpm . It can be preset for any engine speed in between and easily adjusted to a different level.

When changing the ignition system, don't forget to install new high-voltage spark plug wires. Not only do they come in nifty colors, but also they keep the sparks traveling down to the plugs where they belong instead of cross-firing between the wires. If the insulation on the wires breaks down, or if the wires are closer than 1/2 inch, one wire can induce a voltage in the other, causing the other plug to fire. This puts you back in the same place as the factory twin-fire stock system, negating all the benefits of the new ignition.

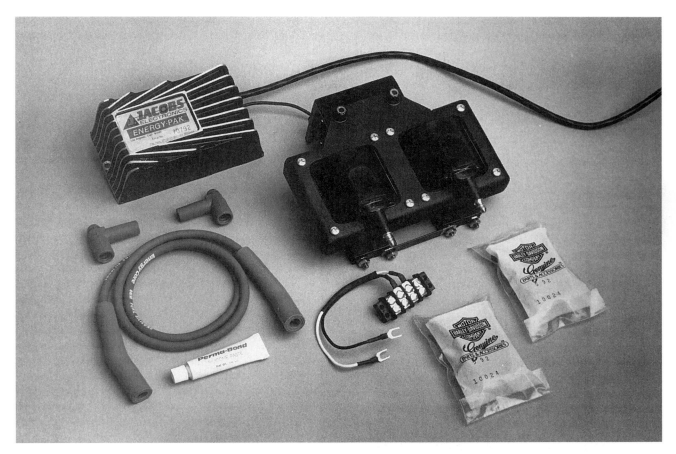

Jacobs Electronics has a complete, single-fire "Energy Pack" ignition system for Harleys. It's a bolt-on affair, done in less than two hours. Be sure to use the silicon paste for a proper electrical bond. *Jacobs Electronics*

MSD offers a set of helical-wound, solid conductor wires for all Harleys. These wires have their conductor wound around an inner fiberglass core, creating a radio frequency (RF) choke. This feature prevents the high voltage from creating problems with radios, which isn't much of a concern on a race bike; it also ensures that the onboard electronics won't do anything weird like quit firing at odd times. As mentioned, they also come with a five-year warrantee against people like me leaving the boot and terminal on the plug when removing the wire.

Jacobs Electronics (800-627-8800) is a company usually associated with cars, RVs, and boats, but they have branched out into the motorcycle ignition business. They guarantee their "Energy Team" ignition system will upgrade your Harley to higher performance levels than any other system. The brains behind the brawn is their "Energy Pack" microprocessor which tailors each spark for each cylinder in your engine. The Energy Pack processor interprets feedback from the spark plugs and adjusts the black box to generate the optimum spark.

With each spark firing as needed, Energy Pack will eliminate misfires, rear-plug fouling, rough idling, and hard starts. The voltage to the plugs is computer-controlled from 12,000 volts to a high of 60,000 volts, using computer feedback to determine the spark intensity required to fire the mixture. This way, the processor can detect a fouled plug and up the spark enough to zap through the gunk.

Jacobs states that their system will produce up to 2,550 watts peak spark wattage at the plug while the current through the transistor or points is held to .056 amps. This is below most single-fire systems that run around 0.50 amp draw and the OEM unit pulling 3.50 amps .

The company recommends that all components be installed as a kit. This consists of the processor, two 40,000 volt coils, metal core ignition wires, and a complete set of instructions. Everything plugs in directly; no cutting of wires or changing connectors.

The Energy Pack was tested by *Hot Bike* in their June 1992 issue. Buck Lovell, the editor, said, "It'll blow your b_ _ _s off!" Perhaps not the most professional analysis but Mr. Lovell succeeded in conveying his high regard for the system. Personally, I would rather see the Energy Pack make my scooter run better as opposed to disposing of certain parts of my anatomy to which I'm particularly attached .

Jacobs also has a number of tools and other products you'll find fairly useful when working on your bike. They have a set of plug-gapping pliers capable of setting gap from .025 to .085 while keeping the side electrode centered over the plug. Set the required gap, drop a plug into the recess, and squeeze the handle. It will adjust both long- and short-reach plugs.

While the plug is out of the head, you might want to index the side electrode before installation. This will allow you to install the plug with the electrode pointed away from the incoming fuel mixture, ensuring complete combustion. Jacobs has brass plug indexing washers to space the plug properly. Mark a line on the plug body with a felt pen on the side of the plug where the electrode is attached. Then use the washers to align the electrode so that the center electrode isn't shrouded. Jacobs includes thirty reusable washers of assorted size in the pack—more than enough to set both plugs.

Spark Plugs

First off, the most important tip about spark plugs in a performance Big Twin is to keep them fresh. It makes no sense to outlay a lot of money for cams, carbs, or pipes, just to let the performance suffer because the plugs aren't doing their job. A plug with a rounded electrode can take 25% more voltage to fire. Most of the new high-performance ignition systems discussed above can fire a plug through a tub of wheel-bearing grease, but there's no reason not to spend the money to ensure that the plugs are fresh. The automotive manufacturers have gotten their engines to run fairly well for 30,000 miles between plug changes, due

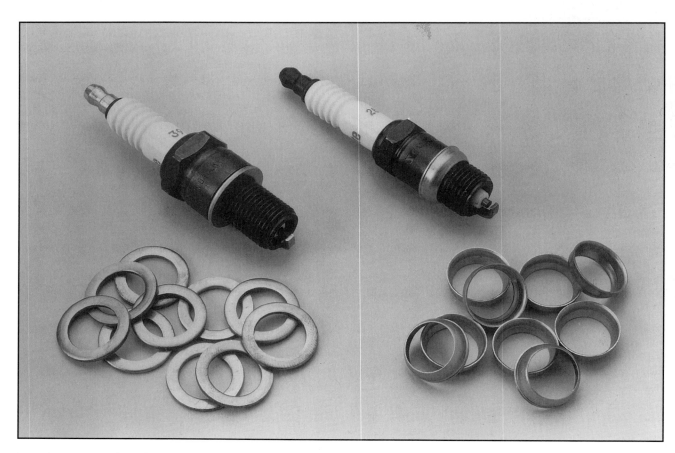

In order to properly index a spark plug, mark a line on the ceramic parallel to the side electrode. Use spacers to line up the plug so the electrode doesn't shroud flame propagation. Every little bit adds at the finish line. *Jacobs Electronics*

Jacobs also makes a plug-gapping tool to precisely set electrode gap without applying force to the side electrode. *Jacobs Electronics*

in the combustion chamber. The piston is starting to melt and will burn a hole through the top if the timing isn't backed down and/or the mixture fattened.

The mixture also needs to go rich if the plug looks like the ceramic is getting glazed. Neither electrode should turn color or have any rounded corners. At the bottom of the ceramic insulator there should be a brown ring of fuel. A cold plug can foul while a hot plug can cause pinging and lead to damage to the engine. Better to start on the fat side with cold plugs than to try to go lean and hot and fry an engine. No engine ever cooked off because of a fouled plug (I'm not talking about blown fuel motors that can go into low earth orbit for many interesting reasons, fouled plugs included!).

Timing

The ignition timing is preset at the factory and usually won't have to be adjusted until the engine is torn down. If for some reason you think the timing is off, it is relatively easy to check on a stock electronic system. The hardest part is to figure out how to rotate the engine on an electric-start-only bike. First, remove the timing plug located between the cylinders on the left side of the engine. Next, remove the front plug wire and install a plug with the electrode grounded to the engine. Turn on the ignition, then rotate the engine until the plug sparks. If you are holding an ungrounded plug when this happens, you won't have to guess when the plug fires. Check the timing inspection hole to see if the front cylinder timing mark appears in the center. If not, then the pop rivets holding the timing cover on the cam case will have to be drilled out before the timing can be adjusted. The sensor mounting plate can then be loosened and moved until the mark coincides with the spark.

Trying to push the bike forward without help while watching for the timing mark to come up is a good way to find out if you can dial 911 while wearing a 700lb iron suit. Better that you have someone with a lift capable of hoisting the rear wheel help out. As the timing on my bike hasn't changed enough to be noticed since 1986, I don't foresee that this procedure needs to take place very often.

The best way to time an engine is with it running. After setting the timing mark in the proper position, connect a timing light to either the battery or a 12 volt DC source. Today, most of the timing lights, like Jacob's "dial back to zero" light, work by induction. The timing is set by referencing the timing mark in the middle of the hole, with the degrees read off the dial. The cords plug into the base of the light for easy replacement if they get cut or frayed. The

to electronics and unleaded gas, and most people change them at least once each century or so, but this doesn't mean that you, hero race driver, should run them until they rust. I know some riders who change plugs before each race. And no, the old ones don't go back in the bottom of the tool box as "spares"—throw them away!

When you first start racing, or when running a new engine, you want to check the plugs after every practice or run. Learning how to read plugs doesn't require a long white beard, black robes, and a magic wand, but it does take a bit of knowledge to figure out what's going on at the electrode.

If the plug has spatters of aluminum on the ceramic or electrode, things are literally hotter than hell sensor needs to be clamped over the front plug, with the arrow pointing towards the plug.

Make sure the timing light wires aren't touching anything, put on some old clothes, and start the engine. Right, oil does spit out the hole. There are a couple of companies who make transparent plugs to go in the timing hole; however, I haven't seen them advertised lately—best to check with your local dealer.

Run the engine up to full advance, somewhere around 2000rpm, and look at the position of the timing mark in the hole. If it's at the back of the hole, the timing is advanced approximately five degrees. If it's at the front—five retarded. Again, adjust the sensor plate until the mark rides in the middle. Afterwards, go wash the oil off. Easy, huh?

Summary

Now that we've covered some of the methods, manufacturers, and parts used to improve the performance of a Big Twin, let's see how they go together.

All these combinations are based on a stock 1994 Big Twin weighing 775lbs with rider and three gallons of fuel. In the quarter mile, this bike should run between 13.8 to 14.4 around 92mph, depending on rider's ability and whether he rides like he makes the payments or like the ET is more important than money.

A dresser will be considerably slower, say in the 15 second bracket. Most touring riders won't be found crouched below the windshield firing off burnouts at a race track, so ET isn't as important as lower acceleration time in the higher gears and torque increase over the operating range. These engine changes will enable an 850lb tourer with rider aboard to cut the 50–80mph time by 3–5 seconds. This might not seem like much to you until you find yourself in the wrong lane, going uphill, watching a twin of the semi next to you approaching. Three seconds and twenty more MPH could become real important real quick.

One benefit that hasn't been mentioned very much is better mileage. Keep the throttle less than ful-

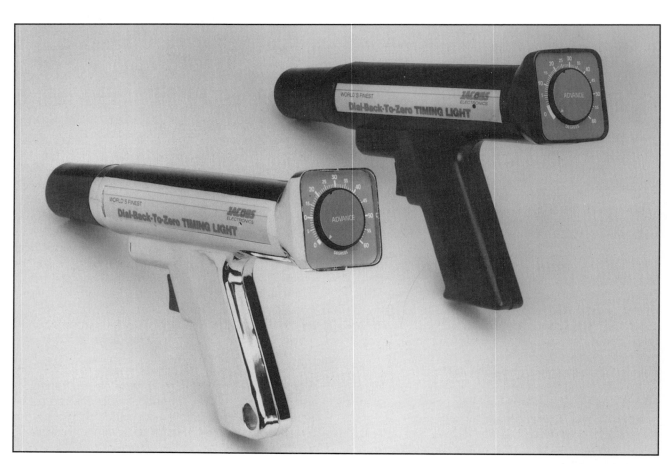

This type of timing light allows you to set the advance back to zero when setting timing. That way, timing is always set off the TDC mark. No more trying to figure where the mark is in the timing hole—works slick on any internal combustion engine. *Jacobs Electronics*

ly open, the bike will go farther on a tank of fuel. You'll also notice that it runs a lot smoother and crisper.

All performance mods will be considered as a package deal. You can gain a little by just installing different pipes or better breathing alone, but to really wake up the engine, all the changes shown in the packages should be done at once. Prices change so much that when a dollar figure is shown (rarely), it's only for comparison.

All modifications apply to the California screaming 39–41hp bike as well as to the 49-state Federal engine. Both engines' ignitions will be changed to allow them to turn 6200rpm or higher, taking advantage of better breathing without letting the motor wind to the point where it will encounter excess wear. Any rev limiters should be set for no more than 6250–6300rpm. because above that piston speeds get too high for the stock parts, with the end result that you are just thrashing the engine while standing a good chance of breaking something.

One last caution. I know you need someone to tell you how to ride like a fish needs a bicycle; however, when you first take your new, improved, faster bike out for its maiden voyage, things are going to happen much faster than before. You might want to find someplace other than the freeway at five PM for the first full-throttle run. I'd even recommend taking the bike to a racetrack first where you can spend your time figuring out what does who to where without watching for those black-and-white sports cars with whip antennas. It's much easier to work out bugs when you don't have to watch for the state racing team.

Package Specifications
Stage One Engine
(65–70hp)
Can be done for $800 without cam—
$1,200 with cam change (1993 dollars).

Kit #1
1. S&S Super B Carb
2. S&S Teardrop Air Cleaner
3. Crane Hydraulic Cam Part # 1–1101
4. Jacobs Part # 379126 Energy Team Ignition
5. SuperTrapp two-into-one

Kit # 2
1. Mikuni HS-40 Carb
2. K&N Air Filter Part #ML-092B
3. Competition Cams "V-Thunder" EVO-3020
4. MSD MC1 Ignition
5. White Bros. Porker Pipes w/ Medium Baffles

Kit # 3
1. CCI (Custom Chrome) RevTech Carb #58–155
2. CCI RevTech Accelerator Air Cleaner (comes with carb kit)
3. CCI RevTech #20 Cam
4. Accel Super System Ignition System
5. CCI AR II 1-3/4" Staggered Duals

Kit # 4
1. S&S Super E Carb Kit
2. S&S Big Twin Cam #502 or
3. Sifton #143-EV
4. MC Power Arc II Ignition
5. Drag Specialties Python II Pipes

These are but a few of the ways parts can be combined for a 20–25hp gain on a stock 80 inch bike. Other companies market products that can be substituted in building the stage one engine. Some are shown below.

Cams
Andrews EV 3, EV 13, EV 46
Bartels BP20, BP40
Crane 1–1000 (check piston clearance)
Sifton 140-EV, 145-EV

Coils
Andrews
Dyna
Exhaust
Bub Enterprises Bad Dogs
Carl's Speed Shop
Rich Products two-into-one
Kerker

Because every rider has a different idea as to what performance he/she wants to see out of his/her bike, any of these kits can be used as good starting points for pumping up a Big Twin. Any combination of carbs, cams, and pipes, with a good ignition system thrown in, will light up an Evo motor. Only by working with the combination of individual components will a particular rider be able to extract the most go from the engine.

If all work is done properly, if the carb is jetted to the right mixture and the bugs are worked out before you meet your riding buddies to go profiling, you should be able to let them observe the diminishing size of your taillight without a great deal of effort. Or, if you can refrain from massaging your ego, it might be possible to recoup some of the expense through a bet or two. I, personally, would go practice somewhere, like an industrial park on a Sunday morning, until I had the bike pretty well dialed in, then go look for sheep to shear. Be gracious—but hold the money!

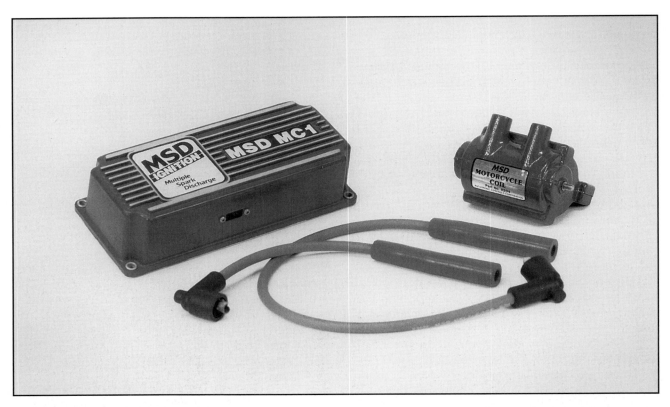

MSD's Motorcycle Ignition comes with an adjustable rev limiter and an air shifter ignition-cutoff feature. The MC1 comes with a tach output to mount an electronic tach. *MSD Corporation*

Accel's Mega-Fire ignition module can be set to one of four different timing curves, depending on what bike you ride and how you ride it. A longer wiring harness is available to facilitate mounting in remote locations. *Accel*

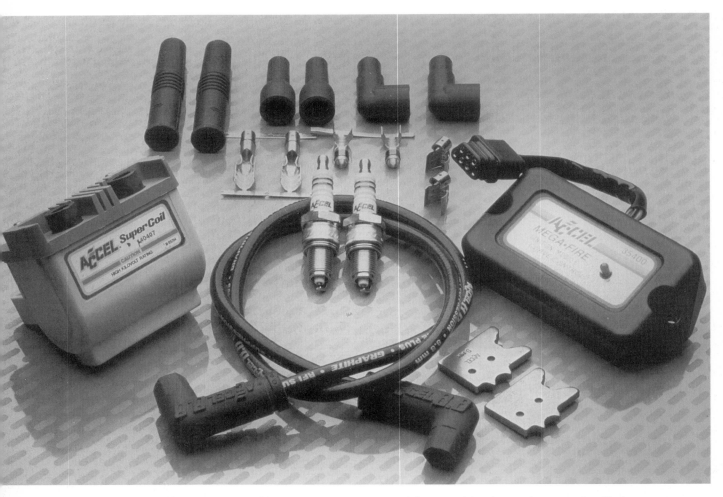

A complete, single-fire, programmable ignition system, down to coil, wires, and plugs, will replace the stock Harley dual-fire ignition. This will smooth out a rough idle caused by the stock system. It will also put out more zap for working with higher compression engines. *Accel*

Were I to take delivery of a new Tour Glide, the carb would find its way into circular storage and a fuel injection unit appear in its place. The Accel unit takes a little fitting to get it to work, but the improved performance is well worth any problems. Horsepower goes up by five, torque moves up 8lb-ft, and fuel mileage really jumps. The best part about EFI is starting problems, or the lack of said problems. Hot, cold, or anywhere in between, touch the button and the engine's running. Accel's unit is also set up to run nitrous oxide with little work. *Accel*

Chapter 3

Stage Two: Super Street

I first went drag racing back in 1977. One of my friends owned an early Doug Schwarma drag racing frame, stuffed full of an ex-GP Kawasaki 500cc H2 engine that didn't do much except set his right boot on fire from the exhaust. He managed to convince me that I should build a bike to go racing with him. This whole drag racing bit looked like something I'd like to get into, but my only bike at the time was an early Panhead FLH. With the wisdom of the young and foolish, I thought that I could turn my bike into something suitable for racing with a lot of work and money. Welllll, it didn't quite happen as I had planned. It took a lot more time and all my money to make either a slow drag bike or a fast anvil—depending on who was asking.

I took off everything not needed to make the bike run in a straight line. Front brakes? Didn't do much anyway—off they went. Headlight—not needed. Pull the front fender, it just adds weight.

Mayhaps not the most controlled approach to building a racer. I ended up with a lot of spare Harley parts on the ground and barely enough left on the bike to keep the engine turning—a very unprofessional approach to competition.

Then it was time to build a faster motor. I had once owned an English sports car, a Triumph TR-4 with a four-cylinder, 2500cc engine, equipped with a set of SU carbs. The car had lost an argument with a large tree late one night (actually, the entire car would fit in a four-by-five trailer after the wreck), and I had a box of spare parts lying around, including the recently rebuilt carbs. Using semi-twisted math, I figured that if two carbs made 2500ccs of Triumph engine work, then one carb with a larger main jet needle would make 1200ccs of Harley engine really fly.

I picked up a manifold for the SU from a guy who said he had only run it for a short time prior to going to something else. Right then the light should

Everything on this motor's new, from the nut on the compensating sprocket to the tabs under the primary case bolts. The primary chain adjuster can be seen bolted to the back primary case. Note the ring compressor that has just popped off the piston. Don't drive a cylinder head down with a hammer. If everything is well lubricated, the piston should slide down with a steady push.

have gone on but didn't. He let the whole kit go for less than half of what he had spent six months ago. I sure got a deal. I was ready to bolt it on and go racing.

Right!

Bolting on the SU was no problem; replacing the mufflers was no problem; getting the bike to run as well as it did when it was stock *was* the problem. Seems as though I had a ways to go before I got mixture and jetting to where the fuel spent most of its time going through the carb into the engine, instead of through the carb onto my pants leg. See, a

58

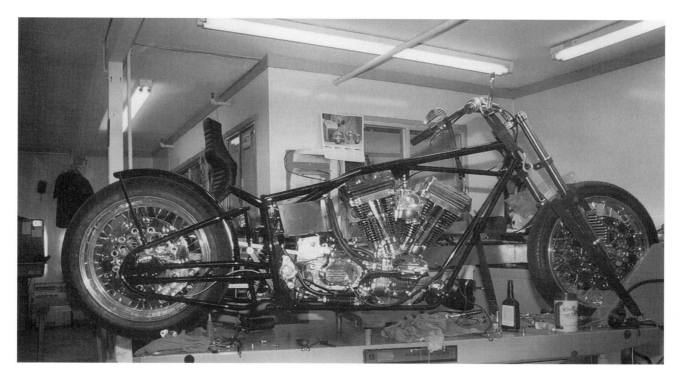

The hydraulic lift even gives you a place to set your coffee cup where you won't have to move to reach it. Some of the lifts are on wheels, enabling them to be rolled into any position. When you do this for a living, this becomes important. It's not easy to turn out a custom product from an uncomfortable position.

carb doesn't care which way the air flows through it. It's perfectly happy adding atomized fuel to the backfiring mixture as easily as to the stuff going into the engine. By the time I got the engine to run, the timing was so far out that it backfired a lot and didn't want to run too well. Of course, I had installed one of the velocity stacks off the old TR-4's race engine on the SU—no sissy air cleaner for me! So a lot of the fuel charge ended up on my Levi's right leg. Just getting faster by the minute!

With this fine setup, I was able to either bang my knee or set it afire just about every time I tried to ride that bike. Lucky for me, an older mechanic, wiser in the ways of fools and Harleys, took pity on me and showed me how to set up the motor so's it ran well enough to finish the quarter.

Now it was time to go race.

Before I go through any trials and tribulations, a question to all you riders who have never drag raced a bike: have you ever thought about what it's like to be the focus of attention for a grandstand's worth of spectators while you launch a large motorcycle off the line?

You're in line, about six bikes back from the lights. The guy in front of you fires his up—he's either warming it up or making some noise to cover the pounding of his heart. You figure you might as well do the same.

The first four racers burn out and go. Soon there's only two in front of you—better start thinking about how hard you're going to have to leave at the start to put some distance on the dude in the other lane.

The staging official points at you and then up to the burnout box—you're up! Ease the bike forward into the water. Bleach burnouts used to be the norm, but now it's only water on the asphalt. That's OK, water is slippery enough, thank you!

Both feet out behind you, toes touching the ground, ease the bike into the center of the wet pavement. Pull about 4000rpm and hold it. The last two racers in front of you are gone; you're facing a long empty stretch of rubber-streaked pavement.

The starter motions you up for your burnout.

Peg the throttle, drop the clutch!

The rear wheel disappears in a blur of smoke and steam. The front tire slowly moves forward, while the rear wheel tries to walk around you to the left. Back off the throttle a bit; the spinning tire grabs, kicking you 50 feet down the track before you can get shut down. Clutch in, fight the gearbox into neutral. Slowly walk the bike back behind the lights. Funny how quiet it gets—can't hear the bike next to you, the crowd, or

The cams are installed, the rocker boxes are bolted on, the polished cone cover is on, and the engine is ready to go in the frame. Sitting on the bench is the best place to degree-in the cam.

your own engine. If it wasn't for the tach, you'd have a hard time telling the engine was running.

Back up ten feet behind the lights. Toe it into first. Yank the throttle open, drop the clutch, light the rear tire, and stop two feet before the staging lights!

Throw a quick glance at your competitor—he's already staged. Good—let him wait! He needs to practice patience.

Keep the revs up. Ride the clutch enough to roll the bike into the staging area. The first yellow light turns on; roll another six inches and the second yellow jumps to life.

It's all going to happen real soon!

Watch the starting light tree, you're only going to get one big yellow and one green. You better have the clutch out before you even see a green, or you'll be on the line all by yourself.

Now, bring the revs up to 4500 and wait the longest 1-1/2 second in your life.

The yellow jumps out at you! Pin it! Drop the clutch! Just as the bike leaps forward you see the green light out of the corner of your eye—good start, no red light!

First's all done, grab second. Try to keep the rear wheel pointed in the same general direction the rest of the bike wants to go. That's it for second.

Shift! Feet up on the pegs. Now shift again. Hold it open. Don't look at the other guy; you've got your own race to run. Besides, what you going to do if he's pulling you—get out some oars and row?

Time for the last shift, don't let up. Through the lights, it's over! Let the power drop off, sit up on the bike and start feeding in the brakes. Who won? Who cares? Let's get this pig turned around on the return road and go do it again!

Stop for your time slip. You beat him by .015 second. Beat him, hell, after the start you never even saw him again—way too busy just trying to run your own race.

Sound like fun? Well, if you think this is a good way to spend a Sunday, and you want to run harder than all the other stockers with pipes, carbs, and cam jobs, all similar to yours, then it's time to think about building the stage two engine.

This time you are going to get a little more involved; open up the engine and see if you can't stir up some important horsepower. Get serious about building a 90hp+ bike, capable of turning in the high 11s to low 12s. Cut the lights at 110mph or better.

Motor outlay is going to run around $3,000 or so, depending on how deep you delve into the engine. Reliability should be close to a stock engine if some restraint is used with the throttle. That said, let's deal with reality. If you build a Big Twin capable of putting the hammer on Sportsters, Hondas, Ducatis, and the like, chances are you're going to use it. After all, you aren't building a bike with over twice the horsepower of a stock bike just to go on Poker Runs.

I didn't—I went racing!

I learned that a 100hp Harley is largely wasted on the street. It can't really be utilized on anything other than a drag race track or running for top end at El Mirage or Bonneville. Some people enjoy their speed fix a quarter mile at a time. I prefer to run for top end. Whatever route you take for racing, be prepared to do a lot more initial modification and future maintenance on the entire bike.

Heads

One of the most serious impediments to making horsepower in an Evo motor is the breathing. As said before, an engine is an air pump. The more air that can be pumped, the more power that can be developed. The air (air-fuel mixture) enters through the intake valve mounted in the head. On the front cylinder, it's located at the rear of the head, nearest the carb. The rear intake valve is mounted nearest the carb at the front of the rear cylinder.

The exhaust valves are located in the head, closest to the exhaust pipe outlet. Ideally, the valves

The exhaust ports are clean, but not polished. Many builders differ on how much polished ports help. This is what your engine should look like when being built—clean and freshly painted. Baked-on crud can be removed by a bead-blaster. Fiberglass beads won't hurt the parent metal, but will remove everything except the shadow.

in any engine would be sized so that all the air possible could flow through the engine with the least amount of interference. Due to engineering requirements and space considerations, this isn't possible to achieve on a narrow-angle V-twin engine and still make it fit within something resembling a frame. Incoming air must turn almost continually, from the time it enters the air cleaner until it is compressed by the piston. Then it has to start out an exhaust port, begin turning, and make its way to the atmosphere.

In the process of flowing through the head, the air-fuel mixture's speed will be slowed by any roughness encountered on the way to the combustion chamber. Areas where the valve seats are pressed into the head cause roughness. Valve seats are made of a different, tougher metal than the surrounding head. They are pressed into place using mass-production methods and tolerances. This usually results in a ridge where the seat and head meet, causing power-robbing turbulence. Even if the seat is cut so as to remove this ridge, after enough miles, the seat will wear enough to form another ridge, diminishing any flow advantage. Valve-to-seat contact areas need to be renewed more frequently in a racing engine. The seats must be ground smooth enough for the valve to touch all around its face. This is what's meant by the term "valve job."

There is more magic, mystery, and misinformation about heads and their modifications floating around the racing world than about practically any other part of a racing engine. Single plug, dual plug, bathtub chambers, stock pattern, two-valve, four-valve, modified stockers, or new heads completely—which way to go? How do you go about increasing airflow and efficiency and still stay legal in class?

If a tuner is going for maximum airflow with good heat transfer, he will shape the seat so that there is .060in contact area with an intake valve. The exhaust's contact width should be .010in wider, due to its hotter operation. The intake valve is partially cooled by the incoming mixture, but the exhaust valve doesn't have that advantage. Some exhaust valves have a hollow stem, filled with some low-boiling-point metal, like sodium, to help transfer heat away from the valve face. Exhaust valves can actually get so hot that they will turn cherry red. If not properly cooled, a valve can burn partially away, causing rough running and power loss.

To ensure long life, good aftermarket valve manufacturers, such as Manley (908-905-3366), produce their valves out of stainless steel. The stems are chrome-plated for wear resistance, the tips hardened for the same reason, and the underhead angle and radius is smoothed for maximum airflow. All Manley's valves, including their lower-priced "Street Master" series, are compatible with unleaded fuel.

Buy the best valves available. Saving $10 just to lose a valve 100 feet from the finish is a hard way to economize. All it takes is one valve to pull off its head to send you home with a lot of expensive parts in the bottom of the engine cases.

Good valves, like any other high-quality parts, aren't inexpensive. One set of two stainless intakes lists right at $69.70 (for Manley severe duty Evo 1.850in valves). The titanium version, 1.90in or larger, will set you back $260 and require larger seats cut in the head. For a "racing-only" engine, titanium valves are well worth the investment for their increased strength and lightness over stainless steel counterparts.

Manley has two types of valve guides: silicon-aluminum-bronze for the race track; and cast iron guides for the street. They recommend .0015–.0020in intake valves to guide clearance and .0020–.0025in exhaust valves to guide clearance when running on the street. Their Teflon/metal or all-Teflon oil seals should be installed on all street engines. These seals will keep oil from running down the valve stem into the combustion chamber and reduce deposits on the back side of the intake valve.

The intake port delivers the incoming mixture to the combustion chamber from the intake manifold, the amount of air roughly determining power. Port size and shape go a long way towards determining where and how an engine produces horsepower.

The stage two engine will entail purchasing a set of professionally ported heads or modifying yours for the best available flow. Usually, porting heads is better left to the people who do it for a living. Not that you, a hand grinder, and a lot of time can't produce heads that flow lots of cubic feet per minute (CFM); however, you should have on hand a number of heads to work with, as the chances of doing one wrong far, far outweigh the possibilities of doing one right. Now I know Evo heads are cheap and you are

a whiz at working cast-iron with a Dremel tool, *but—* you might give some thought to approaching a professional like Air Flow Research (AFR, 818-834-9010) to see about letting them do the heads before you screw them up.

AFR will do a basic port, polish, and valve job for $695, labor only. If you want the full-tilt-and-boogie racing setup, they will install larger valves, titanium retainers and locks, and do all the welding and machining for $1,500. $2,500 will get a set of STD Development (818-998-8226) aftermarket heads, along with an intake manifold—all work done—all hi-po parts installed.

Dan Umstead putting it on the ground. This is why we spend all that money and all those late nights. Lots of noise, wide-open throttle, and the wheel spinning— burnouts are almost as much fun as the actual racing. *Barnett/Auto Imagery*

Prices for some of AFR's other work are as follows:
1. Unleaded fuel conversion $175
(mostly Shovelheads)
2. Flow test and head calibration $150
3. Mill head deck $80
4. Valve job $85

Other services and estimates are available on request.

AFR's been building small-block Chevy heads for roundy-round racers running in the 2500 to 7500rpm, 497hp range for a number of years, so they know of what they speak.

Ken Sperling, the owner of AFR, took a Big Twin with his heads, an S&S carb, an aftermarket cam, and a set of pipes, out for a run one day, going 11.50 and 115mph in the process. Not bad for a guy who owns the company, as opposed to being paid to ride for it.

A lot of heads have been turned out with the intake and exhaust ports polished smoother than the front doorknob on a Victorian house of ill-repute. So far, just about everyone disagrees whether this really does any good for airflow or just makes the owner think he's got something special.

There is no doubt cleaning up the port runners will help some; however, having a mirror finish hasn't been proved to improve airflow. Leaving the surfaces coarse, said to improve atomization, has its share of defenders also.

If you compare flow bench rates from different manufacturers, find out if the flow readings are taken bare-head, intake manifold installed, or with the carb bolted up. Everything in front of a port will cause the

Look at the wrinkles on Dan's rear tire as it hooks up. In the bad old days, this much torque could actually rotate the rim inside the tire, making for a flat tire and a few anxious moments. *Barnett/Auto Imagery*

Ron Fringer, caught in a relatively quiet moment. The Shovel engine drives the trans from the left. The trans drives the rear wheel from the right. The final drive sprocket is supported by a large bearing to help keep things from shifting or bending. *Barnett*

CFM to be lower. A stock H-D head with 1.850 intake and 1.600 exhaust should flow 228cfm intake, 159cfm exhaust at .500 valve lift. An AFR port/polish job on the same head should bump the figures to 273/192 at the same lift. Going to a trick head with porting and polishing, 1.940 intake, 1.625 exhaust, expect to see 297/198 for flow.

Earlier Shovelheads have a few top-end idiosyncrasies of their own. One of the more common problems that plague the 1966–1984 80ci heads is in the exhaust pipe connection to the head. Harley, in its somewhat questionable wisdom, set up the exhaust port with just one stud to mount the head pipe flange to the head. This usually held the pipe fairly securely to the head—until you were 500 miles from home, sitting in the parking lot of a motel surrounded by a town whose 1,200 occupants didn't know what a Shovelhead was, to say nothing of a Grade 5 bolt that you needed to get past the worn-out threads in the head so that the pipe could be tightened back up at least enough to stop the exhaust from warming up your Levi's or spitting hot gasses onto your oil tank.

Should you wonder, I was in a small town in Nevada on a Fourth of July ride. I was so far from civilization that you had to be seriously lost for over half a day just to get to the city limits. My bike of choice was a 1982 FXRS with under 15,000 miles on the clock. My brother and I had left Silicon Valley, thirty miles south of San Francisco, on July 2nd to escape all the drunks, semi-drunks, and ordinary crazies that would descend upon the California freeways with the start of the four-day, 1989 Fourth of July weekend. We spent two days on the road, heading through the Yosemite Valley on our way to Lund, Nevada, population 1,578—not counting goats.

After we were nine or ten zip codes from home, we stopped for fuel and drinks in a small convenience store in the Sierra Nevadas of California. As soon as both the scooters and we ourselves had taken on a large quantity of necessary liquid fortifications, we lit the fires, planning on covering another 150 miles that day, heading for cooler parts of Nevada or at least an air-conditioned room. The ambient temperature in the shade was a balmy 102 degrees, and there wasn't a great deal shade at 70mph. It was the kind of heat that made you think of steel smelters and blast fur-

FOR THE HELP

Here's everything needed to install CCI's RevTech dual-plug heads. Various combinations of valves and springs can be specified, depending on what cam is run. *E. Chris Wisner/CCI*

naces. Traveling for any time without a helmet and long-sleeve shirt would ensure that burn ointment would feature heavily in the evening's entertainment.

As I rolled out of the store parking lot back towards the road, the bike made noises like a old Chevy Six with a bad muffler. I rolled right back to the side of the building, and, with the bike idling, removed my helmet for better hearing and revved the engine. It wasn't too hard to see that the noise was coming from the exhaust port/head pipe connection. Evidently, the wind and road noise had covered up the sound of the exhaust leak as the stud slowly pulled out from the head while I rode, allowing the hot gasses to erode what was left of the gasket and leaving a 1/4in gap for the exhaust to leak out. After 110 miles of 70mph riding, the steel stud had pulled halfway out of the aluminum head, taking the threads with it.

I had a tool pouch, with enough tools to repair the problem slung under the headlight, and I had fortunately included some drilled socket-head bolts,

this not being my first cross-country, nor my first Harley (I started taking trips on a collection of loosely connected spare parts called a 1963 FLH that was so temperamental that it only started once every St. Middlemas Day, but that's a story for future late, well-lubricated nights). I figured to let the engine cool down (in 100+ heat—HA!), then see if there was enough thread left to hold a bolt.

Harley-Davidson used socket-head bolts to hold on a lot of parts like side covers and handlebars on my FXRS. I always carried a few spares on any ride—what with the Shovelhead's slight engine vibration and all, I figured they might come in handy one day.

I used to restore airplanes a few years ago, amassing a large collection of high-tensile-strength, Grade 8, socket-head cap screws over the years, so I included a selection, along with washers and nuts, whenever I went farther than the local bar. I found that the easiest way to pack them was to fill the longer bolts with washers and a nut or three, then wrap them all together with .030 stainless aircraft safety wire. This way they all stayed together at the bottom of my tool pouch. I carried sizes ranging from 1/4 to 3/8in , all assorted lengths. In this case, everything I had was either two threads too long or two threads too short. Enough washers would take care of that, I hoped.

After thirty minutes, some *expletive-deleted* language, and numerous burns, I managed to remove the old one and install a new socket-head bolt through the pipe into the head. A normal hex-head wouldn't fit because the bolt hole sat too close to the pipe. Removing the worn-out stud proved to be little problem for a man with my masterful skills—it fell out in my hand. Locating something to use as a gasket became the next problem.

In the back of the grocery store, I found an old round port exhaust manifold gasket off a car engine that I cut up to kinda/sorta fit between the pipe and the head. I trimmed it to fit and hoped the flange would pull down enough to create a seal. The bolt was only able to grab three good threads deep in the head. Even at that, I had to use four washers to take up the slack on the longer bolt shank. Everything seemed to tighten up OK. When I revved the engine, no leaking gas could be felt. Time to pack up the tools and hit the road.

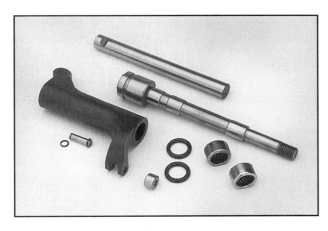

Crane makes a set of roller rockers for high-winding engines. The shaft rides in the two roller bearings shown on the right. The tip of the rocker has a hard roller to ride across the end of the valve instead of sliding, as on a conventional rocker. *Crane Cams*

When I returned to what passes for civilization around my neighborhood, I decided to see what type of permanent fix was available. B.C. Gerolamy Co. (916-638-9008) makes a Shovelhead three-bolt exhaust conversion kit to replace the factory single-bolt port. I had to remove the heads and ship them UPS so that Gerolamy could install the new flanges. They cut off the old flanges, welded on the new three-bolt setup, blended the welds into a smooth-flowing line, and sandblasted the heads. Included in the kit are new steel exhaust flanges with gaskets and mounting hardware to weld on whatever pipes you use. My old pipes had more holes than a brass flute, and the only thing keeping the mufflers together were rust molecules holding hands, so I picked up a set of Bub Enterprises (916-268-0449) FXE Shovel Duals, whacked off the flanges, welded on the new three-bolters, and hung them on the engine. These pipes are one-piece, with integral mufflers, eliminating one source of leaks. They don't use the factory cross-over pipe, but the stock heat shields can be mounted on them if you want to keep from frying your right calf like I did. Ouch!

Gerolamy has been in the cylinder head business since 1966, making high-performance heads for automotive and motorcycle use. Their products have sat on many racing engines from Nissan, Acura, Ford SVO, and Honda Racing. They offer up to five levels of modification for Shovel and Evo Heads. They will weld and recontour intake ports and chambers, install oversize intake seats for 1-5/16' valves, and weld the chamber to 80/81cc with a head milled .060.

There is a long list of head modification and repair work available, from dual plug installation to big port cylinder heads. Gerolamy has a new Evolution "D" exhaust port design capable of flow 20% better than on a stock Evo. The exhaust port floor is welded up, then recontoured to a "D" port shape. This port is available with their complete Evo welded "bathtub chamber" head packages. It's best to give them a call first to discuss your personal performance needs and prices.

Dennis Manning, owner of Bub, has been around Harleys since they had side valves, and has been operating as Bub Enterprises for over fourteen years. He comes with a fairly respectable set of credentials. In 1970, Cal Rayborn rode Manning's Harley-powered streamliner to a new Absolute Land Speed Record for motorcycles of 265.492mph. This machine, after a starring appearance in the movie "On Any Sunday," now lives in good company at the Indianapolis Motor Speedway Museum in Indiana.

In 1986, Dan Kinsey rode the Manning-built "Tenacious" over 290mph. This single-engined Shovelhead is still the fastest single-engined motorcycle in history. Dennis is currently involved in building another bike with an engine of his own design, based on a V-Twin, that he hopes to set some new records with down under in Australia. By the time you read this, he's probably run it for the record.

His Shovel pipes run around $135 in black, $155 in chrome. He has a whole selection of exhaust systems for Evos, from $105 Drag Pipes to his $280 "Bad Dog" pipes, advertised as good for ten more horsepower than the stockers at 4000rpm.

While building pipes, Manning ran into an interesting happenstance along the way. The test bike was a 1986 FXR with Andrews EV3 cam, 8000rpm spark module, K&N filter, stock carb with 160 main and 50 needle jet. He found out that his engine made two more horsepower with a full tank of gas. He contacted Branch Flowmetrics (714-827-1463), a specialist in head flow and porting. Jerry Branch told Dennis that the same thing happened on his own test bikes. Branch used an electric fuel pump to guarantee a steady fuel supply, ensuring consistent runs. Make sure your tank is close to full and the venting system isn't clogged. It's possible to starve the engine to the point it misses just from an inoperative fuel tank vent. A sign of a defective cap or vent system is a hissing noise heard as air fills the partial vacuum in the tank when the cap is removed for refueling.

Compression Ratio

A lot of people talk about compression ratio (CR), but not everybody totally understands what it is. CR is the ratio between the volume of the combustion chamber of one cylinder when the piston is at bottom dead center (BDC) and when it's at TDC. This is called the "mechanical compression ratio."

Operational compression ratio is the actual CR reached when the engine is running. The volumetric efficiency (VE) of the engine will cause this ratio to change in direct proportion to the change in VE. If the cylinder is filled to its maximum, then the VE will be 100%. A street engine, turning at its torque peak, will operate at a VE of approximately 80 to 85%. Running at horsepower peak will show a lower VE, because, at higher rpm, the cylinder will not fill as completely as it will at the lower torque peak.

As the engine's intake system is improved, the cylinder will achieve higher VE. A racing engine, with a tuned intake tract and an exhaust system operating at maximum efficiency, will compress the fuel mix and produce a VE in excess of 100%.

Once the VE begins to drop off, the cylinder fill begins to decline from 100%, causing the torque to drop off. When the torque drops faster than the rpm climbs, the horsepower peak has been reached.

In a theoretical engine, the intake valve would close just as the piston begins rising in its compression stroke up from BDC. This ensures maximum compression when the piston hits TDC. However,

Florida Caliper has a set of roller rockers for Big Twins. These will operate above 7000rpm without binding. *Florida Caliper*

the incoming mixture has mass and momentum, so it takes time for the cylinder to fill. As the rpm climbs, there is less time for this to happen, so the intake valve has to open sooner and close later, after the piston has started up on the compression stroke. When the revs are down low, the rising piston pushes some of the mixture back past the valve, resulting in reduced fill and subsequently less power. Higher revs take advantage of momentum and cam duration to push the air-fuel mixture past the valve during part of the compression stroke.

Using a cam with a long intake duration will allow the cylinder to fill better at high rpm because of the length of time the intake valve is open in comparison to crank rotation. This will also cause a loss in VE when the revs are low, with a resulting power drop.

More bang through increased cylinder pressure (compression) is the key to power. Everything you do to modify your engine is aimed at increasing power through more efficient breathing and improved combustion by more efficient cylinder-filling and raising cylinder pressure on the power stroke.

The mechanical compression ratio of Harley's Big Twin runs between 8.35 and 8.5 to 1, depending upon tolerances. Ideally, a raise to 9.5:1 is needed to make any kind of reasonable power. For racing purposes, ratios above 10.5:1 can be used as long as you realize that parts will go away much faster. If you are freshening up the engine fairly frequently, then this isn't a problem. Trying to make a high CR motor live

Air Flow Research (AFI) welds up a figure-eight tub in the head's combustion chamber. They have also O-ringed the head for better sealing. *Air Flow Research*

on the street brings on its own share of problems. Looking for fuel with a high enough octane rating to keep the engine from dissolving under severe detonation is a problem in itself

Gasoline

Today's gasoline refiners provide a "Super," "Extra," or some other aptly named 92 octane fuel to the pumps . Without playing Chemistry 101A, lets say that 92 octane will run in a 9:1 engine without much problem while higher ratios will require a higher octane fuel. A compression ratio of 9.5 can be handled by most modified motors without rattling pistons and with no more problem than perhaps pulling some of the advance out of the timing. Still, running much more compression in a street motor will entail filling five-gallon cans at your friendly, local airport, with all the attendant hassles, or buying racing fuel at $4.50 per gallon.

ERC Racing Fuel (800-445-1479) sells four or more different types of racing gas, from their ERC 110 fuel, rated at 104 octane, to ERC A-8A way up at 111 octane. They also have a fuel, custom-blended for drag racing, called ERC A-11, which contains a small, highly concentrated, leaded fraction. The fuel stocks blended for this gas have high hydrogen/carbon ratios and elevated resistance to heat and pressure as the main criteria. You won't get as many miles per gallon with it; however, if you're just going a quarter mile at a time with the drive back done on the end of a rope, mileage probably isn't much of a

concern. In order to achieve proper air-fuel mixtures, more gas will have to be burned for the same power output.

A-11 is only recommended where the engine will be producing power for a short time. It really shouldn't be used in air-cooled engines where the fuel is relied upon for cooling due to the higher heat load; however, if you can keep the V-twin from cooking, power gains of 1.5–2.5% can be achieved. A-11 is made in smaller quantities than the ERC 110 racing fuel and is more costly. Most H-D racers won't be using this fuel except in very special circumstances. ERC 110 is a better choice for most applications.

ERC 110 is a bulk-blended product constructed out of high-grade alkanes with tetraethyl lead-sensitivity and high resistance to heat and pressure. It will provide cooling to extract heat from the combustion chamber during overlap flow. This helps lower the heat load the engine produces at high power and high rpms. This fuel will give you good lean mixture function and the best power settings during sustained operation. Its research octane rating is 110, while the motor method rating comes out at 104.

What's really important to you is that it will keep a 10.5 or better engine from detonating while racing. If you run on the roads and only race occasionally, then you're better off not to go above a 9.5 ratio. This won't compromise reliability, and can be operated on what laughingly is passed off as "high octane" 92 gasoline.

Back in the bad old days of no smog and muscle cars (say around 1965 or so), Chevron offered a "Custom Supreme" fuel, packing an octane rating well in excess of 100.

Needless to say, pinging wasn't much of a problem on those early 389 GTOs and Dodge 426 Hemis. Harley was producing the Panhead up to 1966—then the Shovel on to 1984. During the 1960s, both motors didn't have enough pop to make use of the available high octane fuel. Also, go-fast parts weren't readily available, so most H-D owners stayed fairly stock on the street; detonation never became a problem.

Alas, those days, that fuel, empty roads, and $25 speeding tickets are long gone. Today, we have to make due with 92 octane, lots of traffic, and don't even ask what the judge nailed me for the last time my throttle hand overpowered my brain.

Pistons

Changing the compression of a Big Twin engine entails opening the engine for a piston swap. Companies like Axtell Sales Inc. (1424 S. E. Maury, Des Moines, IA 50317), Wiseco (7201 Industrial Park

Compare a stock Evo chamber to the figure-eight modification in the last picture. *Air Flow Research*

Blvd., Mentor, Ohio 44060), and CCI, along with many others, have pistons in various sizes and compression ratios for all Evo and Shovel engines.

Axtell specializes in building large displacement, 97ci "Mountain Motors" out of Evo engines, using forged flat-top pistons in conjunction with Pro-Street cast-iron cylinders and Speed-Pro rings. The cylinders are standard length and flywheels are factory, so no clearance problems arise. These pistons are also available in an angle-top design. Axtell fabricates the piston dome with a 30 degree angle on top, as opposed to a flat surface. The head has to be modified with a similar cut for clearance in the squish area. The idea is to use the air in the combustion chamber more efficiently. Turbulence is maintained, but the in-and-out paths are better with a 30 degree angle rather than the normal flat top. Angled domes also force the air-fuel mixture towards the spark plug. Compression ratio bumps up to 10:1, gaining horsepower in the process. Timing and jetting will have to be played with for optimum results.

This piston is available for everything from stock motors to 4-5/8in strokers.

Bores run from 3-1/2in to 3-13/16in. Various piston coatings can be specified—ceramic on the dome and composite film lubricant on the skirts, for example.

Axtell offers Teflon buttons to fit over the keeper clips holding the wrist pins in the pistons. These ensure that the keepers can't come out of the piston

and damage the cylinder walls. Retail is under ten dollars for four buttons—cheap insurance.

As of mid-1994, the piston sets have a price range of $215 to $310, depending upon bore and stroke. Piston coatings will add another $8 to the bill, but, in terms of wear and durability, it's money well spent.

Axtell can set you up with everything from a cast-iron Pro-Street 81.7ci cylinder kit, including 10:1 pistons, cylinders, rings, wrist pins, and keepers, to a giant-killer 114.1ci kit with a 3-3/16in bore by 5in stroke—definitely not for the timid and meek. They make four- and eight-head bolt hole finless barrels in all sizes for racing purposes only. Compression runs from 8:1 up to 11:1. Installing the big 3-13/16in bore cylinders will require stock bolt holes to be downsized and heads counter-bored. Axtell also recommends a 30 degree compression relief be cut into the heads.

As in all engine modifications, be sure to check clearances before firing up for the first time. When you bolt everything together, rotate the crank to see that the pistons don't touch the valves on the up-stroke and that they do clear the flywheels as they turn through the bottom of the stroke.

If Harley engine builders are few and far between where you live, or you would rather let the pros put the motor together, Axtell will assemble a short block on a set of Delcron or STD cases with S&S or H-D flywheels. Standard package includes iron cylinders, forged pistons, Speed-Pro rings, bearings installed and line-lapped, breather opened up, and lower end balanced and trued. Standard short blocks are 97ci—larger sizes available on special order.

When you reach the point of buying custom engines or building the one you ride into something with bores the size of your average train tunnel, then a call to the guys who do it for a living should be first on your list. A complete short block will eat up most of $3,000 without headwork, carb, or exhaust, so it's a good idea to spend a few hours with a calculator, working out different ways to go for the money available. Then talk to a specialist about how to proceed. Involving the pros at this time can save a lot of grief in the future.

Remington's corollary to Murphy's law states that: "Budgets for racing will always exceed at least twice your expected outlay." Murphy says: "Fast engines, slow horses, and old whiskey have made a poor man out of me!"

Another source for piston kits is Wiseco (800-321-1364). They have been in the business of popping out pistons for everything from snowmobiles to Harleys for quite a few years and have the aftermarket arena pretty much covered. All Wiseco H-D pistons are forged from high silicon aluminum alloy for high strength and are available with rings, wrist pins, and circlips as a kit. The piston shape allows tight piston-to-wall clearance, making for a quieter-running motor than normally found with forged pistons.

Cast pistons are quieter-running than their forged brothers, but they have the tensile strength of tomato juice cans when it comes to holding up under increased compression. Early forged pistons were built with more clearance than cast pistons, and you could hear them rattling around in the cylinders when cold. If you're going racing, the pipes, your helmet, and all that adrenaline in your system will probably keep you from hearing any piston slap. Profiling the local streets on Saturday night might be another matter. Like most every other engine modification, there are some tradeoffs involved—you make the decision, cast or forged.

A Wiseco 10:1 kit for the Evo runs $189.98. Sizes range from standard bore to .040 overbore. If you need a top-end gasket kit, one's available for just under $60. Shovelhead kits, from 7.0:1 for burning peanut oil or running a turbo to 9.5:1 for a little more bang on the street, are also available through Wiseco for $155.80.

Unless you are breaking down a new, zero-mile engine, any piston change will require that the cylinders be pulled and at least honed to break the glaze on the walls. If they are egg-shaped, a boring bar will be needed. It's fairly easy to go .010 to .020 overbore without making the cylinder walls too thin, but if you are looking for more cubic inches, then aftermarket cylinders might be the way to go.

Some of these modifications include some machine work, but the types of machining—boring or fly-cutting the stock heads— aren't anything trick. Any good shop will be able to do the necessary punching of cylinders or other work required whereas the stage three engine will have to be massaged by a custom shop with lots of experience working on hard-core race motors. The actual costs for stage two shop work should be small in comparison to the overall expenditures.

When you step on the compression, the engine will require more fuel for a given rev range. Running too lean can fry pistons. Too rich makes less power. Always err on the rich side when first setting up an engine. Dialing in too much timing can also build excess heat, causing problems similar to lean operation.

Take the time to set the engine up right during the first few hours of operation—get the jetting right—and check and double-check the timing. Road test the bike and do a few plug checks. Take the bike

AFI gets 360cfm through this port. The head has to use a larger custom manifold to match the huge ports in the heads. *Air Flow Research*

down an empty road for five to ten miles (I know, I know, empty roads are few and far between where you live. Try running when the sun comes up—not a lot of traffic out at 6:00am on Sunday). Pull the clutch after running through the gears. Hit the kill button; let the bike roll to a stop. Remove the plugs for a color check. Light brown indicates a good mixture. If the plug is black, you will have to back down the jetting. If the plugs show white with a blistered look, you'll have to go bigger on the jets.

Compression is one of those things where some works OK, more is better, and a little more can put the pistons down in the cases. An Evo motor for the street will do all right with 9.5:1 or thereabouts; a Shovel responds well to another .5 point bump. Any stock Big Twin can really benefit from a compression ratio increase, along with better breathing. If you are riding a touring bike, or pack two up a lot, detonation can become a problem when pulling long grades or hammering the throttle, so keep any compression increase below 9.5:1 on real heavy bikes.

A long-duration cam will generally tolerate more compression but make less power at lower revs. You will have to come up with a better fuel than pump gas if you go for a big jump in ratio to 10:1 or higher. ninety-two octane pump gas can be mixed with Avgas or racing fuel for a higher octane rating, but, in any case, if you feel missing or hear detonation, back off and check the plugs.

Expect to shorten the life of rods, bearings, pistons, and rings if you squeeze the compression and use all the new-found power.

Cylinders and Strokers

Well, what if 80 cubic inches is getting to seem a little small? You're looking for more displacement 'cause you're a firm believer in the American way—"If it won't go, make it bigger." You feel that pushing up the compression and helping the breathing on an 80 incher is fine for your average, everyday throttle turner, but you'd rather have more authority under you when you open the carb. How does 25 cubic inches more authority—available on demand—sound?

How do you make it bigger? One place to start is with Axtell's Mountain Motor mentioned above. This is a large-bore engine built with reliability and dependability, along with high performance, ready to bolt in place. Piston speed is held to stock specs by staying with the factory 4.25in stroke. This ensures long engine life, providing some sense is used when picking a redline.

Larger motors take more air to make use of their increased size. Usually, this means some fairly trick heads will have to be incorporated into the rebuild. Remember, maximum power results from matching a complete set of components, building a complete engine package. The NASCAR and roundy-round guys use engines built and tailored for a specific purpose. Engine builders know exactly how long given engine combinations will survive using different redlines for shift points. A 355in Chev might live for 501 miles of a 500 mile race when spinning 8000rpm. It might run two qualifiers and the entire race when held to 7000. It will probably last until you're tired of looking at it if it never sees more than 5000.

Porsche and Ford build excellent endurance motors. Back when Ford was actively campaigning in endurance racing, they designed their motors to run wide open for twice the period of the race. When they built motors for the 24 Hours of Le Mans, they hung a motor on a dyno and ran it until something let go. Then they improved that part until it stopped breaking. When the engine would run forty-eight hours at racing speed, the design was finalized and the engines installed in their 240mph GT cars.

In 1970, the late Pedro Rodriguez, driving for John Wyer in the Gulf Porsche 917, ran at Le Mans, a track where the fast cars exceeded 200mph in three different places. The 1970 race, much of it in heavy rain, was a fiasco for almost everybody, and only seven cars out of a starting field of fifty-one were counted as finishers.

Later, Pedro talked about running at speed in the driving rain. He said he'd be traveling down the long Mulsanne straight at 240mph without being able to see anything through the windshield except spray off the wheels of a car he was overtaking, sometimes at a closure rate of over 100mph. He tried

slowing down to a "tortoise-like 220" (his words), but still couldn't see the track except out of his side windows. So he kicked it back up to a reasonable 240 and went on with the race.

The cars were expected to take this kind of running for over 3,000 miles. This averaged out to 125mph for twenty-four hours, counting fuel and driver changes. Both Porsche and Ford gained a reputation for building reliable racing engines that would finish this type of long-distance race without problems. Porsche still continues to dominate the endurance racing scene today.

Technology has progressed a long way since the Le Mans cars of the 1970s, and it has worked its way down to the motorcycle arena. A properly built 96in or larger engine will be as reliable as the stock motor. A high-performance engine will require more maintenance, but if you do your part, there is no reason it won't last for many thousands of miles.

Racing is a different story, though. Drag racing motors measure their lives in number of passes, as opposed to thousands of miles. A good gas engine,

Compare the stock manifold to the rough casting on the right. When finished, this prototype will flow 360cfm to the head in the above picture. *Air Flow Research*

treated properly, can run an entire season without being torn down. A blown fuel motor, full of nitromethane, will usually last an entire pass before having to be opened up.

Axtell's Mountain Motor uses 96ci so that the stock cylinder length can be retained, along with factory flywheels. Stock-appearing cylinders, coupled with an appropriate cam and carb change, maintain a factory look. This can be an advantage if the opportunity for engaging in a speed contest should arise. Otherwise known as a sleeper, to all outward appearances Axtell's 96 incher looks fresh

After all is up and running, find a rear-wheel dyno and go check actual horsepower. This enables you to tune the engine while the bike's stationary. *Air Flow Research*

from the factory. This is part of its charm. If you've ever had the pleasure of owning a sleeper, you know what I mean.

Some of us derive immense pleasure by educating our less enlightened brethren aboard Oriental motorcycles by showing them the error of their ways and leaving them for dead with an apparently "stock" Harley. Not that I would advocate entering into a performance contest where there is a possibility of money changing hands, but it is a tidy way to provide that odd dollar or two, and it is immeasurably rewarding.

For those of you who think too many cubic inches isn't quite enough, or a .44 Magnum is a good starting point for a real gun, Axtell offers a set of 4in bore cylinders. Working with a displacement chart, we find that using a 4in bore by a stock 4.25 stroke, 106.8 cubic inches appear.

For those of you who want to wade into taller engines and longer strokes, a five inch stroke lets you play with 125.7ci. A stock piston just lays down in the bottom of such an engine, looking like a thimble in a quart oil can. Some, like me, think engines this size are great fun. Big engines (96in or better) don't require a lot of revs to make a lot of power. It's real easy to drive one on torque alone—shifting at 3500–4500rpm and letting the engine do the work.

An old friend of mine subscribed to this principle with his 427 Cobra. He has a real one, built in the early sixties by Carroll Shelby. It has the short track gears installed, limiting it to around 125mph on the top. He delights in standing on the gas next to a Corvette of current vintage when the stoplight turns green. Gary winds the 427 all the way to 3000rpm, in first, then shifts directly to fourth. Another loud roar up to a stratospheric 4000rpm and we were over 100 watching the 'Vette recede behind us. Sometimes it was sort of hard to see him, though, as all the laughter made our eyes water.

The same sort of approach can be used with a big-inch Big Twin. Unless you are really working hard on winning a brass ashtray at the races, you don't need to wind a big motor much past 4500 to enjoy its pleasures. ninety-six inches can take the worry out of being close. An excess of cubic inches comes in handy during those little tribulations that life throws at you from time to time—like showing your taillight to the guy on the rice rocket next to you.

Larger motors can also make shifting optional. No longer do you have to reach down in the transmission for a lower gear when another 15–20mph is needed. Just roll on the throttle and watch the speedometer unwind. You can justify the cost of the large cylinders to yourself by thinking about all the stress your left hand will avoid by not having to pull in the clutch lever so often.

For those of us who feel that we can't take off for a minor 800-mile jaunt without packing a laundry list of items ranging from a small color TV to a curling iron, a bigger engine will definitely perk up a touring bike. Like the commercial says, "Don't leave home without it."

S&S has a comprehensive instruction manual covering the installation of their "Sidewinder" 3-5/8in big bore cylinders for all Big Twins from early 1936 to the present. The cylinders are comparatively easy to install by any well-equipped Harley Davidson repair shop. Note they say "shop." The tools and equipment used for installation are beyond what is normally found in the average home garage.

S&S has designed some special tools to make cylinder installation a little bit easier. A degree wheel heads the list—this should be a standard tool for any H-D mechanic who tunes engines or changes cams. A connecting rod checking pin helps align pistons in the bore. Crank pin nut clearance gauges set crank pin nut to crankcase clearance. Then there is a cylinder head and crankcase boring fixture and Evo motor crankcase boring spacer that sets up most boring bars to punch heads and open crankcases to take the bigger cylinders. And if you're going to be really accurate, you will need a 100ml Burette, a graduated tube used for measuring liquids by milliliters, to calculate the compression ratio. As you see, this is more than the average wrench keeps in a toolbox. This machine work is where a stage two engine begins to differ from a stage one.

Installing a set of S&S 3-5/8in cylinders will open a stock bike, with a 4-1/4in stroke, up to 87.6ci. The largest engine that can be built by just changing the cylinders and leaving the stroke stock is obtained by going to a 4in bore. This necessitates using aftermarket cases and expanding the head bolt pattern. By the time you change cases, mount big cylinders, install stock or stroked flywheels, drop in a set of big pistons, and change

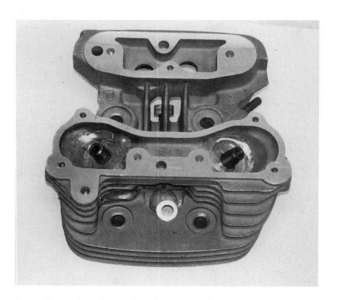

In order to fit a larger intake valve, the spark plug had to be relocated. At the same time, the spring pedestals were welded up so the port roof could be raised to make bigger ports. Kids, don't try this at home. *Air Flow Research*

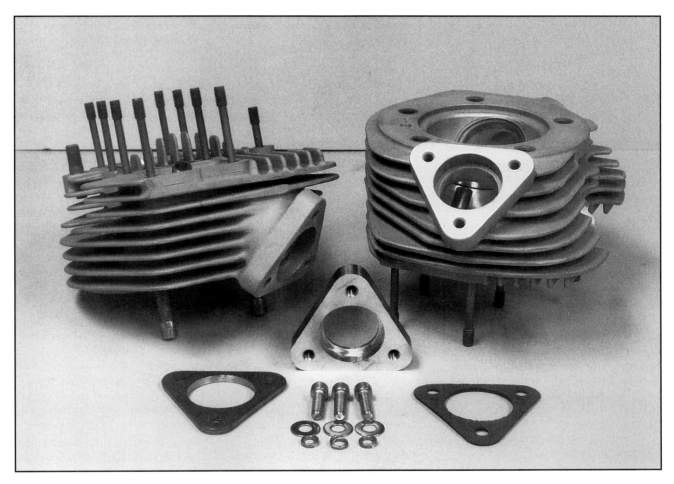

B. C. Gerolamy's three-bolt conversion for the Shovel-head is shown finished on the right. The factory flange has to be cut off, the new one welded on, and every-thing shaped for fit and appearance. The flanges at the bottom have to be welded on whatever pipes you use. *B. C. Gerolamy*

the heads, about the only thing left of the Harley engine is the oil on the frame.

If you have dreams of a 100-inch motor, you'd be better off to start from nothing and build a complete aftermarket engine from outside parts or buy a $3,000 short block assembly from one of the after-market go-fast people like Axtell. three thousand dollars might be a lot of money up front for parts, but it does save you all the hassles of building a motor up from stock—especially if you're like me and don't know what end of the screwdriver to pound with.

Standard cylinder length is 5.550 inches. A 3-5/8x4-3/4 stroker motor, 97.9ci, will have cylinders 5.625in long. Not a lot of change, but still enough to where engine-to-frame clearance can become a problem. Engines with up to .125in longer cylinders will clear most Big Twin frames, although a dresser might pose some difficulties, depending on what ac-cessories are installed. Some clearances have to shrink in order to build bigger motors. All S&S Sidewinder kits with tall cylinders require careful checking for frame interference.

Say you want to build your own motor; where do you start? Whether you go for a CCI Revmaster kit, an Axtell short block with STD or Delkron cases, or a complete S&S stroker kit, the first place to start is with the directions included with the kit. Now that you've decided to build a big motor yourself, farm-ing out all the machine work, you need to know what goes where before picking up a wrench. It's much easier to unbolt parts and forget where they went than to remember what goes where six months later when you get down to putting them back to-gether. A comprehensive set of directions, nailed to the workbench wall, will go a long way towards helping reassemble your engine.

The top head shows the conversion to a "D" port. The existing port is welded up to this configuration, increasing flow 20% over stock Evo heads. This port modification is available with B. C. Gerolamy's welded bathtub chamber, shown on the bottom head. *B. C. Gerolamy*

Always allow more time than you think necessary to do the rebuild. That way you won't fall off schedule if the machine shop takes an extra week to bore the crankcases. Plan on building the engine during the winter. Staring at a kitchen table full of Harley parts when the front yard looks like the place penguins play is a lot easier on the nerves than trying to hurriedly assemble an engine after the sun comes out. Estimate thirty to forty-five days from the time you start to work until the motor roars again. That way nothing will get rushed and half done. There's an old adage in the engine-building business that "you never have enough time to do the job right the first time, but there's always enough time to do it again." I'm not in the habit of writing trite homilies; however, after twenty-five years in the racing business, I've found this one truer than most.

Opening the Engine

Going to a larger engine is one of the more common methods of increasing horsepower without compromising reliability. Cylinders and pistons in numerous sizes can be purchased as a kit from many manufacturers. Here we will walk through a typical rebuild using S&S parts.

First, take a couple of pictures of the stock engine while it's still in the bike. I know you have more talent than a factory-trained Harley mechanic, but it never hurts to have a picture of where everything was before you've reduced the engine to its component parts. Every step should be planned prior to taking anything off the engine.

To build a big-inch motor, S&S lays out the instructions for installing its 3-5/8in. big bore kits in sixteen steps. Some of them pertain to certain models of engines and won't be used on an Evo motor. Others cover Knuckleheads, but are included for general instruction.

1. On Shovels and Panheads, the heads need to be bored to match the cylinder diameter.
2. Knuckleheads need the head bolts relocated.
3. Align the crankcases and install the new cylinder studs, if provided. Otherwise, clean and reinstall the stockers.
4. Bore the crankcases.
5. Check frame clearances using the engine with the new parts in place.
6. Modify crankcases for oil return lines (Knuckle, Pan, or Shovel).
7. Rank pin nut, connecting rods, piston/flywheel, and piston-to-piston clearances.
8. The crankcase breather timing must be modified (more about this later).
9. Install the cam, lifters, and lifter blocks.
10. When connecting rods other than S&S' are used, they will have to be set up for proper oil feed and machined for proper clearance.
11. Assemble and true flywheels. Mount mainshaft and con rods. This can try your patience, depending on your experience. Flywheels assembled improperly prior to being dynamically balanced can damage the mainshaft and crank pin tapers. Be careful at this point. If you do it wrong, S&S won't send you another set for free.
12. After the flywheel assembly is installed in the crankcase, the rods must be checked for alignment.
13. Modify Knuckle engine heads for oil return conversion kit (S&S).
14. Check and set piston-to-valve clearance.
15. Finish engine assembly and install in frame. At this point, add oil (you'd be surprised at the number of fresh engines turned over for the first time without any oil).
16. This is the hard one. Set the timing, install the pipes, bolt on the carb, and start 'er up. The first five minutes are the most critical in an engine's life. Run at 1500rpm while cylinders and heads warm up. Don't let the head temperature go above 250 degrees. Ride it for the first fifty miles like you pay the bills. Up to

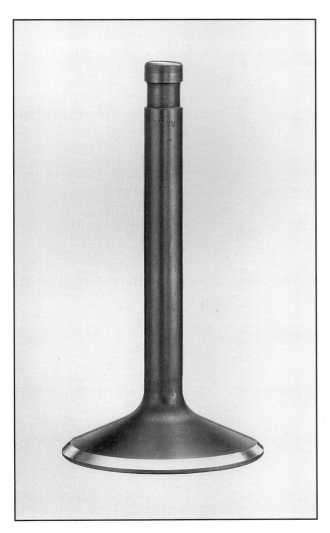

Manley produces a severe-duty stainless steel valve for 74 & 80 cubic inch Shovelheads. The stems are nitrided for wear resistance. The nitride process imparts a hard, semi-self-lubricating surface coating to the stainless steel valve stem. *Manley*

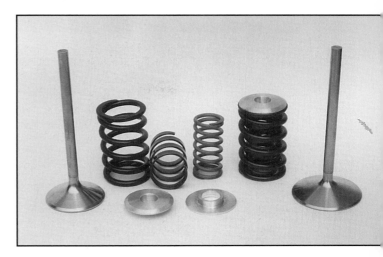

Manley's valvetrain packages includes titanium valves, severe-duty stainless valves, stainless valves with chrome-plated stems, all the necessary keepers and retainers, plus a matched set of springs. Almost every Harley engine application is covered . *Manley*

1,000 miles, don't let the engine lug or sit at the same speed for any length of time. Keep revs below 3000. Change the oil at 1,000 miles.

Some owners change the oil after the first fifty miles. They also check all the nuts and bolts at that time for proper torque, paying close attention to the cylinder base nuts and head bolts.

Engine Breather & Oil Pump

To keep oil from building up in the bottom of the crankcase on a high-performance Big Twin, the oil breather and its timing need to be massaged a bit. This ensures that the hole in the cases is lined up with the hole in the breather gear at the proper time during rotation and that the engine won't build up excessive pressure or hold oil in the cases. An engine can lose a lot of power by excess oil in the bottom of the cases dragging on the flywheel.

The Harley oiling system is built as a dry sump oil supply and return; there is no oil sitting in the bottom of the engine, as in most passenger car motors. Race cars and Harleys use a pump to scavenge all the oil from the bottom of the crankcase and return it to a tank mounted in the area of the back seat on a race car. If we have to point out where the dry sump oil tank is on a Harley, perhaps you would be happier with another hobby—say, knitting.

Setting the breather timing is another case where a degree wheel comes in handy. Pull the engine up to TDC on the front cylinder. Rotate crank to 10 degrees before TDC. Always turn the engine in the normal direction of travel. Look through the lifter block opening to check the relationship between the breather and case opening. Now rotate the flywheel to 10 degrees after TDC. At this time, the edge of the breather cutout should appear in the hole. If not, the cases will have to be opened up by grinding to the proper dimensions. Again, be careful. Cases improperly ground can be heli-arced back to proper dimensions with a bit of work by a very good, experienced, heli-arc welder; however, it's not something you want to have to do.

Now rotate the wheel to 55 degrees after BDC and check the breather/case hole relationship. Push

Bub's "Bad Dog" pipes. Bub's owner, Dennis Manning, comes with a fairly impressive background in the world of go-fast Harleys. He built the fastest single-engined Harley in the world—278mph+. Currently, he is constructing a new bike, running his own 3000cc V-4 engine design. Plans are a trip to Australia to shoot for a world record. His street pipes take advantage of all the technology learned through building record-setting machines. At 6000rpm, a 1986 FXR wearing his pipes, modified with a cam, filter, re-jetted carb, and better ignition, made eleven more horsepower than the nearest competitor. *Jim Bush/Bub Enterprises*

the wheel to 75 degrees after BDC and check to see that the back edge of the hole in the gear disappears from view. If not, then the closing side of the case hole will have to be cut in the same way as the other side.

CCI makes replacement breathers already set up for maximum breather time. This alleviates the necessity of grinding the cases. The part number is 58-076 for stock duration and -077 or -078 for 10 and 20 degrees more duration. This enables you to dial in the exact timing needed to ensure proper scavenging and improve the performance in the process. Their breathers come with a complete selection of four different thrust washers to set proper end clearances. The cover screen on the breather has larger holes than stock, for better flow. This is a lot better than removing the screen completely, as dirt or strange crud can pass through the unscreened opening and do a real number on the oil pump.

Next modification to consider is improving oil distribution. The existing pump can be modified, but rather than opening up a stock oil pump for increased flow, S&S has an oil pump kit, including a steel breather that replaces factory parts. Installing it will improve crankcase scavenging and oil flow. CCI also has their chromed RevTech series oil pump, with improved pressure regulation. S&S doesn't recommend chroming their pump, due to the very real possibility of introducing buffing compound and other crunchies into the passageways. Also, it's very difficult to just chrome the outside of the pump without getting plating on the gasket surface and inner pump body. S&S states—in bold type—that chroming their pump will void the warranty. So if the engine has to be chrome, go with CCI.

Whichever pump is selected, follow the instructions closely, as installation will differ depending on year of the bike. Pumps fit all models from 1936 to present. S&S has ten different parts numbers for the pump and CCI has two, covering 1936 to 1991. You will need an oil-drilling jig to modify the pressure-relief valve hole on pumps for 1970 to 1980. Either supplier can provide the necessary fixture. All drilling operations have to be undertaken VERY CAREFULLY, or oil won't go where it should, or it might bleed off into the gear chest cavity. This will result in loss of oil pressure, followed by loud screeching noises as the engine quits in protest.

On your racing engine, you might want to intercept the oil line going from the oil tank to the oil pump in order to install an oil cooler. It usually depends on the amount of time the engine is producing high horsepower as to whether or not an oil cooler is a good investment. Running an ET of under ten seconds won't let the oil get hot enough to worry about. Holding the throttle open for a record run at El Mirage Dry Lakes or Bonneville (info through Southern California Timing Association [SCTA]. Secretary Warren Bullis 714-622-2146) will require a cooler to keep the oil below 250 degrees.

Cam

Now that you've bumped the compression and maybe opened up the displacement a bit, the engine can deal with more cam. Cam selection is based on the other modifications and intended usage. Sifton splits its cams into two categories: performance—for fairly stock, primarily street engines; and high performance—for people who want to have a lot of go on the street or are seriously going racing and are willing to put up with degraded low- to middle-speed opera-

tion. Low power at low revs, lumpy idle, and higher maintenance will all become more of a problem when installing a cam with a lot of lift and duration.

The advantage of running a big engine with a performance cam is being able to watch a lot of headlights in your rearview mirror while the other dudes wonder why their bikes have such a bad case of the slows. Might be more work to build, but it's sure fun.

Let us be reasonable: the reason we go through all this time, effort, and money in building a fast engine is to either take down one sort of a record or another or to leave some duck for dead when the light turns green.

In my past, evil life I was wont to build bikes that were absolutely stock-appearing outside their 100+ cubic inch interiors. Perhaps I might even have let them get a little dirty around the edges—even let a little rust appear on the parts that don't count. That, coupled with saying to the other rider, "Gee, that sure is a pretty bike—your dad let you ride it?" was usually enough to get some money laid down and a contest of speed proposed. I always had someone I knew hold the money, as the loser's attitude wasn't real good after a quarter mile or so, and I didn't relish the chore of locating him again to extract my winnings.

I didn't do this a lot—mostly when I felt like educating the unwashed or adding a little excitement to life. Didn't win them all, but paid for more than one engine. 'Course, there was the time I ran into a guy with an uglier scoot than mine—with a turbo hung off the right side. I punched it, he punched it; his boost went positive and I thought I'd lost a plug wire or shut off the kill switch. Told myself to never play the other guy's game. Especially when that's how I had been operating. There's always someone faster. That incident taught me not to let my mouth write a check that my bike couldn't cash.

Back to cams. Sifton specs-out their #142, #146, or #147 grind for engines with improved carburetion, open exhaust, a bit of porting to the heads, competition valvetrain, larger bore and stroke, and stepped-up compression. The 142 grind has an rpm range from 3500 to 6500+ and is not intended for the novice engine builder. Total valve lift is .540; duration is 264 intake, 270 exhaust. As on all cam changes, spring bind has to be checked, along with free travel and ignition drive clearance.

Most hi-po aftermarket cams with .540 lift or better will need more valve-spring operating distance. Coil bind occurs when the cam lifts the valve farther than the spring can compress. When this happens, something has to give. The springs can absorb the additional travel by compressing, or the cam can drive the valve through its keepers with the possibility of planting it in the piston. This *will* have a detrimental effect on performance.

Stock Evo heads can't use more than about .500 lift. Going to a Sifton #142 will require modified or different heads or most of the cam's power range will be wasted.

Sifton's #147 cam is aimed at big-inch drag racing motors. Lift is .640—duration: 268 intake, 275 exhaust. This is definitely not a street motor cam. The springs need .670 to coil bind and .720 of free travel. With this cam and any other high-lift aftermarket cam, it is normal practice to put clay in the piston reliefs, assemble the engine, turn it through by hand a few times, pull it down, and measure the thickness of the clay. If there is no clay left under the valve, then the clearances are too tight. Everything must be checked again until the problem is solved. Then button up the engine again for another clay check. Also, there must be .040 clearance between the valves at their maximum overlap. A piece of .040 safety wire can be inserted through the spark plug hole so that it passes between the valves while in the overlap position (five degrees after TDC). Look through either the intake or exhaust port with a flashlight shining through the opposite port. If the valves don't have the proper clearance, their heads must be beveled at a 45 degree angle.

Installing a compatible set of springs, collars, keepers, pushrods, and lifters with any high-performance cam is pretty much mandatory. The stock valvetrain won't even begin to keep up with the new cam. Sifton makes a kit for all their cams that will allow the valves to follow the cam at higher rpm. The pushrods are .095 wall, 7/16in 2024 aluminum tubing. They are lighter than stock, with an expansion ratio sufficient to keep up with the cylinders, maintaining the same clearances set when the engine was cold. The valve springs have about double the 300lbs pressure of the stock springs at maximum lift. This will keep the valves from floating when the revs go above 6000. Too much spring pressure can be as bad as too little. Too much pressure can accelerate seat, cam, or other parts wear. Valve-spring pressure will change after a few hours of operation. Seat pressure (valve closed) can change by 10% from new specs after a run or two. Stock seat pressure is somewhere in the 120lb range, modified runs around 180lbs, with twenty more pounds when used with a high-lift cam.

Most performance kits use double-valve springs, although a few go with three. The two outer springs are made of round wire, while the third inner can be a flat wire spring. The dual springs help reduce spring

A 9.5:1 piston for an 80-inch Shovelhead. The high-compression piston has a tall dome, with deep valve relief. *Wiseco*

surge. The third, flat wire spring is designed to dampen spring frequencies. This helps control surge and keeps the springs from losing tension in a short time.

Sifton uses aluminum collars and keepers, but these can also be made out of chrome moly, which is stronger, or titanium, which is both strong and lightweight. Lifters can be either solid or hydraulic. Sifton uses solid lifters, drilled for top-end oiling. Both the lifters and the roller assemblies are made out of alloy steel. Also available are aluminum lifter blocks cut to fit perfectly with their lifters. The blocks are cut with a spiral groove to aid in lubrication, extending part-life and reducing friction.

If you want to stay with hydraulic lifters, but still want to have a cam with a lot of lift and duration for racing, Crane has a grind—Hi-Roller #101003— ground to .550 lift, 266 degrees on the intake, 276 on the exhaust. Not as much lift as Sifton's #147, but still enough to let bigger ports and larger cylinders do their work.

This cam will have to be installed with performance springs, such as Sifton's new "Thermo-Cool" coated springs. These have a thermal coating applied to the wire to help reduce coil friction and disperse heat. This eliminates hot spots in the coils, which cause oil burn-off and pressure fade. Anything that helps keep the oil from crisping and aids in heat transfer from the valve area will prolong top-end life. Two seat pressures are offered with the coated springs: 155lbs, with 352lbs at open; and 175lbs, with 394lbs open. Each set of springs require different hardened keepers, so it would be a good idea to contact Crane for a catalog outlining cam and kit combinations prior to making a purchase.

Crane also offers a lower-priced "Fireball" series of cams, but none of them have the lift and duration available with the bigger Hi-Roller series. The Hi-Roller can be set up with three cam-timing settings by using their adjustable timing gears. Four degrees of retard and stock timing or four degrees advance can be dialed into the cam just by changing the cam index position when the gear is mounted. It comes with three keyway slots cut in its inner diameter instead of one. Depending on how the gear is positioned on the cam, the cam timing can be advanced or retarded to suit the engine builder.

Howell's H-D, out of Denver, runs this Pro Stock racer. I guess if it has what passes for a headlight and something that looks like a brake light, it falls into the Pro Stock classes. I don't think I'd like to ride it on the street, but the racetrack is another matter entirely—a very well-done machine. *Rich Products*

Setting the cam up with four degrees of advance will lower the power band of the engine whereas retarding it by the same amount will raise it. This might only move the powerband 300–400rpm up or down—not a large change but important enough in racing. For a big touring engine that lives below 4000rpm most of its life, cam advance will add torque down low while racers can gain some top end by backing down the cam timing.

Each cam swap will require that the cam drive gear be checked for clearance. Harley changed

their method of measuring cam gears and gear color-coding in 1990.

The 1989 and earlier gears are measured using .105in roller pins set in the gear teeth 180 degrees apart. With the newer gears, H-D used .108in pins. If in doubt as to early or late gears, look at the grooves in the side of the gear. The early ones have one grove while the later gears have two. Crane uses the same color-coding as the factory: yellow for the 2.7344/2.7354in; red for 2.7354 to 2.7364in; and blue for the 2.7364 to 2.7374in diameters on the early engines. The 1990 and up gears employ the same colors for diameters 2.7460 to 2.7490 inch in .0010in steps while using the .108in pins for measurement.

All this aids when setting up gear backlash. Replace the stock gear with the same color-coded aftermarket gear or punch the original gear off the cam and use it. I'd let the cam manufacturer install the cam gear if I were doing my first couple of cam swaps. The possibility exists that the cam gear can rotate a few degrees while being pressed on the shaft, due to the type of jig used. Manufacturers are familiar with this, allowing for the slippage during gear mounting. If you try to press it yourself, the probability is great that it won't end up where you want it. At the least, this will negate any advance or retard you're trying to achieve.

On a stage two engine sitting on a bench, installing a new cam isn't much of a problem with an Evo motor. Changing a cam while the motor's in the bike is another task completely. The model of the bike will determine the amount of pieces that have to be removed to get at the cam. Big Twins will require the engine to be dropped for clearance. Some say that it's not necessary, but save yourself a lot of hassle and plan on either removing the engine or at least dropping it down. Drag racers don't have as much of a problem opening the engine, as the usual conglomeration of gas tanks, exhaust pipes, and air cleaners isn't in the way. Actually, pulling the engine out of a Big Twin shouldn't take more than a couple of hours, with the right tools. Having everything up on a bench makes performance modifications, like degreeing in the cam, much easier.

Engine stands can easily be fabricated out of angle iron, using the engine case mounting bolt holes to locate the supports. S&S, Crane, and others make a degree wheel that bolts on the end of the crank. Crane's "Tune-A-Cam" kit makes setting up cams easy. It comes with wheel, dial indicator, mounting arms, TDC locator, and lightweight valve springs. This kit can also check cam and crank-end play and other clearances. When you go racing for

S&S' Land Speed Record bike, "Tramp III"—fastest run at Bonneville in 1991 was 239.492mph. It set the AF2000 class record at 226.148mph, running fuel. Next time you think about going fast, you might want to give Dennis Manning at Bub Enterprises a call—he built the bike. S&S built the motor with the same parts available to you today. *S&S*

serious, you're going to build engines for serious and need to dial in the cam properly.

The reason for degreeing in a cam is to ensure proper valve timing. Part tolerances can cause enough differences between engines to make one faster than the next by enough to make one bike outperform an-other, even though both are built with the same parts. How the parts go together will determine how the engine performs. Full-tilt-and-boogie engines will need the cam dialed in for maximum power at the top end.

In order to degree in a cam properly, a degree wheel will have to be mounted on the sprocket side of the engine, with a pointer bolted to the engine center through bolt to set TDC. Different cam companies set up their cams differently, but the end result is the same—install the cam so that the lobes open and close the valves according to cam manufacturer's specifications.

To find TDC with a pin locator, screw it into the spark-plug hole of the front cylinder, then rotate the crank until the piston rests against the bottom of the pin. Set the degree wheel to TDC. Now rotate the engine backwards until the piston is back against the locator. Read the setting off the wheel. For purposes of discussion, let's say the wheel now reads 16 degrees after top dead center (ATDC). Divide the 16 by two to find the halfway point between the two measurements, and that will be the actual TDC. In this case 16 divided by 2 = 8. Without moving the crank, move the wheel eight degrees back from its initial setting and check it again by the same method. The engine will be at TDC when the wheel reads the same in both directions.

Now position a dial indicator on the front intake lifter. If you don't know which lifter is the intake, I advise you to find someone who has done this before and talk nicely to him, in hopes that he'll teach you how to do it right. Doing it wrong can and will bend parts.

Rotate the crank until the lifter is on the bottom of its cam lobe. Turn the face of the dial to zero. Rotate the crank forward to maximum lift, when the lifter is on the top of the cam lobe. Now go past top until the dial indicator reads .053in of lift. This is the point where the factory sets the camshaft's intake valve closing. Your readings should correspond with the cam manufacturer's. Setting the inlet lobe to a late closing position will cause poor compression and poor performance. Early closing will give good low-end performance at the expense of the top end. Semi-late closing will give good mid-range but not peak top end. A cam ground with a semi-late closing inlet and a semi-early opening exhaust will give the best performance.

If you need to change the camshaft gear position relative to the cam, and it doesn't have a multiple keyway setup like the Crane Hi-Roller, then the gear will have to be pressed off and repositioned. This gets more than a little involved, so double-check all measurements prior to moving the gear. It takes a special fixture to set the gear properly, as it can rotate when pressing it on the shaft. On a street motor, two degrees either way is close enough. Skipping a couple of meals will give about the same performance gain as one or two degrees of cam timing.

A racing motor is different. Cam timing has to be spot-on. Some engine builders measure the rear cylinder along with the front. Then, if the two values are different, they can be split to arrive at the best figure. Here again, to change the cam timing, the cam gear will have to be moved on the shaft.

Latest neat trick is to set the Big Twin engine cases up to accept cams similar to Sportsters. This way each valve event can be individually dialed in, insuring accurate valve timing for both front and rear cylinders.

A few things to watch for when installing an aftermarket camshaft:

1. Be sure to check the bushing in the case. New engines, or those with few miles on them, won't need replacement bushings—older, high-mileage engines will.
2. Use the right side clearances; stock are fine.
3. Hydraulic lifters go with juice cams, solid lifters with solid cams.
3. Any cam change will require that the engine be retuned. Carburetion will change.
4. Be *sure* to check valve-to-piston clearance. Bent valves make the engine run slightly under peak (i.e.: not at all). Use the clay method previously covered.
5. Check the valve-to-valve clearance through the ports.
6. Don't buy more cam than the engine can use. Not too many big-inch touring bikes need a power range from 4500 to 7500rpm—unless you tour a whole lot faster than the rest of us.
7. Take your time during assembly, or the evil gremlins that break parts might come visit you.
8. Use break-in lube on the cam and lifters. It increases the load-carrying capability of the engine oil to prevent scuffing and galling between moving parts. Use it on hydraulic and solid lifters. It's very important to have engine protection during the first few minutes of operation—especially on a racing engine. I use Ford Motorsports Camshaft and Lifter Prelube, part #M-19579-A991, to coat the lifters and cam on any surface that comes in contact with metal. One four-ounce bottle will easily cover the cam and lifters on a two-cylinder engine. Most cam manufacturers recommend a specific type of prelube; some include a small amount in the kit. Wherever it comes from, make sure it's on the cam.

Carburetion

S&S Super "E" and "G" carbs are designed for Big Twins that have been extensively modified with cams, strokers, displacement changes, and head modifications. Both carbs are butterfly-type, with an adjustable idle system. The accelerator pump and mid-range and high-speed jets can be set to complement many different stages of tune.

The Super E has a 1-7/8in throat at the butterfly and a 1-9/16in venturi. It can be identified by an "E" cast into the carb body next to the throttle linkage. The Super E is recommended for use on any Big Twin. The Super G is a larger carb, with a 2-1/16in throat and a 1-3/4in venturi. It has a "G" cast into the carb body in the same place as the Super E. The G is intended for 74ci motors, or larger, that have had serious motor work done. S&S recommends it not be installed on low-pop motors.

Both carbs are not legal for use in California for scooters ridden on the roads. If you live elsewhere, you're OK so far, but the smog police will come get you sooner or later, so bear that in mind when building an engine.

The two carbs come as a kit that includes:
1. one S&S carb—Super E or G;
2. one Teardrop air cleaner;
3. manifold;
4. mounting hardware;
5. fuel line and clamps, including overflow line;
6. one extra intermediate jet and two main jets;
7. instructions.

A Super D, with a 2-1/4in throat and 1-15/16in venturi, is also available. As part #11-0119, it

Axtell builds short-blocks in many sizes—97ci, 102ci, 105ci, and 108ci. Axtell mounts their cast-iron cylinders and forged pistons on a set of Delkron or STD cases. The bearings are installed, the breather modified, and the lower end balanced and trued. A little under $2,900 will bring one to your house. *Axtell*

is an alcohol carb, not capable of running on gas (more on fuels in a later chapter).

As with their oil pumps, S&S does not recommend chroming their carbs, for the same reasons. Even CCI, the Khrome Kings of the Known World, don't offer a chrome carb.

One thing I've learned the hard way (I think most of my general body of knowledge came this way) is to change the manifold O-rings, rubber bands, and clamps whenever pulling the carb. The stock ones on my Shovel lasted less than 15,000 miles before growing air leaks. And don't skip installing the carb support brackets, or everything will slowly rotate downward (yes, I did that too!).

Both S&S carbs require dual-throttle cables like their near relatives, the Super B and Super D. S&S offers different cable kits, with throttle cables running from 38in to 48in. With some Harley models, it's easier to change carbs with the fuel tanks pulled. Make sure the engine is cool and all gas valves are turned off. Better yet, take the time to drain the tanks completely before removing them. When I swapped carbs, I ran the bike down to low reserve before draining the tank. This way you don't have to hold a five-gallon can under the gas line until your knees go soft. Usually, a one-gallon can, like where you keep the lawnmower gas, will do. Sounds simple, and it is, but every little bit helps when working on your bike.

On an older bike, this is a good time to pull the throttle apart and clean and oil everything that rubs. A little cable lube down the top of your old cables will do a world of good, too. Tape a small piece of paper in a cone around the top of each cable. Elevate the cable and squirt the lube into it. Wait about five minutes—this way, the lube can run down inside the cable and reach the other end. After reassembly, check the throttle for smooth, free action.

The old Harley carb didn't have a return spring, so the throttle would stay in any position—sort of a budget cruise control. All the new bikes have a throttle-set screw that accomplishes the same purpose. You don't want to have this installed on a serious racing bike. Not too much of a quarter mile is covered in cruise, and this is just one more thing that can cause problems at the wrong time.

After a new carb installation, make sure that the float needle shuts off the gas flow 100%. Fuel that leaks by can fill a cylinder and bend rods when the engine's turned over. Liquids can't be compressed, but engine parts can. If you are in the habit of firing the bike on a set of rollers driven by the rear wheels of your truck, a cylinder full of fuel can easily hydraulic the rods. Not only does this lower the compression ratio severely, but it also will stop the engine from rotating and can damage other parts. Plus, the stuff can burn if it overflows the engine—presto: instant crispy critter. Turn the fuel valve off when not running. Be sure to check it prior to racing. It's very easy to forget to turn on the gas valve when the adrenaline starts to rise—makes for a very short run.

S&S offers two air horns for drag racing. Part #17-0485 is a 2in horn while #17-0486 is a 4in horn. These look real good on a race bike; however, they never should be used on a street engine. Bugs, grit, and what passes for air in California will raise unmitigated hell with the cylinder walls if allowed to enter unfiltered. The perceived increase in performance on a street bike (none) isn't worth the added wear. Drag racing engines might only cover fifty miles, including testing and racing, prior to tear-down. Wear isn't a factor when the engine comes apart so often, but anything that improves performance needs to be used, so that's where a velocity stack belongs, not on the street.

Fuel delivery can be improved by installing one of Pingel's petcocks and fuel filters. Two are available, 3" and 1-1/2" long. A new filter is a necessity on any new motor and is an excellent idea on any motor. Something else to watch for while working around the carb: most pump gas these days is oxygenated by the addition of alcohol. This affects us in three ways. First, it helps clean the air. Second, it can decrease mileage slightly. Third, it can intensify the wear on rubber O-rings and other parts on an older bike's carb. Some rubber parts on Shovel carbs can be damaged by too much alcohol. So if your pristine 1978 FLH-80 Electra Glide begins to do some strange things that can't be adjusted out by tuning, look for deterioration in the carb .

CCI sells their RevTech Carb Kit for all Evo and Shovel motors except the Ultra model with cruise control. Not too many racers will need the advantage offered by the Ultra's cruise, so lack of an aftermarket fuel mixer shouldn't be much of a problem on that model.

CCI's carb is designed expressly for Harley-Davidson high-performance applications on modified, or big-inch engines. It has a number of unique features that improve rideability and serviceability and is adjustable over a wide range of applications.

The RevTech carb has an accelerator pump pushing 1/2cc of fuel directly into the center of the intake venturi when the throttle is opened. This helps ensure an even shot of fuel to both cylinders, giving quicker response times from the first twist of the throttle. Unlike carbs without a pump, the Accelerator, the S&S, and the Mikuni HSR 42 all give a quick squirt of gas to pick up the engine speed when the throttle is cracked and air begins to flow into the cylinders. Without this feature, the engine could stumble for a second before the airflow speed through the venturi picks up enough to create a vacuum to lift gas through the jets.

There is no choke, per se, on the RevTech carb. A three-position enrichment lever allows additional fuel to smoothly enter the carb without having the obstruction of a choke plate in front of the butterfly. The gas line fitting can be rotated through any position for easy hookup to any tank. Also, the rotating fitting gives you the room to install a fuel filter without having the gas line kink or extend so far that it can move against the engine at speed.

As your engine changes cam, displacement, pipes, or all the above, the RevTech carb can grow to fit the situation through the use of interchangeable venturis. It comes with a 42mm tube; sizes 38 to 45 are available, covering a wide range of applications.

As with the S&S, all the jets are replaceable. A tuner's kit for the Evo is available, containing:

a 1.60 high-speed jet;
a 1.80 high-speed jet;
a .64 low-speed jet;
a .68 low-speed jet;

Rather than cutting up your stock crankcase breather, CCI offers an adjustable valve, permitting the engine builder to match the breather timing to the engine displacement. Four different-sized thrust washers are included. It can be ordered in various durations, from stock to +20 degrees. *Custom Chrome*

Above and next page: A set of Shovel cylinders on the left, compared to Evo cylinders on the right. As you can see, they won't interchange—no matter what your friends say. The Evo cylinders are bored to four inches, requiring aftermarket cases and moved-out bolt holes on the head. *Axtell*

a 1.85 high-speed air jet;
and a 2.00 high-speed air jet.

A similar kit is also available for the Shovel, with slightly different-sized air jets.

Actually, many more high-speed and low-speed jets are available, ranging from .56mm to .84mm, for the low-speed, to 1.40mm to 2.80 to fit the high-speed. If you can't find a combination that works for your particular application, it won't be from lack of parts.

The carb kit comes with a one-piece manifold, air cleaner, and twin-throttle cables but no breather kit—necessary for installation on 1992 or later Big Twins. A short plenum manifold, extrude-honed for better flow, moves the carb 7/8in closer to the motor, increasing flow and power at higher revs. Longer intake manifolds, giving up to .200in additional length, are available for taller cylinders

In September 1993, Mikuni introduced its HSR 42 carb for H-D. As the name implies, it's a 42mm venturi smooth bore, second-generation racing carb, designed specifically for all-out performance applications. The throttle slide runs on eight roller bearings, ensuring smooth operation even at high-flow rates. Stiction, caused by high manifold vacuum on the other side of the slide, was handled by a big spring on the smaller Mikuni. On an 80in motor this worked OK, but the throttle pull was heavy, and final closing of the slide could be a problem on bigger engines. The stainless steel bearings and slide housing go a long way in eliminating throttle slide problems on the HSR 42.

The HSR 42 flows 20% more air than its smaller brother, the HS 40. Mikuni states that the new smooth bore actually flows more air, with its 42mm venturi, than other types of big-bore carbs equipped with larger venturis. This, they say, is due to the absence of any throttle butterfly disrupting airflow when wide open.

The HSR's accelerator pump can be tailored for specific applications, giving instant response from off idle throughout the full rpm band on any engine.

Taking care of the higher end of the rpm range, the float bowl is larger and the needle valve has a greater gallon-per-hour rate to keep modified engines happy at full throttle.

The bigger HSR 42 will greatly enhance engine operation on motors that have been pumped with longer duration cams, stepped-on compression, and free-flow pipes. It's a little bit of overkill on stock motors. The HS 40 will flow 155cfm, which is more than adequate for a stock or stage one motor. The HSR 42 will pass just under 200cfm, enough for large engines like Axtell's 96in "Mountain Motor." This isn't to say that the new carb won't help a stock motor. On a dyno, four to six HP were gained over the stock, lean-running factory carb. However, it will produce better performance on a modified engine with big pistons.

The HSR 42 is physically larger than the HS 40 in order to engineer the larger venturi. This shouldn't pose any problem for fitting it between the cylinders and under most any fuel tank. The front-to-back dimensions are 8mm smaller than its little brother's, enabling it to fit within the "V" of the Evo motor.

The HSR 42 kit can be hung on a 1990-to-present Evo for $395. Shovelhead or earlier Evo installation will lighten your checkbook by $495. The kit for pre-1990 bikes includes a new manifold, along with a K&N chrome air filter assembly. All kits come with cables, and, for those of us who ride Shovels, a new throttle grip is in the box. All kits are ready to hang on the engine, right out of the box. Jetting should be close, but be sure to run a plug test before hitting the track.

Fuel Injection

Personally, I think that electronic fuel injection (EFI) is the way to go on future engine modifications or new bikes. I wouldn't be surprised to see it sprout up on all motorcycle engines in the near future. Ducati's new 916 comes with it installed from the factory. They must know what they're doing, as they are currently dominating superbike class in this country and in international competition.

EFI gives control over fuel metering that carbs can only dream of. Cold start, throttle response, precise fuel delivery, and tight smog control are only some of the benefits of EFI. Automakers no longer use carbs on any of their engines, being unable to control emissions without computer-managed fuel delivery systems.

EFI also offers the LARGE advantage of on-board, real-time engine monitoring and tuning. A

display unit, like the one on WhiTek's Engine Control System (805-481-7710; FAX 805-481-090; or write PO Box 337, Arroyo Grande, CA 93421), is capable of providing:

engine rpm; battery voltage;
engine temperatures; settings;
and operating/tuning instructions.

It can be used to adjust: mixture;
timing; "choke" (none on EFI—enrichment only) and prime; accelerator pump function;
cruise lean-out; and altitude compensation.

The WhiTek EFI was built specifically for Harley-Davidson air-cooled engines. It's not an adaptation of an automotive system, cobbled up to sort of work on a motorcycle. The electronics utilize the Motorola 68HC11 microprocessor, developed for small engine control. In the world of internal combustion motors, a 96ci Evo is a "small" motor. The EFI provides adjustable, independent cylinder mixture control to both cylinders. It also contains a single-fire ignition system with an adjustable advance map. Dual coils will have to be installed to run the single-fire system.

All operating parameters can be changed without resorting to an external computer. Say you change the cam to something with more lift and duration—the computer can be reprogrammed to new timing and fuel-flow specs by input through the display unit. Should you get bogged down trying to input new data, the programmer has a sub menu with "help" functions.

Actual operation is fairly easy. Spend some time on-line with the display unit, and all the operations become easier than setting up a carb/ignition

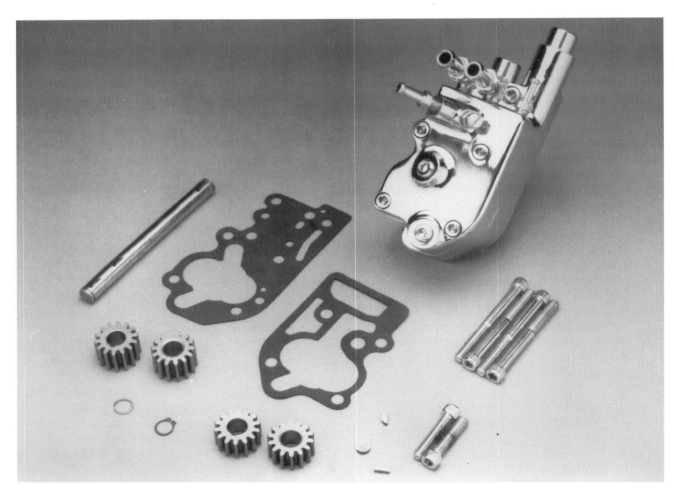

CCI's RevTech oil pump can be retrofitted to most Big Twins from 1936 to 1991. It has adjustable chain oilers that can be blocked off with plugs for use with belt drives. Some early engines will require a bit of drilling to fit.

The pumps are chrome-plated while under assembly, making sure no flash or grinding compound gets in any orifice. *Custom Chrome*

The oil pump mounts behind the engine, as seen from the right side.

engine. The EFI doesn't care if it's on a Shovelhead, Evo, Sportster, or any other H-D engine—theoretically, it could be set up to run a Knucklehead with little difficulty. Normally aspirated or supercharged makes no difference. Jean White told me, recently, that sales were much higher than expected. So much so that another run will have to be started pretty soon. She said that she's hearing nothing but positive feedback from customers using EFI.

Add thermocouple probes (additional cost, but well worth it), and the display will show exhaust gas temperature (EGT) and individual cylinder head temperature (CHT). Aircraft have been using these gauges to set mixtures for many years. All this info is presented while you ride from the bar-mounted display panel.

Installation is as easy as pulling the carb. The EFI unit is self-contained in the same machined billet case as the air intake. Mount it on any intake manifold mounting fanged carbs, hook the wiring to power and spark, install fuel supply and return lines, hang the display monitor on the bars, and light it up. Take my word for it: if your total knowledge of computers is confined to the TV remote control—you still won't have any problem understanding the setup. You don't have to know hard drive from hard rock to make this work, just be able to follow directions. Right now there's an S&S mixing the fuel on my '82 FXRS. I won't change it over to EFI 'cause I like the way it looks; plus, I only have 21,450 miles on the scoot and don't plan on accumulating many more, making EFI kind of a waste. However, a new FLHR Electra Glide should be in the garage about the time you read this, and the plan is to change the cam and pipes and go to EFI before it has

1,000 miles on the odometer. If all goes to plan, the Glide's going to travel around the country doing research for the next manuscript, giving me a chance to use EFI in a real-world situation.

List price is $2,195, direct or through a dealer. The system is available in 42mm and 46mm. One of the sizes will work on whatever you are building. If touring is your bag, the lean-out-in-cruise feature, improving mileage without losing any performance, will be your favorite feature. Better mileage, instant throttle response, no lag or flat spots: EFI is the way to go.

Exhaust

Any good set of free-flowing pipes will let the bigger engines breath. Drag Specialties' Python II anti-reversionary pipes show a significant gain in the top end, without having the mid-range or low end suffer. The pipes are of 40in equal length, 1-3/4in header, 2-1/2in muffler single-piece manufacture. Dyno tests show a 12hp gain over stock pipes at 4500rpm. Mounted on an Evo sporting a 44mm Mikuni, high-lift cam, and large amounts of head work, the Python IIs made more power than any other staggered-duals.

Rich Product's Thunderheaders two-into-one setup far outperforms the stock pipes throughout the rpm range. Their patented Thundercone dissipates the negative wave from the pipe, increasing power. Like most semi-open systems, this setup is louder than stock, even with the fiberglass baffle, so watch the throttle in built-up areas. On a drag bike, they will perform to the max.

Bub Enterprises' "Bad Dogs" staggered-duals on a 1986 FXR, cammed and rejetted, showed a major gain over stock pipes throughout all rpm ranges. They put out close to Thunderheader's power at all ranges except at 6000 and above, where the Bad Dogs showed an 11hp gain, to 71hp.

For those of us who have to ride through housing developments, sound levels can be a real problem. It's been a while since an angry neighbor threw a two-by-four at me when I made a full-throttle run down the block, but I remember it well enough to keep it from occurring again. My 1963 Panhead had straight drag pipes on it. No way was I going to run no sissy mufflers on *my* bike. As I remember, the headache would start after thirty minutes of riding. No helmet, no mufflers, no brains.

Stock pipes put out 82dBa at 5000rpm. H-D Offroads are good for 94 at the same rpm. The loudest are Rich Product's two-into-one, at 96dBa. Bub's pipes are close, with 93 at 5000. The loudest set was Rich Products', recording 99dBa with the engine turning 6000. Pink Floyd rock concerts put out almost 100dBa and can leave you partially deaf for hours. . Any exhaust noise above 96dBa can do permanent damage over long periods of time. Wearing earplugs under a helmet while racing is a good idea. The yellow disposable type can be purchased at any sporting shop for less than a buck per pair.

I had the rare privilege to witness a series of dyno runs at CCI's distribution/research center in Morgan Hill, CA. The bike and dyno were behind thick glass walls, which attenuated the sound to a great degree, but the floor shook for 100 feet in all directions during full-throttle runs. Inside the dyno room, we all wore hearing protectors while the run was made. The engine was held at 3000rpm; then, when the run began, the throttle was abruptly wound full open. There was a split second's hesitation, then it sounded like a top-fuel dragster coming off the line. The sound could be felt as much as

heard. Without hearing protectors, anyone inside would be driven deaf in short order. I pulled the muffs away from my ears for a second just to see how loud the pipes were. Dumb trick—I can still hear ringing.

Sound is what you hear when the throttle is opened; noise is what the neighbors hear. All of the pipes made under 90dBa below 3000rpm—'nuff said.

Just Add Money

Sometimes the quickest way to the racetrack is to buy an engine ready to bolt in the frame and run. This way, the people who build motors for a living build yours, instead of you having to go down the trail of broken parts on the way to finding reliability and horsepower.

Zipper's Performance Products (8040 Washington Blvd., Jessup, MD 20794; Hotline 301-799-

S&S does not recommend plating their oil pumps, due to the possibility of ingesting foreign bits and pieces. Different drive gears, breathers, and shims are available.

The exact year and model of your bike must be stated when buying a pump, as oil pump bodies differ depending on year model. *S&S*

8989) offers a series of engines in various stages of size and tune, ready to run. Zipper's has been developing racing engines since 1981, gathering a large amount of knowledge about what works and doesn't work on V-twins.

They offer three flavors of motor modifications, starting with stock displacement and climbing through an 88in stroker motor to a Pro Street 96in thumper. All their motors run S&S cranks and kits, Axtell pistons, Zipper's heads, Red Shift, Crane, or Andrews cams, and other high-quality components. Complete engines can be had, or, if your motor has a bad case of the tireds, they can rebuild it to any state of tune.

Other products, from heavy-duty cases to custom carbs, can be worked out with them. Once you have a specific idea as to what you want the engine to do, let them work out costs on your particular needs. All their work is done in-house, so they can handle just about anything on a custom-build, rapid turn-around basis.

Summary

The stage two engine should be capable of producing ETs in the mid-eleven- to high ten-second bracket. Engine size runs 87ci, with a stock stroke and 3-5/8in bore, to 114ci, using a 5in stroke and a 3-13/16in bore. Horsepower ranges from 92 on pump gas to 145 on racing gas. The modifications outlined below aren't suitable for a touring bike unless it's being actively raced. Stick to a Big Twin that earns its keep at the track or is ridden for fun and profit on the street. The bigger engines will be reliable for thousands of miles, providing maintenance is kept up. Where the additional wear and tear appears is when all the power between your legs gets unleashed on a regular basis. If you're going to race, you're going to see the insides of the motor more often.

S&S provides a drilling fixture to adapt their oil pumps to various engines. The crankcase must be drilled to provide a pressure valve relief hole, crankshaft feed hole, and primary chain oiler supply hole on different models. Here, the fixture is being used to drill the primary chain oiler passage on earlier motors. *S&S*

One-hundred and fourteen cubic inches is definitely harder on components than 96. It is possible to go through an entire season without splitting the cases; however, expect the heads and cylinders to come down at least twice during the year. Street 96in motors, kept in a reasonable rpm range, will last until you're tired of looking at them, providing the oil gets changed regularly and the engine is kept tuned (reasonable rpm means 5500, not 6800—even though it's more fun up high).

Package Specifications
Stage Two Engine

(92 to 145hp). Figure on $3,000 to over $5,000 depending on size, cam type, and heads. The upper limit will depend on each individual engine combination.

Kit #1
1. S&S Super E or G carb;
2. S&S Air Cleaner;
3. Crane Hydraulic Cam Part #1-1003;
4. Jacobs Energy Team Ignition;
5. Bub "Bad Dogs" Pipes;
6. Axtell Cylinder Kits, 86ci to 97ci;
7. Aftermarket Rods—Carillo;
8. Ported Heads—AFR;
9. Adjustable Pushrods.

Kit #2
1. Mikuni HSR 42 Carb;
2. K&N Air Filter;
3. Competition Cams #EVO-3050;
4. MSD MC1 Ignition;
5. Rich Thunderhead two-into-one;
6. S&S Sidewinder 3-5/8in Bore Cylinders;
7. B.C. Gerolamy "D" Port Bathtub Chamber Heads;
8. One-Piece Chrome Moly Pushrods.

Kit #3
1. CCI RevTech Carb;
2. CCI RevTech #40 Cam;
3. 5in Stroke by 3-5/8in Bore—103.1ci, or
4. Sputhe 104ci w/ 4-5/8in Flywheels;
5. Sputhe Cases & Heads;
6. Drag Specialties Python II Pipes.

Kit #4
1. S&S Super G Carb;
2. Andrews Cam;
3. Dyna Ignition;
4. Sputhe 95ci Street Engine;
5. S&S Crank & Rod Assembly;
6. S&S Oil Pump;
7. Crane Roller Rockers;
8. Rich Thunderheaders.

Kit #5
1. S&S Super G Carb;
2. S&S Cam;
3. S&S Oil Pump;
4. Axtell 97ci Mountain Motor (Stock Cases);
5. Carillo Rods;
6. Staggered Dual Pipes.

Shovelheads can use most of the above parts to run serious drag racing times of 10.8 to 11.2 seconds. Some parts will have to be unique to Shovels, but availability isn't a problem at this time.

With Shovels out of production since 1984, you might want to think twice about ripping apart a stock motor. Although Shovels don't command high prices, there's a possibility that they could go the way of the Panhead. Five years ago, Pans could be found easily for $5,500 in semi-stock condition. Today, $5,500 will get you boxes containing most of the big parts. These days, it takes $14,000 and up to acquire a nice stock Panhead.

Shovels are still common, but you don't want to rip apart an FX Super Glide only to find out that it's worth $15,000 eight years from now. Doesn't sound possible, does it? My '82 FXRS sold new in January 1982 for $6,200 out the door. It's still box-stock, under 22,000 miles. Last month (May '94), I turned down $8,500 cash for it at a Harley Owners Group (HOG) rally. A new 1994 replacement would run $14,000, providing one could be found at this time of the year. A 1995 will be more. If the new bikes are as hard to get in the future as they are today, in California anyway, the clean older Shovels will do nothing but appreciate. Should you still find reason to doubt, write me—I'll put money on it.

There are many other possible combinations of aftermarket components that will deliver a sub-eleven second bike. Go to a few drag races and check out what the competition is running. Talk to engine builders—people like Axtell, S&S, or Sputhe can help you plan an engine. Figure everything will cost more, take longer, and provide more fun than you think.

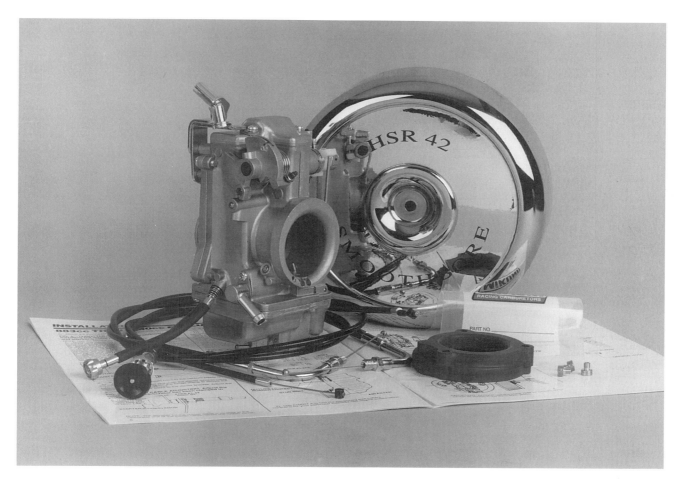

Above and next page: Big engines need to be able to flow a lot of air to make maximum power. Mikuni's HSR 42 will move as much air as a 52mm butterfly with 45mm venturi, due to its slide function. When the carb's wide open, nothing impedes the flow of air. The chart shows the HSR 42 flowing more air than the bigger carb when both are bolted to a manifold and head. *Mikuni*

FLOW TEST RESULTS
CFM @ 12" water/.600" lift

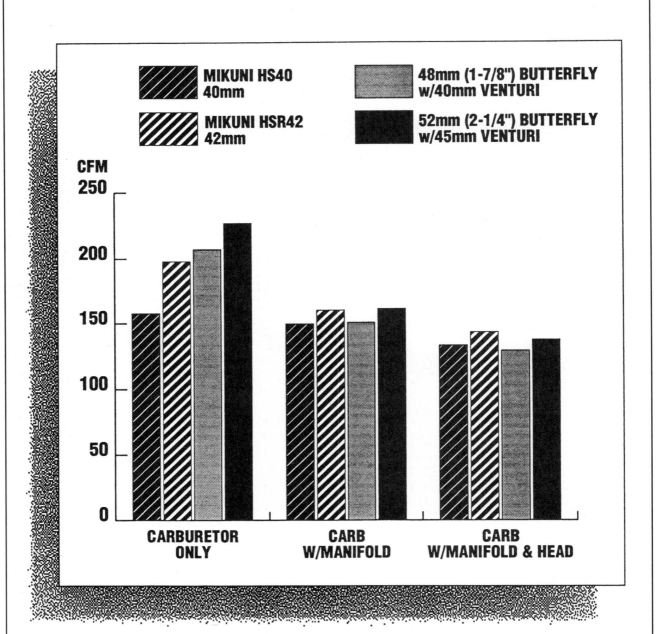

A thunder jet will improve the performance of S&S' Super E. The Thunder jet is a self-adjusting third-fuel circuit, allowing you to increase horsepower mostly in the top end through additional fuel flow. *Zipper's*

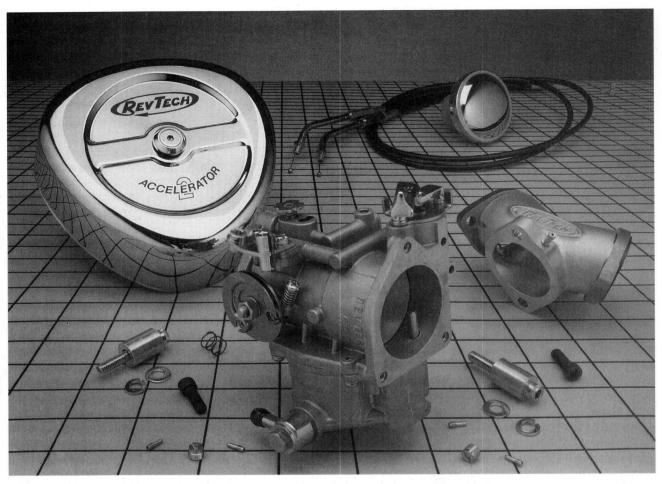

Above: The RevTech carb from CCI comes as a kit, with everything needed to bolt on your Evo or Shovel. Extra jets enable you to set it up for your particular installation. As with S&S, dual-throttle cables are required. *Custom Chrome*

Right: The entire unit takes less space than the factory carb and air cleaner. It has the same fit as a Bendix or Keihin and is available in two sizes, 42mm and 46mm, to cover most applications. The unit can be mounted on everything from Knuckleheads to Evos. (Be the first one on your block with an EFI Knuckle.) The Motorola 68 HC11 Microcomputer is controlled by the display unit mounted on the bars. It's self-prompting and can be set to run over a wide range of parameters. And all the trick words aside, it's fairly easy to install. All the wiring plugs into existing plugs and the rest of the cables hook up to power, ground, coils, and points pick-up. If you know nothing whatsoever about computers, it'll take about two hours to install. If you're a wizard with a hard drive, it still takes two hours. At $2,300, it's a bit expensive; however, once you try it, you'll never switch back to carbs. Save your old carb so you can take the EFI to your next bike. *Whitek*

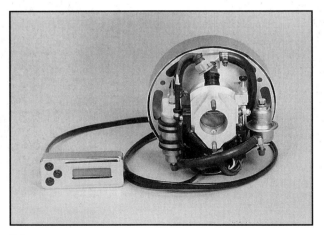

Left: Some day all motorcycles will have fuel-injection instead of carbs. Emissions regulations, if nothing else, will force manufacturers to adopt it as a better method of fuel control. Whitek already has developed an Electronic Fuel Injection (EFI) for H-D. This is a unit made specifically for motorcycles, not an adaptation of an automotive unit. It's a good-looking system—installs in place of the carb, with a readout mounted up on the bars. *Whitek*

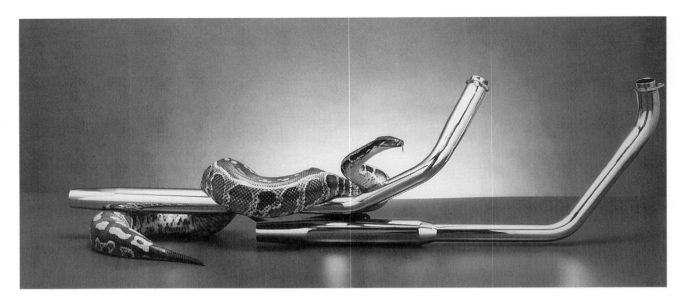

The snake's optional, but the Pythons from Drag Specialties can be purchased at a nominal price. When the picture was being set up, we were assured the snake *had* been fed recently, but it was decided to employ a slightly longer lens. These single-bolters fit Shovels. *Edge Advertising/Drag Specialties*

Going to a four-plug, single-fire system requires mounting two coils where one used to sit. Custom Cycle offers a bracket and chrome cover to make the job easier. Two Dyna coils are used. The horn must be moved behind the rear cylinder; Custom Cycle makes a bracket for that purpose. *Custom Cycle*

Chapter 4

Stage Three: Big-Inch Race Motors

This chapter deals with engine combinations developed strictly for racing. Displacement will run from stock to 125ci. We'll also take a look at alcohol- and nitro-based engines. Anyone contemplating building a 150hp, or better, racing motor should have a lot of prior racing experience. All these motors will take much more than average maintenance, and large infusions of money. A 125ci Evo motor *can* be run on the street; however, the idea is to build it, as the disclaimer says, "for racing purposes only." By this point in the book, it's to be assumed that you know enough about building engines to be able to handle the additional work involved in building big-bore stroker motors running on 110 octane racing gas, alcohol, or nitro.

The best place to start building a racing motor is at a desk with a pencil and paper. Before anything gets ordered, be it parts or a complete engine, your budget needs to be worked out with some sort of cap figured in to limit expenditures. As covered elsewhere, Murphy's Law will add at least 20% to the total outlay, so it might as well be figured in now.

A very rough idea of dollar outlay for the big parts in the engine goes as follows:

Heads, complete $2,200
Cylinders, pistons, rings, wrist pins $1,100
Cam, lifters, pushrods, rockers, springs . .$547
Flywheels, crank pin, rods $1,023
Cases $895
Cam cover $295
Complete Evo short block $3,400
   (97ci Pro-Street)
Oil pump w/ gears $440
Ignition, plugs $185
Carb $469
Machine work (depends on who your friends are) $1,500

Axtell's 97in "Mountain Motor" uses the standard-length cylinders and factory flywheels to keep the Evo engine looking stock. Inside hide forged pistons, Speed-Pro rings, and all necessary wrist pins, O-rings, and gaskets. *Axtell*

Flow-testing— $700
port & polish, if necessary
Gaskets, break-in lube, sealants $45
Oil & filter (at least two changes) $45
Motor mounts, fasteners, ...$120
   specialized hardware
Hi-Vo primary chain $150
Complete Sputhe 95ci engine $8,000
   (Pro-Street)

Or, if you want to go all out, try a Sputhe 60 degree, 125ci engine. If you have to ask how much, you can't afford it (last price from Bill Chappell, manager at Sputhe's, was $8,000+).

And I'm going to take an out here—prices *can* vary dramatically. Best you call all manufacturers to get current prices. My prices might be out of line one way or the other, but this is what I was quoted as of May 1994. Figures don't take into consideration spare parts or any expendable bits and pieces—spares depend on you. Might as well buy two sets of gaskets, oil by the gallon, a box of spark plugs and fuel in five-gallon cans, as you will be amazed and amused at how fast these goodies disappear.

All the rest of the bike—frame, trans, tires, suspension, etc.—will be covered in later chapters.

Heads

Here's where you are going to definitely have to take advantage of a flow bench. You're going to

eleven years. *Cycle World* tested a street version of the bike and pronounced it "the fastest motorcycle of any kind that this magazine has tested" (July 1980); pretty impressive credentials when it comes to building speed parts.

His modified Evo heads take advantage of all the prior racing information gathered while Sputhe raced Open Superstreet and Open GP. His engines won both classes in 1980 and 1981, along with Allen picking up first place in the SCTA Dry Lakes Championship in 1981. This manufacturer has definitely learned the speed business from the rider's seat.

Leo Hess begins to turn ethanol into noise on his dragster at El Mirage. You have to be there to believe the sound this bike makes. The rear wheel's turning faster than the front, and it will do it up to 200mph. *Full Blast Engineering*

want the flow from the carb to the piston to be slicker than greased duck feathers. Airflow should be at or above 250cfm, measured at .560 lift, through 1-15/16 inch intake Evo heads. Sputhe or STD 2.100 heads should flow 260cfm, or better, at the same lift.

Sputhe has been producing aluminum heads for the XR-750 racer since 1979. Allen Sputhe built a Sportster-based 1300cc bike that went 176mph at Bonneville, taking home a record that stood for

All the products use computer-aided design—computer-aided manufacture (CAD-CAM) technology and CNC machining centers to design and build the aircraft-grade aluminum heads. No offshore vendors are relied upon to produce parts, so Sputhe is able to exercise better quality control over all their products. They are also able to respond to your needs quicker, whether they be for a complete engine or a 25mm layshaft bearing for a 5-speed transmission.

On the heads, the inlet port is raised for better flow. The intake and exhaust valve guides have fairings to help move the air into the cylinders, transferring heat away from the combustion chamber in the process. Guides can be spec'd out as aluminum-bronze or magnesium-meehanite. Valve sizes, on the intake side run from 1.937 on stock 80in cylinders to 2.100 on finless racing cylinders. The exhaust valve diameters span 1.710 to 1.875, depending on usage. A complete set of heads, valves, and springs will run $1,495.

B.C. Gerolamy will take bare STD castings, port, polish, and raise exhaust ports, incline valve angles, and cut the seats to accept 2.100 intakes and 1.750 exhausts. Gerolamy has done a lot of work on Shovelheads—getting 232cfm to move through ported 1-15/16 intakes at .550 lift. They can weld and shape intake ports and chambers, install Rowe guides, install larger valves, port and polish the manifold—all for increased airflow on Shovels. They began working with H-D cylinder heads, initially welding and raising intake ports on Shovels, over nine years ago, and now doing the same on Evo heads, with excellent results.

Gerolamy formed Cylinder Head Abrasives in 1983 to provide porting and polishing supplies for professionals who wish to do their own head work or for amateurs who are feeling adventurous enough to try to hone their own. They do all sorts of racing head work for cars as well as bikes and are more than willing to provide help in setting up your heads for whatever type of event you run.

Cams and Valves

When it comes to installing valves and guides, Manley recommends using silicon-aluminum bronze guides in all racing engines with either chrome or nitride finish on the valve stems. The nitride process imparts a hard surface on the stem, aiding in lubrication and durability. Their valves are available with "severe-duty" stainless steel construction, chrome-plated stems, hard tips, radiused and dished in sizes from 1.850 to 2.000 intake, matched with 1.615 to 1.650 exhaust.

The valvetrain can be ordered as a kit composed of valves, double-spring assemblies, steel top collars, and machined keepers. For racing use, titanium top collars should be substituted for steel.

The Evo kit can be used with any lift cam up to .600in. Cylinder heads don't have to be milled for clearance, as with Shovel heads. The spring load at full open is 380lbs; 170lbs at rest.

For those of you who run lots of revs, Manley has titanium valves available up to 2.100 on the intake, 1.80 exhaust for the Evo. List price for a set of two runs $263.30. Stainless valves are $72.20 per set of two, so you can see there is a significant price difference between the two types of metals. The advantage of titanium is lower weight. Every time the cam turns one time, a valve has to accelerate from 0 to maximum lift, stop, then reverse direction back down again. Lower weight means less inertia to overcome. Less inertia = better valve control. Titanium also has a higher tensile strength than stainless—less chance of pulling the head off the valve at high spring pressures.

S&S .630in lift valve spring and collar kit will control valves up to 7500rpm without float. Their kit

Leo's fuel engine. As it's sponsored by the South Dakota Corn Utilization Council, I highly doubt he will run out of fuel any time soon. Lots of corn in the Dakotas.

runs 460lbs open-spring pressure, needed if you are going to turn the motor at high revs. For cams with up to .780 lift (about the height of your average front step), they make a .780 racing-only kit. This is one case where "if some's good–more's better" won't work on the street. Any lift above .550 will be just about as useless as a football bat, below 4000rpm.

Electric starters aren't very compatible with tall cams in large motors with stepped-on compression. What happens is that the starter gives it one good spin before surrendering. If everything is perfect, you get a running motor—if not, you get hot battery wires and strange noises from the starter. Long-duration, high-lift cams will lower cranking compression in a stock, or close to stock, displacement engine, but

Tator Gilmore's twin-engined Top Fuel Harley sits in the pits. Under the engines is written "Feel the Difference." I imagine with two engines running on nitro, you could do just that. Ready to try? *Rich Engineering*

big motors still pose a starting problem when the displacement climbs above 98 cubes.

Because big-lift cams have such radical specifications, expect valvetrain wear to be higher than usual. High spring rates will wear out seats quicker. High revs will wear out everything quicker, especially if you miss a shift or two. A rev limiter is good insurance. Blow a one–two shift when the engine's turned so tight that it sounds like a gas turbine, and you will probably gain a whole new collection of very hot, bent parts. The strip owners will make you clean up all the oil, too!

S&S cam #631 is a good grind to use for big-inch racing motors. All the horsepower is made between 4500 and wherever you feel comfortable. Usually, 7500 is the upper limit for any-sized Evo motor. You can turn it higher, but you're only thrashing parts above this speed. The valves can get confused and smite the piston heads a mighty blow should the revs go high enough to let the valves actually lose contact with the cam. Kissing the piston can bend the valve enough to go from maximum horsepower

to zero in .001 second. At 6000rpm, the engine is rotating 100 times a second. Even if you have reflexes quicker than an 1880s gunslinger, the valve will open at least 200 times before you can kill the engine. I can admit, from personal experience, that it makes a terrible (expensive) noise.

Back a few years ago when I was building engines by the torque-it-and-hope method, I sneezed a motor just as I was shifting into fourth at about 6000rpm. The problem was, the shift forks in the tranny would flex enough to where the gearbox would grow a whole set of neutrals if shifted too hard. I was six inches behind the bike in the other lane and trying to stretch another 300rpm out of third gear before going for fourth. Either that, or I just plain forgot to shift. When I noticed the engine wasn't making any too much more power, I snagged the clutch lightly enough to let the gearshift lever go for the next gear. Notice I didn't say that I let off the throttle. Well, the shift forks did their dance, and the box went from third to never-never land. This was back in the bad old days before rev limiters, so the tach needle disappeared off the right side of the dial. The valves floated off the cam and proceeded to embed themselves in the piston tops. The rods bent from the impact. All of a sudden I had lots of noises, parts leaving the engine, and zilch power. The engine died immediately (in front of 3,000 or so people and numerous racers), leaving me to coast off the track in dead silence. About that time, I figured I should start really learning how to build engines, as this wasn't the first one to get air-conditioned.

The S&S #631 grind has .630 lift, 275 degree duration on the intake side, and 276 on the exhaust. Because of the extreme lift, additional piston-to-valve clearance will be necessary. All the related clearances—valve-to-valve, valve-spring spacing, and rocker arm-to-spring collar—need the same checking. One place a lot of builders forget to inspect is the rocker box cover-to-rocker clearance. Prior to bolting the engine into the frame, wrench down the valve cover, including the gasket, and slowly rotate the crank. If the engine quits turning, or if you hear strange noises emanating from within, loosen the valve cover, then spin the crank again. By watching the cover rise, you can get an idea of how much clearance must be cut in the cover.

Any S&S cam, especially a high-lift one, should be installed with the S&S valve spring kit. On the .630 lift cam, the valve spring kit comes with three springs per valve, two round wire, one flat, for harmonics control. Collars are lightened steel, or titanium—recommended for high revs.

Early Evos, equipped with "shoulder"-style valve guides, will have to be fitted with "shoulderless"-type guides, as on the newer heads. This kit has been run to 7500rpm without any float, but, as described above, the open pressure of 460lbs will increase valvetrain wear.

A titanium collar kit contains four collars, four collar-friction reducing washers, four outer valve springs, four inner valve springs, four harmonic springs, four steel bottom collars, and eight valve keepers.

Kosman Specialties builds a frame to take a four-valve-head Evo motor. You probably won't find too many H-D parts numbers on that motor. Cases, cylinders, heads, and most everything inside come from aftermarket suppliers. *Kosman*

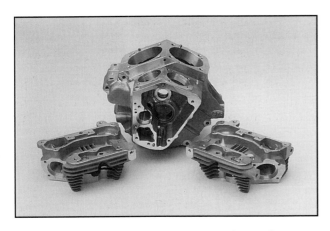

Building a big-inch Big Twin requires aftermarket cases and heads like these from STD. The heads are available as unfinished castings, for you to try your hand at finishing, or as complete units for custom engines. Zipper's can provide you with either type. *Zipper's*

For those of you who think a .630 cam is nice, but something with a little more lift would be appropriate, S&S will oblige you with a .780 lift, racing only, kit. Same type of parts as in the "little" .630 kit, just set up for more travel. The heads will have to be fly-cut to fit the larger diameter springs.

Both high-lift kits are set up to use solid lifters. The lifter roller-to-lifter block clearance must be checked because of the greater lifter travel with the taller cam lobes. Juice lifters can be adapted to a limited travel lifter by installing an S&S HL2T kit. It keeps the lifter from going to sleep at elevated revs while retaining the benefits of hydraulics.

Stock pushrods go limp when asked to run much over 5500rpm. Spin the stockers hard a few times—you get U-bolts instead of pushrods. Most hi-po cams require solid lifters, necessitating the use of adjustable pushrods. Adjustable pushrods not only are stronger, but also give the flexibility required to make up any increase in cam-lobe diameter. High-lift cams change the angle of the pushrod from lifter to rocker because of their increased lobe rise, sometimes causing interference between pushrod, pushrod tube, and/or cylinder head. All S&S 7/16in rods will work with any of their cams without problems in clearance. The longest rod fits the front exhaust—farthest from the cam. The next longest goes in the rear exhaust. The remaining two short rods fit both intakes. Different angles leading to the pushrods from the cam make for longer or shorter rods.

The individual factory pushrods can be identified by color-coding and length. Front exhaust is green—11.325in. Rear exhaust, purple—11.210in.

Front intake, yellow—11.090in. Rear intake, blue—11.045in.

To check stock Evo pushrods for straightness, roll them one at a time across a piece of glass. Bent rods will flop up and down. After checking the stockers, throw them away. They just aren't suitable for racing.

Some books advise using non-adjustable chrome-moly pushrods, with solid lifters set up with adjustment screws. Personal preference is for solid lifters and adjustable rods in all racing engines. Non-adjustable pushrods have to be cut to size, then fitted with the ball ends. Any benefits possibly gained through solid pushrods are negated if one gets bent at the track, leaving you either with a one-cylinder drag bike or trying to figure out how to cut chrome-moly to fit, using a hacksaw and file. Another corollary to Murphy's Law states that the part that fails will be the one you didn't throw in the spares box this time. It will also fail at the track farthest from your home—usually at least two time zones away. All four pushrods only differ by .280—a long distance with non-adjustable rods, but no problem with the adjustable type.

Years ago, some adjustable pushrods occasionally had the bad habit of backing out of adjustment, with the usual power-loss problems. These days, the aftermarket parts don't have any such problem. You can bend them if you try hard enough (you can bend anything! I have a friend who could break an anvil in a sandbox and lose two of the pieces. And he's my engine builder), but they won't come loose. They really won't bend without something being seriously wrong in the engine. You start bending aftermarket pushrods below 7500, you better take a hard look at your valvetrain—something is real wrong.

When using adjustable pushrods with stock hydraulic lifters, you will have to collapse the lifter for proper operation. Start with a cold engine. Rotate the crank to the lowest lifter position. Set the adjusting screw so that all free-play is taken up. Then turn the adjuster out 4 to 4-1/2 turns to set the lifter all the way down. Remember that the oil takes time to bleed down, so don't hurry this procedure. All remaining pushrods are adjusted the same way.

The HL2T limited travel kit sets up a little differently. Crank down the pushrod until the lifter bottoms. Back off the adjustment enough to let the pushrod turn freely between your finger and thumb. Tighten the lock nut and recheck the clearance. Do the same for the remaining three. Again, turn the crank through slowly to make sure valve clearance is adequate—now's not the time to have something bend due to lack of room.

My choice of hydraulic lifters for a race motor is Competition Cams' "Velva Touch" juice-roller lifter kits. Their technology won't allow the lifter to bleed down, as the stocker does. Lifters can be ordered either black (with a hard coating) or polished chrome. Seeing as how they're out of sight inside the engine and you're not watching them while racing, chrome lifters serve no purpose except to wear faster than the coated black ones.

If chrome makes you happy, spend the bucks on chrome lifter blocks—at least they show.

Velva-Touch lifter bodies are cut from tool steel to very precise tolerances. The walls are thick enough for strength at high revs, while not being overly heavy.

Above and right: A swirl-polished, stainless steel valve and a set of valve springs with keepers and retainers can usually be purchased for less money if bought as a package. The Manley valve spring set shows all three springs in their proper position. Each spring is slightly different. *Manley*

Where high-quality hydraulic lifters come into their own is in controlling expansion. Cylinders grow—heads expand. The cases change as they warm up. Everything conspires to change dimensions. Increased noise from the valvetrain means increased wear. Juice lifter bodies let the oil enter to take up extra clearance as the engine grows. After a few runs, pull and check the pushrods for any shiny areas. Marks can be caused by alignment interference or bending. Use the "piece of glass" method to check for bent pushrods.

Right now my street FXRS picks up lifter noise when warm. As soon as this book gets put to bed, I plan on calling Competition Cams, with the hope in mind that a #SHV-4000 cam and #8000-KIT lifter kit might

find it's way into my mailbox. I even might try for a price break, seeing as how I said nice things about them (fat chance! I get parts the same way you get parts—except you probably don't beg as much as I do).

Installing high-lift springs might require that the spring pocket on the head be cut out to accept larger-diameter springs. Lower collars have to sit absolutely flat on the head without the spring touching any part of the casting.

The heads should already be off the engine, facilitating checking installed spring height. This is the distance from the top of the bottom collar to the bottom of the top collar, or the height of the installed valve spring. This should be 1.490in to 1.520in for Shovels and 1.800in for Evo motors.

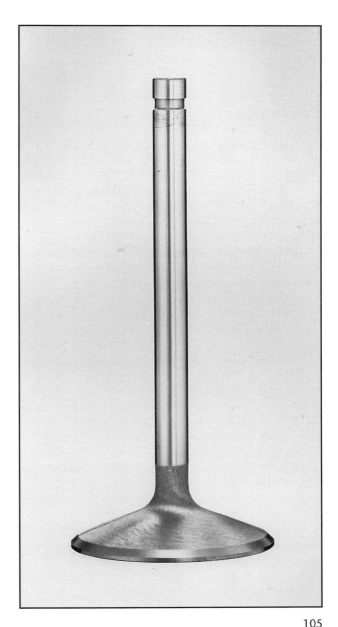

Install the valve, two collars, and keepers. Hold the valve against the seat while checking dimension "B," as shown in the drawing below. Do the same for all the valves (be thankful it isn't a twenty-four-valve motor). The shortest distance is the dimension to use for installed spring height. All the other valves will have to be shimmed to give the same height. S&S can provide additional shims where necessary.

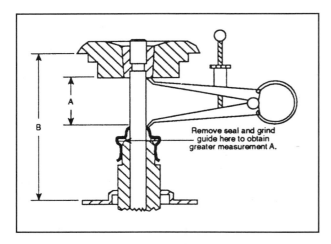

Next up, measure the distance from the bottom of the top collar to the top of the valve guide. This height has to be at least .060in greater than the total lift of the valve. Otherwise, the collar will hit the guide, possibly punching it into the combustion chamber. Normally, clearance problems will wear out valve seals rapidly and turn the cam lobes down to circles.

After the springs are installed in the head, you have to check for spring coil bind. Raise the valve fully open, then check for additional travel of at least .060in before any coils contact. To increase the clearance, the valves can be sunk deeper in the head by grinding the seats. Don't let the total spring height get more than .040in above the 1.520in Shovel or 1.800in Evo installed height.

Once the head's bolted to the engine for final assembly and rockers are installed, rocker arm/valve spring retainer clearance has to be checked. Rotate the engine while watching the rocker arm's relationship to the collar. Too long of a valve stem, or poor rocker arm geometry along with wrong rockers, can result in the arm hitting the collar during its stroke.

As in checking valve-to-piston clearance, all valvetrain geometry and operating clearances must be checked thoroughly during assembly. This ensures that everything will operate without interference when the engine fires for the first time.

There are many reasons not to run the motor at anything like high revs when everything is shiny new, but, as far as the valvetrain is concerned, the springs need to warm up to operating temperature to take a set at their operating pressure. Running the engine until hot, then allowing it to cool to ambient will break in the springs, helping to eliminate early breakage.

Exact costs for valvetrain will depend to a great deal on what components are selected. Buying everything as a kit will give you a better price than purchasing the individual pieces one at a time. Figure on a 20% difference on some parts. Not that any of these parts is going to be cheap, though. But if you wanted cheap, you'd be racing slot cars, not Harleys.

Set aside $350 for a cam, $150 for springs with titanium keepers, $25 more for racing high-lift springs,

S&S offers an adjustable pushrod kit, along with springs and retainers. Titanium retainers should be used with high spring-tension and high revs. *S&S*

and $80 for pushrods and lifters. Real nice roller rockers, for lifts over .600in, run $370 per set. Right around $1,000 will go into making the valves do the right thing at the right time.

Gasoline and Fuel

Now, with a stage two engine, it becomes a matter of how much compression you can run and still operate on available gas. Stock Evo engines have

If you decide to stay with juice lifters, Competition Cam's "VelvaTouch" hydraulic roller lifters give all the benefits of solids without noise or constant adjustment. The sides of the lifters can have a special coating applied to cut down rubbing friction and extend lifter life. Evo lifter kits come with lifters, lifter blocks, pushrods, covers, and bolts. Even an installation video is included. *Competition Cams*

8.5:1 pop. Shovels run anywhere from 7.4:1 to 8.5:1, depending on year and what kind of peanut oil Harley thought was going to be available for gas.

We're not talking street use now—92 octane won't work for racing. Whether you are at the drags or Bonneville, 104 to 110 octane is all that you will be using for racing. Playing with exotic fuels is a whole different game, requiring a great deal of knowledge and no little magic. Strange terms are overheard from racers mixing nitro and/or alcohol. Words like "specific gravity" and "ambient temperature," "stoichiometric ratio" and "percent of pop" float in the air. You hear someone say, "the engine sneezed when we ran too much squeeze behind the turbo." This means an owner gets to build another engine—this time without so much nitrous oxide injected on the other side of the turbocharger.

Nitro-methane stinks good, makes the eyes water, grows horsepower, and is possibly the rastiest fuel known to man. Alcohol comes as methanol—derived from wood—and is real hard on your system if you drink it, or as ethanol, from corn, as used by Leo Hess' twin-engine, 207mph+ Bonneville racer (see sidebar). The South Dakota Corn Council sponsors his bike. Sounds like a good use for agriculture to me.

Back in the late 1700s (1790 or 1794), Secretary of the Treasury Alexander Hamilton initiated through Congress a tax on distilled spirits. Some of the very first Federal revenue officers were tarred and feathered when they tried to collect this tax on alcohol.

These days the Feds don't let much happen to their BATF officers when out chasing "revenuers" and honest, gun-owning citizens. However, they do ensure that the Federal tax is paid on each gallon of alcohol sold. This boils down to one of the reasons why the cost of filling the tank with alcohol or nitro & alcohol costs so much more than pump gas. Also, nitro is costly to produce and semi-dangerous to handle. The hazardous waste people extract their pound of flesh every time it is transported, helping run the cost up. ERC (800-445-1479) has nitro for $35/gallon, $1,300 per fifty-five-gallon drum.

Alcohol costs in more ways than one. Especially if you shoot at tax collectors when under its influence—it tends to make you miss. Buying it for the engine as opposed to the stomach still means you have to pay tax. Either way you consume alcohol gives the government lots of your hard-earned dollars in tax. This is money that has nothing to do with producing, distributing, or consuming methanol or ethanol. As a matter of fact, some of the tax money gets returned to the ethanol growers as subsidy. Methanol is $1.95 per gallon, $1.80/gal in larger quantities.

As far as racing gas prices, ERC 110 gasoline sells for $4.15 per gallon—their A-8B is considerably more, at $7.15 per, but you get 118 octane, as figured by the Research method. We are more used to seeing octane listed by the "Motor Method," which gives a lower reading than the Research rating. 110 Research octane equals 104 Motor octane. 118 Research is the equivalent of 111 motor octane. Either way, ERC's 110 or A-8B will let you carry a lot more advance and compression in a racing motor than you could possibly use with what passes for pump gas.

Compression Ratio & Pistons

Once you've decided to only run the bike on the race track, using higher compression becomes easier. Although 110 octane gasoline can support a 15:1 compression ratio in Shovelheads, usually the ratios are between 13.5:1 and 14.5:1 in the real world of racing. Above these ratios, performance tends to lay down with gas motors. To get a Shovel up to these ratios, high-domed pistons are required to fill the large hemispherical combustion chambers. S&S, and others, make racing pistons for this purpose.

An Evo makes excellent drag racing power with a 12.5:1 ratio, running on racing gas. Higher ratios can be used, but then other factors come into play. How much maintenance are you willing to do to keep the parts together? What type of detonation control will be used? Does the volumetric efficiency warrant such a ratio? How much more go are you

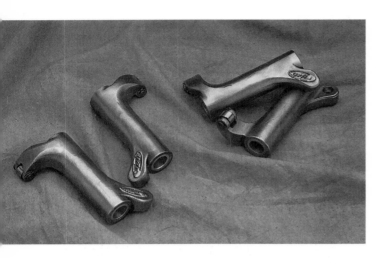

RevTech's roller rocker arms are made from 8620 chrome-moly and normalized to HRC 35. This makes for long life without being brittle. They are made to use stock rocker shafts. *Custom Chrome*

getting by stepping on the compression so hard? Engine life usually isn't a problem to racers, but it would be nice to be able to run the engine more than once before the pistons melt through.

In general, Shovel engines run better with higher compression ratios than Evos. Either engine will benefit from setting up the heads for dual spark. For the same octane gasoline, dual plugs will help an engine function better with more compression before the old devil detonation steals power. Shovels, with their large, high-dome, semi-inefficient combustion chamber can make excellent use of dual-plug heads.

Evo combustion chambers are way ahead of Shovels. They can get away with running more pop than a Shovel without going to dual plugs. However, when the ratios climb above 13:1, Evo motors need the added benefit of that second plug. B.C. Gerolamy can set up a stock head for dual plugs—top or exhaust side. Or you can spring for an aftermarket head, like CCI's RevTech, already set up for twin plugs.

By the way, twin plugs aren't something that came out of a hat three days ago. Race cars have sported them since the early 1930s. People who build those funny little open-wheel cars that go so damn fast at places like Monaco and Surfer's Paradise treat dual plugs almost as a given. About the only engine that couldn't benefit from dual plugs would be one of those last-manufactured 7.5:1 Shovel engines of the early 1980s. It's an engine with a compression ratio so low that you'd think it could run on cooking sherry, but it doesn't have enough power to pull the skin off a chocolate pudding.

One thing you don't want to do is let the compression ratio get ahead of the engine's ability to breathe. The carb, headers, and cam must allow high enough volumetric efficiency to make maximum use of high compression. Too much compression, or too much piston head sticking up into the combustion chamber, can cause a power loss through breathing interference at high rpm. Better to run a lower ratio than try to compensate for poor airflow at too high a compression ratio.

Long operation at high revs with high compression can increase the chance of detonation. Running for speed records over a long course usually means lower compression than can be handled at the drag strip. *Any* oil allowed to enter the combustion chamber will create detonation. Straight pipes, coupled with ear plugs inside a helmet, can make hearing detonation very difficult. Sometimes power loss is your first clue that all's not right inside the heads. By then, it's too late; engine damage may have already occurred. After spending a year getting ready for Bonneville, you don't want to discover detonation halfway into a three-mile run.

High compression engines can get a better seal between the head and cylinder by using an O-ring in place of a head gasket. Axtell cylinders, in their "BT-EV" Drag Race Kit, come with O-ring grooves already cut. When ordering the kits, specify bore, stroke, compression, and application of your particular engine. The kit lists for $1,088.50, by special order only.

If you're moving to an Evo motor from a Shovelhead, remember that less compression is needed for optimum performance. Something around 12.5:1, or slightly larger, works best. Running at high altitude, where the air is thinner, the engine can use a slightly higher ratio without detonation.

Once the big compression step has been taken, figure the onboard electric starter will be about as useful as an organ grinder's hand crank. Don't *even* think about trying to start it with your foot. A few years ago, a good friend (we call him "Stumpy") had an H-D with a bad case of too much compression coupled with a high-ratio kick starter. Most of the time, his 265lbs could get it to light, but occasionally it took a dislike to him and kicked back. One memorable day, I watched him apply his normal suave technique of leaping up to tank level to use his considerable heft to drive the kick crank through. Only—only—only—this time, either the engine was flooded or the timing had gone south, because when the starter traveled halfway through its stroke, the engine chuffed and backfired hard. It was the first time I ever saw a human being kick himself in his back pocket.

His knee made a sound like coconuts being busted with a pick ax. I think he sold the bike and took up checkers or some other non-contact sport.

Most racers use a set of rollers to start their bikes. The two rollers are mounted far enough apart to let a bike wheel sit in them without touching the ground. The rear wheel of the bike is set in one side of the rollers and a car or pickup is backed on the other side. The bike is put in gear, usually higher than first, if you want the engine to turn over instead of scuff rubber; then the vehicle is started, put in gear, and held at 2000rpm, give or take. Turn on the ignition, open the throttle a bit, and drop the clutch. At first this might resemble a dance for three feet, but you soon get the hang of staying upright on the rollers, two feet from a pickup's rear wheel, which is turning at 25mph. One hand holds the clutch, one hand holds the throttle, and one hand steadies the bike so the bars don't gouge the paint. Easy, huh?

Remember to put both wheels of the truck on the rollers so that there's no chance of launching it into the pits in front of you.

Starting the bike while keeping it stationary lets you, or your mechanic, watch the engine during the critical first few moments of operation. Towing a bike to start it, at El Mirage or Bonneville, gets the job done but makes it hard to spot things like fuel or oil leaks. The engine can be turned over on the rollers, without spark plugs installed, to prelube all the internal parts before actually running the bike. My brother, a thirty-six-year-old, certifiably crazy road racer, runs his bike in third or fourth gear while sitting on the rollers to warm up the engine and trans prior to heading out on the track. This way, if anything in the drive train isn't right, repairs can quickly be made without having to push back to the pits—not something you want to do on a 100 degree day while wearing leathers.

Bumping up the compression increases the burn rate in the combustion chamber. Backing down on the timing (less advance) can show a horsepower gain. Long-duration cams and high compression go together. Power will be down at lower rpm, but that shouldn't be a problem on racing engines.

Drag racing engines only see revs below 4500 on their way to the staging area. Land speed record runs start off at lower engine speeds; however, acceleration off the line with a high-geared bike is slow anyway, so lack of power down low isn't a problem. Too much power on the salt just pollutes the air with white particles, anyway. I watched Leo Hess' twin-engined, alcohol-fueled APS-AF 3000cc (Unlimited Partial Streamlining–Modified Engine: Fuel) bike run El Mirage last year. Halfway down the one mile course,

he was still spitting sand and sliding sideways while trying to get it to hook up in third gear. Traction can be a bit of a problem on dirt or salt. Dropping the hammer at 7000rpm on asphalt with a twelve inch-wide M&H slick will make the bike move forward. Trying the same trick on the salt, through a five inch tire, results in deep grooves and a remarkable lack of forward progress.

The record for class APS-AF 3000cc was set at 231.597 in 1974 by Dave Campos. Interviewed back then, he said that during practice runs

he was encountering wheel spin at the 200mph mark. Slightly damp conditions, coupled

A cam is a cam is a cam, at least to casual appearances. Where the difference shows is in the lift, duration, and overlap. This cam from Competition cams is set up for hydraulics and runs hard to 7000rpm. This is one of their new "High Energy" series of cams just released in 1994. *Competition Cams*

with an excess of horsepower, made for an interesting ride. Picture yourself shifting into third gear about one mile out on the salt—speed over 100mph. Turning the throttle wide open only makes the tach needle rock between 5000 and 7000, while the oiled course centerline weaves back and forth under your tires. Every time the engine roars, the bike moves sideways four feet. Sound like fun?

High compression does have drawbacks, though. More compression = more power = more heat and greater load on the engine's reciprocating parts. Oil has to transfer more heat away from bearings, so an oil cooler becomes a necessity for any engine run more than fifteen seconds under full power. Oil temperature above 250 degrees will hasten wear and help bring on detonation.

Running over 12.5:1 compression will reduce engine life by as much as 80% from stock. This is of no consequence to an engine that makes its living on a race track, but be prepared to replace parts like crank pins, rods, and bearings more frequently. Racing fuel—104 octane and up—will have to be run to develop full power and prevent detonation.

Baird's corollaries to Murphy's Law on compression: "The engine will never make as much power as you think it should. The bike will always be slower than you want. Finally, it will always cost more than you think." And, "Parts always wear out in inverse proportion to their cost."

Cylinders and Strokers

The old adage about cubic inches being king wouldn't have held on so long if it weren't true. Serious horsepower, required to propel a motorcycle down the drag strip in less than eight seconds or clear the traps at El Mirage above 180mph, takes big holes full of pistons. The only thing that can beat cubic inches is cubic dollars. Honda proved this back in the 1960s when they made very small, 125cc motor-

cycles go very fast by filling the head with valves, winding the engines past 22000rpm, and lubricating the whole process with copious infusions of money.

These days, H-D Pro Stock bikes don't turn much past 7500 and usually only have two valves in the head, but they make lots of power with lots of displacement. I think the money part's still the same, though.

There are only two ways of making a V-twin bigger: increase the bore or lengthen the stroke. Big motors, above 106.8ci, take advantage of both. Stock 81.7ci Evo Motors are 3.5in bore by 4.25in stroke. This is referred to as an "undersquare" engine—bore smaller than stroke.

Undersquare engines make maximum torque at lower rpms than oversquare motors of the same displacement. An engine with bigger bore than stroke, like most four-cylinder Japanese rice rockets, is considered "oversquare." It will have to be buzzed hard to make maximum power. My brother's stock

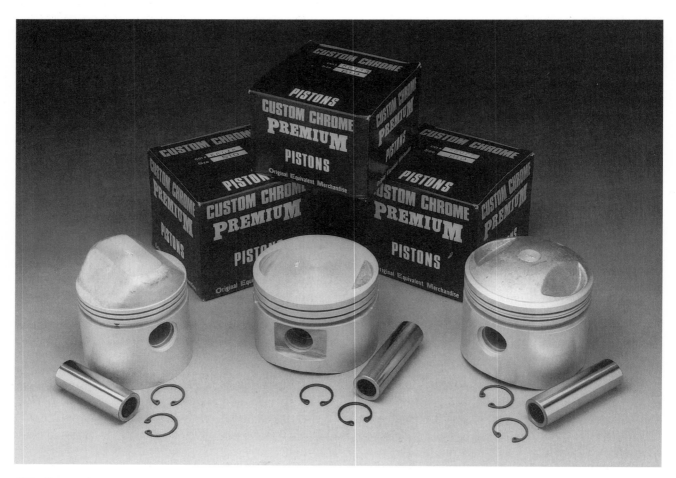

CCI offers replacement cast pistons for Shovels and Evos. Unless your motor will spend most of its time at half-throttle or less, and piston noise is a big concern, stay with forged pistons. *Custom Chrome*

Suzuki GSXR600 has to be turned to over 6000 before the bike even remotely starts to pull. His highly modified 600cc racing bike doesn't have enough power below 8000 for an ant to drive a tricycle around the inside of a Cheerio.

The road to happiness and quicker ETs on a Harley is through bigger engines. Stroking an engine increases the distance the piston travels in the cylinder. Boring makes the hole the piston rides in bigger. Big Twins gain horsepower most efficiently by increasing the stroke. To do this, the distance between the crank pin centerline and the flywheel centerline must be increased. Double this distance is the stroke of the engine, because the crank moves the rod from TDC to BDC, a distance of 180 degrees rotation, for the total piston travel.

Move the crank pin centerline away from the flywheel centerline and the stroke increases. This results in an increase in leverage on the crank, for more torque, plus an increase in displacement, for more horsepower.

Nothing is without its pay-backs, however. As the stroke increases, friction over the distance traveled by the piston increases. Cylinder wear can go up a bit. This isn't a problem in racing engines, as they come apart, sometimes all by themselves, at a frequent rate, but, on a street engine, clearances have to be checked frequently on a stroker.

Excess piston speed can become a problem when a big stroke is coupled with high rpm. Normal piston speed for a stock 4.25in stroke Evo is 3,700 feet per minute (FPM) at 5300rpm. Increase the stroke 1/2in and the piston speed goes up to 4,200fpm. Not really a problem at that low rpm, but it begins to have an effect when the motor is twisted above 7000rpm, corresponding to 5,540fpm. This speed wears out rings, bores, and rods in a relatively short time. Increased wear would be unacceptable on an engine planned to run 50,000 miles or more, but on a race engine it can be sustained for short periods of time. When engine life at full throttle is measured in fractions of an hour, high piston speeds become acceptable.

The best way to take advantage of a long stroke street engine is to shift below 5500rpm, using torque to push the bike, instead of revs. Racing is a different game. The engine makes large power at 7500rpm—use it. The idea here is to be first, not worry about piston speed.

When I first started exercising my H-D for a quarter mile at a time, I was worried whether the engine would last another two–three years without coming unglued. Now if I can get a weekend out of one engine I feel real good. Besides, the first time you see your name in the winner's position, engine life won't mean anything to you. I estimate my first class win cost about as much as a small house on the coast, but it was worth every last, hard-earned, wrinkled dollar bill. Houses don't turn low ETs, anyway.

Long-stroke flywheels, plus big bores, add up to 125+ cubic inch engines, just the recipe for fast passes at the strip. Adding 3/4in to the stroke, for a five inch arm, then bolting on four inch-bore cylinders, gives a total displacement of 125.7 cubic inches, a 44in increase, and a 54% displacement bump (Evos are actually 81.7ci). All these parts don't simply bolt on to any old crankcase, though. Four inch-bore cylinders have to be mounted on aftermarket cases, and the bolt pattern on the heads has to be wide enough to accept the larger cylinders.

After you're through building a 125 inch engine, about the only Harley parts left will be the name on the tank. Heads, cylinders, rods, flywheels, crank pins, cases, ignition, carb, pipes, cam, and kit—almost everything except the rocker covers—will come out of a catalog. Throw in an aftermarket, air-shifted trans, handmade swing arm, racing front forks, and someone else's frame—you see why I advocate starting with chalk marks on the floor instead of a bike.

Save your street scooter for Sundays when you aren't racing. Build your racer from scratch. I tried to run my racing bike on the street when the bike still resembled something street-legal, but it was only an exercise in frustration. The cam didn't want to run below 4500. The suspension (what there was of it) was so rigid that I thought I was going to have to have the seat surgically removed after a fifty-mile ride. When I fired the bike up on Sunday mornings, my neighbors looked at me like I rode a horse, carried a spear, and hailed from the high steppes of Mongolia.

"Ostracized" became a common word in my vocabulary.

People like Sputhe, Axtell, and CCI can help you build big inches. Axtell's fin-less cylinders can be obtained in bore sizes from 3.5in to 4in, and up to 5in stroke. STD big valve heads set up for eight-bolt cylinders, with raised ports and a 30 degree cut for compression relief, are available in the $2,200 range. Rods designed by Jim McClure that stay together for sub-eight second-runs are available through Axtell for $795 a set. These rods are the closest thing to bullet-proof as can be obtained on something that rotates. They are sold as a special order only, with races, wrist pin bushings, bearing cages, crank pins, and nuts together as a kit.

As with the stage two engines, Sputhe will build a few 60 degree, 4in by 4.750in, 120 cubic inch-long blocks for selected riders, set up strictly for

When you are running a lot of compression, a set of rollers is the only way to start the engine. Direct-drive starters can be plugged into the crank, but rollers can rotate an engine slowly for tuning or run-in. Back the bike aboard, fire up the truck, and drop it in first; put the transmission in second or third, light the ignition, and fire the bike.

racing. This motor is designed to be the ultimate pushrod, air-cooled V-twin. It's the best bet for anyone building a Big Twin racer from scratch. Any frame that accepts Evo motors will take this engine, using stock motor mounts. It kinda sorta looks like a Harley motor without using any Harley parts. A 101 cubic inch version is available as a complete engine, capable of being cranked into a street chassis. This would be a great way to amaze and amuse fellow riders. Right around $8,000 will let you run with the big dogs.

Whatever cylinder combination you decide to run, anything with a four inch, or larger, bore will require a set of aftermarket cases. Sputhe's Big Twin crankcases are built especially to take the additional loads brought on by running big inch motors above 7000rpm. Aluminum castings (356A-T6) are CNC-machined with shrunk-in steel bearing inserts, extra case bolts, and increased wall thickness in critical areas. Their chrome-moly, heat-treated cylinder studs have rolled threads (as opposed to cut threads). This prevents stress concentration on the threads, and a high-thread finish allows better head torquing. The studs and cases can be ordered for $864.

When it comes time to climb above the crankcase, Sputhe manufacturers big-bore cylinders to fit their cases. Sizes run from 95.4 to 104ci. Cylinders are cast in 383 aluminum alloy; steel sleeves are an integral part. Aluminum is injected into a steel die at 5,000psi, bonding to a cast-chrome-moly sleeve made out of "Lascomite," for a structure much more rigid, yet less brittle, than factory stock. The cylinders are stock length 3.780in bore, using S&S 4.625in flywheels to give a 104 cubic inch engine. The cylinders

and heads can be removed from the 95ci engine without pulling it from the frame. Solid copper O-rings seat in a grove in the deck, providing a reliable seal. Oil control is provided by Viton seals on the valve stems.

Some heads will need a weld buildup by the head bolt holes to provide a surface for the O-ring to seal against. Cylinder spigots have to be 4.010in diameter to accept the bigger cylinders. Sputhe states that the 95in kit requires re-balance of the crank, because the pistons are lighter than stock. Actually, any engine assembly should take a trip to the machine shop for balance. Any motor later than 1991 must have its cases replaced by Sputhe's or other aftermarket crankcases—one more reason to start from scratch.

Using dished pistons in the 104 kit with Fueling/Rivera or Romanelli heads, compression works out to 12.1:1 at 52cc chamber volume. Ratios of 9.5 to 10.3 are reached with flat-top pistons and stock or STD heads. Other ratios and sizes are available on special order.

Carburetor

When engines grow over 100 cubic inches, carb size, so far as CFM is concerned, becomes of paramount importance. S&S Super G or Super D, Mikuni HSR 42, or CCI's Accelerator II are good choices to sit on big engines. The S&S Super G can be bored out another .100in for additional airflow on 100ci+ engines. The Super G comes with a 2-1/16in throat at the butterfly, narrowing to 1-3/4in venturi. S&S doesn't recommend this carb for low-compression, smaller motors. If your bike is running close to stock displacement, go to the 1-7/16in Super E. If you aren't really sure which carb belongs on your bike, go with the Super E.

As with other S&S carbs, a two-cable throttle is used. All the bits and pieces are available as a kit, making installation easy on any V-twin. Kits contain a manifold, mounting hardware, spare jets, fuel lines, and air filter. The usual disclaimer about California highway legality, or lack thereof, applies to both the Super E and G. But you wouldn't run one on the road, would you?

Pulling gas tanks or other accessories, to aid in installation, won't be a problem on a drag bike because the engine will most likely be built on a bench, then shoved into a frame after everything is ready to go.

Be sure to check that the throttle returns to fully closed before firing the engine for the first time. I've seen more than one motor go from brand-new, cold, zero rpm to 6000 in the first seconds of operation, just because the carb butterfly wasn't fully closed. A very small throttle opening will let an unloaded engine rev quite high. Even if it does no other damage, it can sure take your nerves for a ride.

The Super G has a wide range of adjustment available in all modes of operation. Initial setup works best by setting the idle mixture screw at 1-1/4 to 1-3/4 turns out from the stop. Intermediate jetting will fall between .032 and .036. Main jet, the one you'll be on all the time during a run, is where all the high-speed tuning takes place. The main jet that makes the engine accelerate strongest or rev through the gears quickest is the right one for your engine. Motors over 96 inches want to run between .074 to .086 main jet.

High-speed, or main jet, circuit begins to come on at 3000 to 3500rpm. By 4500, the engine is running fully on the main jet. The best way to determine the proper size is to go make some tuning runs at the drag strip. Tuning runs differ from actual racing in that you're more concerned with how the engine performs as opposed to beating the other guy. Don't shoot for time as much as MPH.

Metering holes on the main jet are identified by numbers, in thousandths of an inch, stamped on the end of the jet. Initial jet size is indicated on a tag attached to the carb, or written on the shipping box. Record this and all subsequent jet changes. Keep track of temperature, event, fuel, run information, and tuning changes for every run. This makes future tuning much easier.

Drag strip tuning begins by warming the engine fully prior to making the first run. Operating temp. will make a difference in how hard the motor launches. Also, it's rather embarrassing to have a cold motor sneeze at the line in front of everybody—cuts into ETs, too.

Make the first run, watching speed and engine rpm at the finish. Bump the main up .004 and run again, recording the same info. Keep upping the jet size until the speed falls off. Back down the main by .002 to gain the best top-end performance. Under racing conditions, this will be where power peaks, then begins to taper off. Shift at this rpm.

Certain cams and exhaust systems can make some engines difficult to tune. Usually this happens only in a certain rev band but disappears above it. Trying to lose this flat spot can make the carburetion through the higher rev range run out of calibration enough to cause the engine to stumble or lay down from too rich a mixture. The idea is to tune the engine for best operation while keeping any flat spots below the speeds where the engine operates on the track. Carburetion, cam overlap, back pressure, or all the above could grow a big flat spot at 3000rpm. Be-

Building the ultimate Shovel for racing will take a set of these finless ductile iron Axtell cylinders. Call out the right part number and you too can have a 132 cubic inch Shovel—over a 60% increase in displacement. Definitely not for street use. *Axtell*

cause the engine will only see this speed once during a run (or the gearing is way too wide), it won't figure in tuning as much as if it were at 4500.

Spark plug color, usually a good source of information on state of tune, won't be as much help in a quarter mile bike as one that runs on the street. 1,320 feet just isn't enough time to develop proper plug readings. Watching the pipes to see the color is nice on a 100 mile run but almost useless on a eight-second pass.

To ensure adequate fuel delivery at elevated rpm, install a Pingel petcock and fuel filter. Engines over 100 inches will burn 300% more fuel than a stocker in a quarter mile run, needing larger lines and a bigger petcock to keep from starving at high revs.

For $395, a Mikuni HSR 42 Smoothbore can be bolted on your intake manifold. Mikuni's airflow rates may not be as high as some of the bigger carbs available elsewhere, but their "smoothbore" feature, or lack of throttle butterfly, makes for more efficient air-fuel mixing. Mikuni's testing shows that the HSR42's 42mm venturi will flow more air than a 52mm (2-1/4in) butterfly carb when both are operating in the real world on a motor. The flow measurements through a manifold and head are 5% better than a butterfly carb on the same setup.

Mikuni carbs are relatively easy to set up for racing. The main jet—your primary concern—controls the mixture from 3/4 to full throttle opening. Up to 75% throttle, the stock jetting should be fairly close. Remember, we're not trying to make this carb operate on the street. Highway bikes can better use the HS40 40mm carb. The smaller venturi speeds the airflow, making for better atomization at low to medium speeds, where most street riding is done.

The main jet, the one you had better be running on while drag racing, is the easiest to get right. Tuning is similar to the S&S in that you need to run the engine over a measured distance and check elapsed time and MPH after each jet change. The jet giving the shortest ET will be the correct one for your particular situation.

The large number of different cam, displacement, and exhaust combinations for Harleys makes it difficult to supply one carb that will work right out of the box for all applications. Mikuni comes close, but close puts you last.

If problems with high-speed operation persist and everything seems right in the tuning department, don't be in a hurry to criticize carburetion. Take a look at fuel tank venting. No air into the tank—no fuel goes out. This is an easy one to check. If you hear a loud whoosh when you open the fuel cap after a run, there isn't enough venting for the fuel used. Keep the tank as full as possible. If you don't want the additional six pounds of weight of an extra gallon of gas, get a smaller tank. Bear in mind that one additional gallon of gas won't change performance as much as having the additional weight of gas to aid in fuel delivery will increase it.

An air leak in the intake system will cause no end of lean-running problems. Don't be tempted to leave off the carb mounting bracket that attaches from the carb to the cases—I did: the carb shifted and the engine ran like a two-stroke diesel.

This may sound real basic, but if you run an air filter, make sure it's clean. One run at El Mirage can build a real sandbox inside the air cleaner. A lot of racers run velocity horns in place of air cleaners at the Lakes. A lot of people rebuild their engines between each weekend at the Lakes.

As an aside, if you've never been to a record run at California's El Mirage Dry Lake, go at least one time. You can learn more about high-speed running in one weekend of asking questions of the friendly folks than you can learn from hanging around a shop for a year. Lakers are also some of the more colorful people you might care to meet. Even if your bike is box-stock, with a windshield and bags, there's a class you can run with just a set of leathers and a Snell-approved helmet. Racers begin lining up their motorhomes as much as four days in advance, so if you want to run, show up early.

Exhaust

Well, now that we've got the gas and fuel to burn, what do we do to get rid of that filthy stuff com-

All those big displacement pistons need a good set of rods to push them. S&S has a rod and pin kit with wider I-beams, heavier radiuses in critical areas, and, on their "Supremes," heavier gusseting. They are forged from 4140 chrome-moly, heat-treated, and then shot-peened for stress reduction. *S&S*

ing out the back? Probably a good exhaust system would help—might buy a little horsepower in the process. For every time 100 inches of engine revolves once, a large quantity of spent gasses will have to be pumped out the exhaust port and through a set of pipes. How the pipes handle the spent gasses can make major differences in power and where it peaks.

Straight pipes offer the most efficient method of moving burnt gasses, due to their minimum back pressure. We're talking high-end performance only—above 4500rpm. The best overall length for pipes is computed using equal parts engine size, port size, cam, carburetion, and magic.

Any 100 cubic inch, or bigger, engine will best perform with pipes 2in or larger in diameter. Particularly in the case of the extreme engines starting to appear on the tracks, pipes larger than 2in are almost a necessity. 120 inches needs a 2.125 to 2.250in pipe to move the exhaust most effectively. Large-diameter tubing helps most at high rpm; however, everything's a tradeoff, and low-end performance will drop off when larger straight pipes are installed. You should only need low end to keep the bike from falling over on the way to the staging area, so it really shouldn't matter.

Total length from exhaust valve face to end of the pipe works out to 42–50inches. When running pipes cut on the diagonal at the end, take all measurements from the side closest to the engine. Appearances aside, straight cut pipes work the best. What's most important is to ensure that both pipes are within .50in of each other in total length for equal operation.

Pipe length for individual engines is a matter of cut and run. Each motor combination responds differently with a given set of headers. Last time I was down at CCI's Morgan Hill Distribution and Performance Testing Facility, I was able to practice being deafened while watching them work out a set of straight pipes on their chassis dyno.

Initial runs used pipes in the 40-inch range. Each two runs, the pipes were cut one inch shorter. The actual power readings weren't as important as finding out where the power peaked in the rev band and how much ultimate power was delivered at the rear wheel.

For drag motors, you want power to peak 10% below shift point. When the revs drop down as a higher gear is selected, you don't want the engine to drop so much speed that it falls out of the power band.

For instance, a big-inch motor will make its best power at 7000rpm—all things being right inside. Ten percent is 700rpm, so shift at 7700. Be sure to set your rev limiter enough above this figure to ensure you're not using the power cutoff as a shift point. This can cause engine damage.

Shovels don't want to twist quite so high. Set your shift point to 7200rpm. Any higher revs just wear out parts faster.

The pipes are the last things to see the air-fuel mixture; they should be the last to be tuned. Get carburetion, ignition, and cam timing right before breaking out the trusty hacksaw. Record every change made on every run. Make only one change per run; that way, you know how each modification affects times. Be consistent with each run. Spending time trying to get the front wheel back on the ground makes it impossible to

The complete Sputhe big-bore kit includes high-tensile-strength aluminum cylinders bonded to cast-in sleeves. Kits range in size from 95.4 cubic inches to 104 cubic inches. Compression ratios can be configured from 8.3:1 with oval dish crown pistons to 12.1:1 when set up with dished pistons for Fueling/Rivera and Romanelli heads with 52cc chamber volume. *Sputhe*

One of Sputhe's neater ideas is a five-speed transmission for the four-speed frames. This allows you to tailor your bike to your own particular driving style. The top ratio is still 1:1, as in the four-speed box, but the lower ratios are better spread out. Materials are better than stock. Every gear turns on needle bearings. The only thing missing would be an overdrive ratio in fifth, using fourth as direct 1:1. An overdrive ratio of .79 to 1 would really drop the revs on a touring bike. You could gear the bike to launch hard with a low first-through-third gearset, then have fifth for low RPM cruising and fourth for passing. I'd much rather be turning 2500rpm on the freeway in fifth overdrive instead of 3100rpm with 1:1 ratio. *Sputhe*

measure improvements. Having a high-speed wobble halfway through third gear will definitely affect your concentration if it doesn't spit you down the track minus the bike.

Back in the bad old days chassis development on some bikes wasn't quite all one would wish to see. My first race engine was in a frame of what you would call "less than optimum" design. I built it. That's why I talk about third-gear wobbles. When I wasn't trying to set my boot on fire from the straight pipes, I was trying to make the expletive-deleted bike run in a straight line for more than 100 feet. One sunny day I managed to run in both lanes on just one pass. Needless to say, some more developmental work (read: new frame) was called for.

We've come a long way in frame design, but it took a lot of development, coupled with a few wild rides, to get to the point that a drag bike can make effortless, straight, 200mph passes.

Every tuner has his magic formula for setting header length. Every engine is different, but not so much that a general operating length can't be worked out as a starting point. What is engraved in stone for one racer might not be used for a lawnmower engine by another. Presuming you're not going to run straights on the street (at least, not after you pass the first cop), noise is a secondary consideration. Maximum power over the widest rpm range is primary.

Without access to a dyno, you have to resort to the cut-and-try method of engineering pipes. By now, the motor and suspension should be fairly worked out.

Sputhe's Big Twin crankcases can run four-inch bore cylinders. They are built with extra case bolts for added rigidity and better oil control. Start with a set of these when building a 100+ inch racer. *Sputhe*

You will have made enough passes to be more than a passenger working the controls down the strip. Most important is not to be behind the bike. Like flying, downhill racing, and other rapid sports, laying down a consistent pass takes a lot of experience before you can begin to notice what's happening underneath you.

Start with a set of pipes that are a little long for what you feel will be the final cut. It's much easier to whack off two inches than weld them back on. Plus, you'll look like you know what you're doing when the pipes don't appear to be baby-food cans welded together.

Above and next page: Last time I wandered through Arlen Ness' emporium, he showed me this set of cases cast with his name in the center of the V. Looks like awful big holes for cylinders. Wonder how big the engine will be?

After getting down to knowing what the bike will turn each run—no sandbagging allowed—try cutting two inches off the end of the headers. Record the results of three runs and compare to the previous times. When the ET begins to flatten out, or climb slightly, you're at the right length. Now go have a professional pipe bender fabricate a nice new shiny set of straights the same length as your test pipes.

When you change displacement, or any other factor, the optimum pipe length will change, giving you the chance to do the testing all over again. Keep good records. You might want to change pipe diameters and see if the times drop. Watch the tach. You should be tuned and geared to pass through the last set of lights right close to redline.

Small tip—when you reach the finish line lights, don't let off the throttle. Speed is calculated by two sets of lights set up in front of and behind the finish line elapsed time lights. If you chop the throttle before clearing the third set of lights, your top speed will suf-fer. Give a two count (not slowly—shutdown area is under 1/4 mile in some cases) before letting off the throttle after passing the finish line. This ensures the highest trap speed, along with the best ET.

Ignition

One Ignition system that wasn't mentioned in connection with stage one and stage two engines is the Dyna Single-Fire. Available through Zipper's Performance Products (410-799-8989; FAX, 410-799-9450) as a kit, the Dyna ignition is set up to use two independent modules, firing one cylinder at a time. Like Dyna's standard system, this unit uses the stock H-D points-type mechanical advance. The single-fire unit draws so much power during operation that it should only be used on engines with a charging system. Total-loss ignition usually doesn't have a voltage source capable of sustaining the amperage necessary to keep the ignition alive long enough to run your bike on the track. More than one racer has been stopped by a dead battery—very embarrassing if it happens to you.

Dyna also supplies coils for single- and dual-plug ignition. A three-ohm, or higher, coil must be used on all bikes after 1985. Figure in the price of a tach adapter for the installation because your stock unit reads both plugs as one spark, and the Dyna has one plug per spark, or half as many sparks per impulse, giving a reading 50% in error.

Summary

By the time you reach the stage three level of engines, you should have a fairly good working knowledge of what makes the pistons go up and down. You've now become seriously bitten by the speed bug, for which there is no cure. The stage three motor is at the far end of the performance curve—strictly a racing engine, with no pretense of running on the street. You've gone so far as to put off buying a new car so you can order a new set of leathers the same color as the bike. The year is

Dyna ignition can be set up with shift indicators, rev limiter, and programmable ignition for street scooters. It's available through Zipper's. *Zipper's/Dyna*

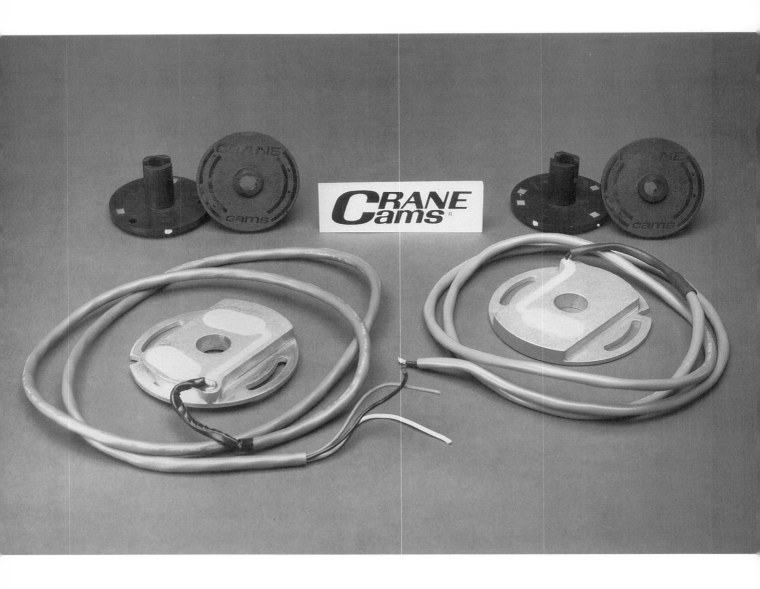

MSD's MC1 won't quite fire a plug through a glass of buttermilk, but it will put flame to whatever passes for gas today. Works real well with high-compression engines. *MSD*

Long-duration running with a modified engine will definitely require the services of an oil cooler. Most come with a thermostatic bypass to keep the oil out of the cooler during warm-up or on cold days. *Storz*

Crane's into the ignition game, too. These are Hall-effect transducers used in place of your points plate. They can be set up as dual-fire (why??) or single-fire. I still run into people who pull the electronic ignition and install points. That's like going back to mechanical spark retard. Single-fire units like Crane's are 100% reliable, never need adjusting, and don't wear, as no metal parts are in contact. And as far as accuracy, transducers beat points and condensers any day. *Crane Cams*

breaking down into two different seasons: racing season, and all the rest of the time.

There are so many different combinations of parts for a stage three motor that trying to list them all would either look like the Manhattan Street Directory or leave a lot of people out. The combinations below only list a few of the possibilities and don't include any of the parts common to earlier stage one or II engines.

Package Specifications
Stage Three Engine
(150–300hp). Can be built for $3,500–unlimited.
Kit # 1

1. Sputhe 60 degree, 120ci racing engine. Bolt in and go.

Kit #2

1. Axtell BT-EV drag race kit. Fin-less barrels, forged pistons, rings, and related components.
2. Stock cases.
3. S&S Super G carb.
4. Competition Cams EVO-3060 cam w/ Velva-Touch lifters (.585 lift).

Kit#3

1. Sputhe 104ci Big Twin cylinder kit w/ Sputhe Heads.
2. S&S 4-5/8 flywheels.
3. Sputhe Big Twin cases.
4. S&S 33-5080 cam (.630 lift).
5. S&S Super D carb.

Kit#4

1. Axtell 4in bore cylinders.
2. S&S 4-5/8 flywheels (116.2ci).
3. Mikuni HSR 42 carb.
4. Crane 1-1003 cam & kit (.550 lift).

Chapter 5

Exotica: Blowers and Hot Fuels

After you have played with the simple things of life, like 125ci racing engines, you might want to explore some of the more interesting ways of making horsepower from the Evo motor. Big engines—harboring cams with more lift than a three-story elevator—make lots of go, but what's a person to do when cubic inches simply aren't enough? What else can be done to give a little more urge?

Luckily, there are other people with ideas similar to yours. People who manufacture performance parts like turbochargers, superchargers, carbs set up specifically for fuel (alcohol or nitro), and horsepower-producing nitrous oxide injection systems.

Some modifications, like nitrous oxide, are "bolt-ons." Others, turbocharging, for instance, will require a lot of re-engineering to function on the bike.

Nitrous Oxide

One of the nicer tricks to come along is nitrous oxide (N_2O). Otherwise known as "tipping the bottle," kicking a load of N_2O through the intake manifold is a sure cure for the horsepower blues.

Hit the switch at wide-open throttle (WOT) for that instant acceleration feeling. It's the best hole-shot since afterburners. If you've ever wondered what it would be like to take a catapult ride off the bow of an aircraft carrier with an F-18 strapped to you, bolt on a bottle of nitrous and hit the switch. Five seconds of punch and you'll feel like you're in a Star Wars movie. The scenery rockets past you like someone tied a rope to it and pulled—hard! One of the quicker ways to take the worry out of being close.

Nitrous Oxide Systems, Inc. (NOS 714-821-0580: Tech Line, 714-821-0592) is one of the predominant manufacturers of N_2O equipment for racing. In motorcycle applications, N_2O and fuel are injected underneath the carburetor, lowering the inlet temperature to produce a denser inlet charge. It increases the oxygen content of the charge, making it capable of supporting more combustion. N_2O also increases the combustion rate of the oxygen-fuel mixture. All this adds up to a major increase in power.

NOS now sells Nitrous Plus, containing trace amounts of sulfur dioxide to prevent it from being used in the same way that your friendly dentist uses it to relieve that nervous feeling during drilling. Sulfur dioxide gives off a rotten egg smell that needs to be experienced to be believed. Not many people will misuse Nitrous Plus—at least, not more than once.

NOS supplies a two-pound bottle for Harley applications. Usually, this will provide a 90—120sec flow at WOT. The full bottle weighs 5lb, 12oz. Best performance and highest flow will be achieved if the bottle weight isn't let go below 4lb or so. Depending on the jet size used in the spray bar, anywhere from 9 to 17hp can be gained with N_2O.

Fuel delivery is very critical with nitrous. Figure on an additional flow of .10 gallons per hour per horsepower. The kit includes a fuel pump capable of handling all jetting situations. Installing a high-flow petcock, like Pingel products, will keep a high-horsepower engine fed during N_2O operation. Fuel quality is also very important. Low octane fuels will allow detonation, with all its attendant problems, so keep the octane rating up when running on the street. You will already be using 104 octane or better for racing, so this won't be a problem on the strip. Running nitrous on the street isn't a very good idea anyway, as it only works well at WOT, engine above 3000. This type of street riding is a good way to get all your meals from the state for an indefinite period—visiting hours on Sunday from noon to three.

NOS recommends only running forged pistons, but this shouldn't be a problem, as that's what

Nitrous oxide—makes better men out of us. Faster, anyway! Here's all the ingredients necessary to bolt on instant horsepower—just add gas. Following directions, a reasonably competent mechanic should be able to mount the entire kit in less than three hours. *NOS Systems*

you have in the engine anyway. You will need to ensure that your battery can handle the load of driving a fuel pump, along with operating a fuel solenoid and an N_2O solenoid, for the duration of the run. If your charging system can run a high-performance ignition with its electrical requirements, adding NOS won't be a problem.

Start with the smallest jet package and work up from there. Instant go is a lot of fun, but until you build some familiarity with N_2O operation, it's better to bump power in small steps. Seventeen horsepower doesn't sound like much; however, remember it all comes on at once, not over a wide power band like a cam. My first shot with the bottle reminded me of riding my old 1969 Kawasaki 500cc, three-cylinder two-stroke. In first gear, it didn't have enough power below 6000rpm to roll a BB across a bowling alley, but at 6001rpm the

Left: One solution to mounting the bottle is to hang it behind your right leg. Just be careful when you throw over the saddle. I might put some foam rubber around the top of the bottle in case it and I should come in hard contact. *NOS Systems*

front wheel lost all contact with the earth and stayed that way through the next two gears.

The bike had anemic drum brakes, a frame that flexed in two or three directions at the same time, and sounded like a rabid popcorn popper, but it sure would accelerate in a straight line. Nitrous will give very much the same sensations when installed on your Harley.

The Harley-Davidson NOS kit consists of a filled two-pound bottle, two solenoid valves, an N_2O filter, electric fuel pump, arming switch, jet assortment, and all the necessary hardware to install it on your bike.

Installation is fairly straightforward. Mounting the bottle is probably the only part requiring any serious thought. As per the illustrations included with the kit, the bottle has a siphon tube, installed at an angle to the bottle. The bottle must be mounted so that the tube is at the bottom and the label facing up. If you mount the bottle upside down, the siphon tube must be removed before use. Be sure the bottle is de-pressurized prior to tube removal.

Positioning the two solenoid valves will take another bit of thinking. They must be mounted above the fogger nozzles in the manifold and kept away from the exhaust pipes. All pipe fittings are to be made with Teflon paste *only* as a pipe thread lubricant. Using Teflon tape for a thread sealant carries with it the possibility of small pieces coming off the threads inside the fittings and causing blockage in the nozzles. The run from the solenoids to the nozzles should be kept as short as possible. Trial-fitting before everything is bolted down will help establish component positions and ensure a proper fit.

The fogger nozzles can be fit into each intake manifold by drilling and tapping a 1/4in hole on the top of both runners, so that the discharge side of the nozzle points down and towards the engine.

The fuel pump should be mounted as far below the tank as possible. Either use a dual-outlet Pingel petcock (preferred method), or cut the main line and install a "T" so that the fuel can be run to the inlet side of the pump. The outlet side will run through the fuel filter up to the fuel solenoid. Hint—if the brass fuel line T supplied with the kit is larger than your stock fuel line, you probably won't have enough fuel flow through the stock gas line—use an after-market petcock. Running short of fuel while the bottle is wide open is a good way to break parts. Also, don't use fuel octane improvers containing methanol. The O-rings in the solenoids can fail, causing leakage and broken engines.

The electrical can be wired through the horn button with a two-position arming switch, allowing the horn to operate in one position and the NOS system to fire when in the other. . With the switch up, the horn sounds; switch down, hit the horn, and hang on.

Most drag bikes don't come with a horn, as honking at your opponent won't do much to slow him down, so another push button must be employed to trigger the system. NOS includes a switch in kits intended for racing, but any momentary contact switch can be used. Just make sure it has a strong, reliable spring to ensure positive electrical cutoff.

There is a micro-switch to be mounted in such a way as to be triggered when the throttle is wide open. This way, the bottle only fires during WOT. The micro-switch needs to be mounted in a place that won't cause throttle interference while still allowing it to make contact at WOT.

Check component operation before every run. Make sure everything fires off properly prior to opening the bottle—especially if you weren't the last person to work on the bike. Having the solenoids open but not close is a pretty remote possibility. Both the micro-switch and the push button have to stick at the same time for the solenoids to hang open. The likelihood of this happening is right up there with winning the lottery; however, the engine will continue to run even with the throttle closed if it's still inhaling N_2O and fuel. The N_2O will supply combustion air and the fuel will fire, so that's all that's needed to make power—throttle closed or open. Invest in a good electrical kill switch so that Murphy can't throw one of his laws at you again—the one that goes: "Anything that can go wrong will go wrong and at the worst possible time."

On initial start, leave the bottle valve closed, run the engine up to 2500 rpm, and hit the button with the micro-switch energized. The inrush of raw fuel should cause the rpm to drop as the mixture goes rich. Let the engine idle down. With everything disarmed, open the bottle. There should be no change in engine sound or operation. Any abnormality in operation will be caused by a malfunctioning N_2O solenoid. Replace and test again. Inspect all the fittings and lines for leaks.

Find a way to hide the bottle and solenoids, mount the arming switch in an unobtrusive place, and no one will know you're running N_2O.

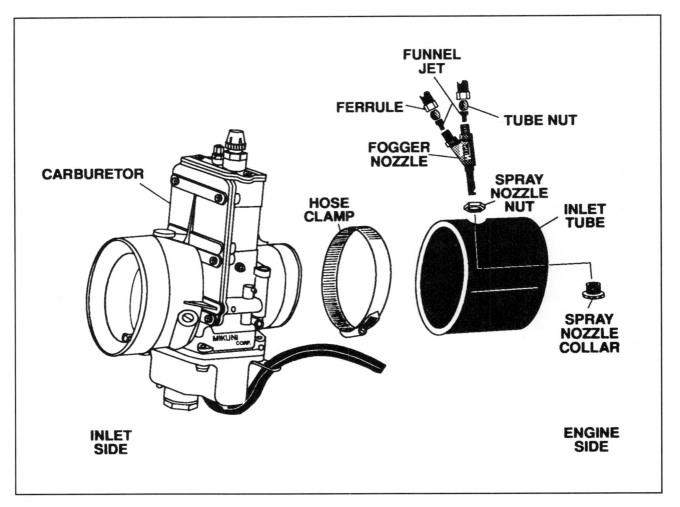

FUNNEL JET

FERRULE

TUBE NUT

FOGGER NOZZLE

CARBURETOR

HOSE CLAMP

SPRAY NOZZLE NUT

INLET TUBE

SPRAY NOZZLE COLLAR

INLET SIDE

ENGINE SIDE

Above and next page: The nozzles locate in the inlet tract on top of the manifold. Might be a little easier to remove the manifold when installing the spray nozzle collars. That way, if they slip away, the head doesn't have to be pulled to get them back. (No, I didn't!) *NOS Systems*

Don't pop the solenoids with the engine off. You'll fill the engine with N_2O and gas. One spark, and some of the parts might not land in the same zip code.

Don't leave the bottle valve open if the bike is going to sit for any length of time. Do remember to turn it back on prior to a run. Hitting the switch only to have nothing happen could give vent to hidden frustrations.

Liquid N_2O is very cold—it condenses at 40 degrees. Getting any on the skin will cause instant frostbite, with all its related pleasures. Inhaling the gas will do more than smell bad—it can cause suffocation.

There is nothing mysterious about a nitrous oxide system. It's simply a way of filling the cylinders with more oxygen and fuel, increasing power in the process. The N_2O molecule contains two parts nitrogen to one part oxygen (36% oxygen by weight.) During the combustion process, the nitrous molecule breaks down, releasing the oxygen. The extra oxygen mixes with the additional fuel injected at the same time, bumping horsepower. The free nitrogen helps control the combustion process by buffering the cylinder pressures. Nitrous oxide also helps cool the incoming mixture by 65 to 70 degrees F, making for denser charges. This effect alone will help increase power.

An average bike will gain from one-half to one full second in the quarter with a 4–10mph increase. Larger, more highly modified motors can utilize bigger jets for even quicker ETs.

A two-pound bottle will last through four or more runs, depending on jet number and size. If you're running for fun, run till it's done, but serious racing needs a different approach to bottle duration. As said above, weigh the bottle before and after the run. When you see a 1lb, 12oz weight difference, it's time to refill the bottle.

All NOS kits contain a list of refill dealers in the U.S. and Canada. Most any industrial gas supply house will be able to refill the tank. Medical grade N_2O won't give any better performance than Nitrous Plus and usually can't be purchased without a medical release.

Engine reliability will depend on a number of different factors. Should the increased loads exceed the ability of the components to handle them, added wear takes place. On a stock engine, a correctly calibrated NOS system won't cause much increased wear. Tip the bottle hard and the power jumps accordingly. More power = more wear. Lots more power, as you can guess, will give you the opportunity to change parts, like crank pins, rods, and bearings, more often.

Stay away from N_2O if your street motor has a lot of mileage on it. Actual mileage isn't as important as how the miles were accumulated during the engine's life. Most racers, though, have a habit of using rather more throttle than absolutely necessary to sustain 55mph. A bike that has been run hard and put away wet will show more wear than the one your granny rides to church on Sundays (unless your grandmother is currently in the points for Pro Fuel Eliminator). Too much mileage might be only 10,000, depending on how the bike is run. You are the person best capable of judging whether N_2O should be used on your existing motor or you need a rebuild before bolting a bottle to the frame. Racing engines acquire wear a quarter mile at a time, and are torn down often enough to catch any incipient wear problems caused by tipping the bottle hard.

Harley has a strong enough bottom end to take more push-button horsepower than most motorcycles. The jets included in the kit will give up to a 40% increase in power and torque. Plus, NOS can provide larger jets for modified motors, giving even larger percentages of performance increase.

It's possible to hold the button down until the bottle is empty, but NOS recommends no more than fifteen seconds of continuous operation. Land speed record bikes will have to run on the bottle longer than fifteen seconds if the button is held down through all the gears. Usually, additional cooling is figured in to take care of the extra heat generated by the longer run times. Some racers only ride the button in the top one or two gears, as traction is enough of a problem in the lower gears without adding a 40% bump in torque.

A progressive controller can be set up to begin to open the bottle at a reduced flow at 2500rpm, increasing to WOT at any set point. This will give a

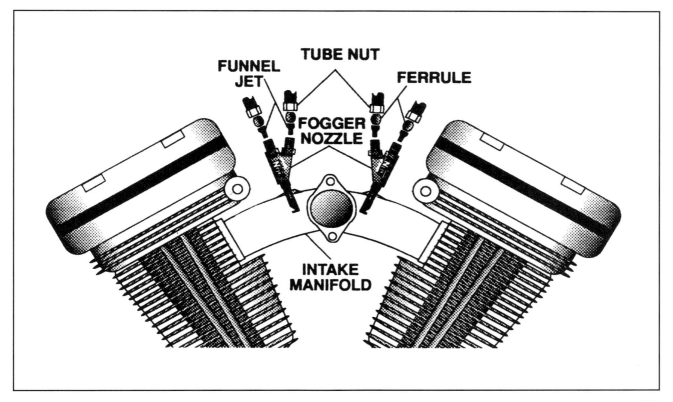

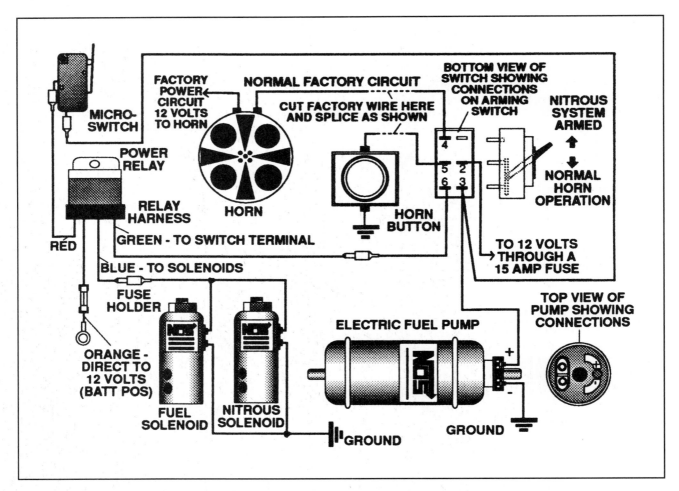

The NOS instruction manual provides a wiring diagram showing how to hook up everything to run through your horn switch. Just be sure where the switch is when rid-ing. You don't want to try to honk the horn with the switch in the armed position. Might be real interesting for a few seconds. *NOS Systems*

steadier power increase, as opposed to bringing everything in at once with a stab of the button.

N_2O works completely independent of the engine's carburetion, so no carb-jetting changes will have to be made when the kit's installed. Detonation should-n't be a problem on a relatively stock street motor, as long as premium gas is used. However, each application is different. Some engine/cam/compression combina-tions will require that the timing be backed down a bit to eliminate any detonation. Racing engines using 104 oc-tane fuel or better could require more ignition retard.

If you are running a turbocharged engine, N_2O can help eliminate the flat spot prior to the turbo spin up. In addition, N_2O will drop the incoming charge temperature by as much as 75 degrees, helping to re-move the heat generated when the air is compressed by the turbo. Boost is increased as well, adding even more power.

High-compression normally aspirated engines can make good use of nitrous, providing the proper balance of N_2O and fuel is maintained. As long as high octane fuel is used and the timing is retarded enough, engines with 12:1 compression or more can handle it easily.

Cams with more exhaust overlap and duration are best suited for operation with nitrous. However, street applications don't need a specific cam tailored to N_2O operation, as most of the time the engine is-n't run at full throttle. Stick with cam manufacturers' recommendations for your particular engine situa-tion. Racing engines can be specifically built with cams having more aggressive exhaust profiling, since all runs will be on the bottle. Gearing and bike weight will be a primary consideration in cam selec-tion, rather than addition of nitrous oxide.

In general, nitrous oxide will return more per-formance for dollar spent than any other single modification. Large performance gains can be had while still maintaining a high level of reliability. Living with high compression and a mega-lift cam in a street motor all the time can be a real chore. For the racer who also rides on the street, N_2O offers the best horsepower increase for the least sacrifice in rideability.

NOS offers a kit, part #03011, for all Harley-Davidson engines, at a price of $502.67. Most speed shops will give you a racer's net price of $427.27 if you make go-fast noises at them and let them know that you will probably be buying more parts as the season progresses. NOS also offers a kit with a smaller,10oz bottle for a $20 drop in price. Lack of space for the 2lb bottle, or infrequent racing, might make this a viable option. On an out-and-out racer, bottle size and placement might not be a problem, and a larger, 5lb bottle can be substituted for a nominal charge.

Octane Boost

Rather than go into a long, complex chemical analysis of octane ratings, suffice it to say that race bikes with highly modified engines need gas with a higher octane number to support combustion without detonation. The quantity of fuel burnt isn't very important when you're only traveling 1/4 mile at a time, so expensive racing fuels can be used. It's when you deal with highly modified street engines that gas capable of defeating detonation becomes a problem. Filling the tank with $4.10 per gallon racing gas isn't very economical, nor is it very practical when distances over 50 miles are covered.

One way around the problem is to buy all your fuel at the local airport. General aviation aircraft with internal combustion piston engines run on 100LL gasoline. This is advertised as a "low lead" fuel, but it contains enough lead and a high enough octane to make a 10:1 motor work on the street. Price per gallon runs between $1.70 and $2.15, depending on where you are and how you pay. Cash will get a better price than credit cards.

Contrary to popular opinion, you don't have to own an airplane to buy Avgas. A few airports will even pump straight into your tank, although sometimes a five-gallon can is necessary. A small number of airports have installed card systems, where no attendant is on site. You pays your money and pumps your Avgas—makes everything very easy. Kind of hard to plan long-range trips, though—unless you plan on taking *The Airport Guide to the U.S.* along with you.

Another way to increase octane is by using octane increasers (see how smart us writers are). Octane Boost Corp. (PO Box 414, Bedford, TX 76095),

manufacturers of 104+ Octane Boost and Super 104+ Octane boost, state that their product will increase fuel rating by up to five points, reduce pinging, and decrease the chance of run-on or overheating. It contains no lead or aniline oil, both of which are rather nasty if inhaled or ingested. I still wouldn't use it for a chaser, but it's relatively harmless if spilled. All sanctioning bodies approve its use.

All that's necessary is to pour it into the tank. Eight ounces treat sixteen gallons of fuel, so it would be easy to carry enough, tucked in a saddlebag, for an extended trip. Also available in gallon cans, 104+ can be stored for extended time, providing the cap stays on tight. 104 won't increase horsepower, but it will allow the engine to develop its full potential without detonating.

The company is so sure of its product that it offers a 104% money-back guarantee if you're not satisfied with the results. The only hitch is that you have to write them for a claim form; still, a guarantee is a guarantee.

While we are on the subject of gasoline and octane, a few words about gas and alcohol blends are in order, as we are going to be seeing more pump fuel with ethanol added. Ethanol is used by petroleum marketers to increase the octane rating of gasoline. Ethanol is widely used and available in most areas of the U.S. It first appeared on the market as "gasohol," extending the stock of fuel products during the late-1970s' fuel shortage.

Later, when it was used primarily to increase octane, the "gasohol" label was replaced by a name signifying the increased rating. Unleaded Plus and Super Unleaded Plus are only a few of the new blends. It's still gasohol, just with a fresh coat of paint and a new name on the door. Now the mixture is touted as "oxygenated fuel," with lower emissions the primary consideration behind its use.

Oxygenated (alcohol) fuels help to clean the air through more complete combustion of the air-fuel mixture, resulting in lower CO emissions. Texaco, Mobil, Arco, Chevron, Super-America, and Union have added ethanol to their fuels to aid in pollution control.

As of fall 1992, our government, with the ongoing quest for cleaner air, mandated forty different metropolitan areas to use oxygenated fuels to help lower CO, especially during winter, when CO emissions are higher due to home heating. Ethanol is limited by law to no more than 10% mixture with gasoline the high cost of alcohol would probably keep this percentage fairly stable, anyhow.

Where the problems arise is in ethanol's reactivity with rubber O-rings, gaskets, and other seals in the fuel delivery system. My bike has been running on oxygenated fuel since late 1992, when the stuff first appeared in the San Francisco area. Lately, my petcock has been dribbling a small amount of fuel around the 'on-off' lever—not around the fuel line, but at the face of the valve. As this just appeared in the last year or so, and the bike is a 1982, maybe the new fuel is eating up a rubber seal. Guess I'll have to take my own advice and buy a Pingel petcock. Newer bikes have a different type of seal, so it shouldn't be a problem.

If any operational problems, such as hard hot-starting, vapor lock, engine knock, etc., appear—go back to unleaded. Take care not to spill oxygenated fuel on the tank when filling. Alcohol will remove all wax from the paint, and, if left on the tank, will damage or remove the paint. As a side note, the old wive's tale of mixing super and regular for an odane increase higher than super is just that—an old tale. It doesn't work, so don't bother.

Valvoline Oil Company tested the effects of gasoline/ethanol blends on various materials for lubricity and compatibility. Although these tests were relatively small in scope, they found that material compatibility was comparable to the reference fuel (straight gas), and that the fuel blend actually performed better on the lubricity test.

Fuel Carbs

Major horsepower gains come by switching from gasoline to alcohol or a nitro-methane/alcohol combination. To get the proper mixture to the engine requires a different type of carb than used on gasoline systems. Flow rates are much higher with fuels than with gas, necessitating larger internal passageways to compensate for the additional volume of alcohol or nitro. Approximately two and a half times more alcohol than gasoline is required. Nitro has to be moved at a rate ten times greater than gas.

Motorcycle gas carbs can't be modified to handle fuel, and fuel carbs won't operate on a gas-fired engine. S&S Super D gas carbs can be modified to flow alcohol only. If you plan on running nitro or alcohol, best that you buy the proper carb at the start, rather than try to make a gas carb work.

To switch a Super D carb from gas to alcohol requires a part kit containing an alcohol float bowl, float, main discharge tube, fuel needle with seat, and a full set of alcohol jets. After changing over to alcohol operation, the carb won't be able to handle gasoline at all.

The Super D is set up for gravity fuel-delivery only. The fuel inlet needle and seat assembly cannot take the additional pressures imposed by a fuel pump, and will leak by if set up with one. Going to fuel will require a larger petcock to handle the increased flow rate.

S&S Super Fuel Carburetors are built to handle alcohol and nitro-methane only. They are set up with two large .380in fuel inlets, one controlled by the

I like the feel of turbochargers. Hit the throttle. The boost goes positive. All of a sudden, it's Mr. Toad's wild ride. Running around ten pounds of boost, you'll run out of revs before you run out of power. Top speed is largely a factor of engine redline. On the left is the exhaust-side turbo housing. The middle piece is called the "cartridge." The right side is the inlet side to the intake manifold. *Turbo City*

When the boost reaches a preset point, the wastegate opens to bypass excess exhaust. It's pressure-operated from the intake manifold. Regulating the opening point, in pounds of boost, will control horsepower. This is a Rajay wastegate. *Turbo City*

float, and one actuated by an adjustable cam mounted on the throttle shaft, adding additional fuel at high rpm. The float bowl is set up with an overflow to handle any excess fuel entering the bowl from flooding the engine.

Super B fuel carbs fit engines up to 115ci. Super D fuel carbs are for any displacement greater than 115ci. They are both sold as complete kits, with jets, main air bleeds, and instructions.

Turbocharged fuel engines require a different carb designed specifically for forced induction motors. High boost and high revs can cause fuel delivery problems with a carb set up for normally aspirated operation. The S&S turbo alcohol and turbo gas carbs are set up to operate with a pressurized fuel-delivery system and fuel pump. The float needle and seat will handle up to 4lbs of pressure without leakby. Auxiliary fuel is handled by the same type of throttle-operated cam as the fuel carbs, providing more fuel under boost and high rpm. Float bowls are fitted with an overflow pipe that is plumbed to return unused fuel to the tank or with a custom-made overflow reservoir. More precise fuel control can be

achieved by setting up the auxiliary fuel-delivery system on a pressure switch and solenoid valve, calibrated to induce additional fuel at a predetermined point.

All S&S turbo carbs must be mounted in front of the turbo, so that the airflow is drawn through the carb by the turbo, instead of pushed through. The throttle shaft and other components aren't sealed, so if the turbo blows through the carb, as in some applications like Yamaha, fuel will be blown out of the carb.

Carbs are available in 1-7/8 and 2-1/4 throat sizes, depending on engine size and turbo application. Turbo gas carbs are also available; they have smaller discharge holes for the reduced fuel flow.

S&S builds special Evo racing manifolds capable of handling throttle bodies up to 2-7/16in diameter. They can also be ordered with oval runner shape to match modified heads with oval intake ports. The bigger manifolds will necessitate special mounting flanges and relocation of the mounting bolts in the head. Round port manifolds can be machined to match intake ports as large as 2.200in.

These manifolds are a special-order item only, due to the different heights of various cylinder/head combinations. Manifolds can be ordered to fit cylinders from 4.650in to 6.950in overall height. Raised intake ports, taller crankcase deck heights, and other modifications must all be factored in when ordering individual manifolds.

None of the carbs set up with auxiliary fuel inlets or set up for turbo has any starting system, so street operation and warm-up will be a bit of a problem. I've only seen a couple of bikes running turbos behind S&S carbs on the street. Both owners say starting is a little more difficult than stock, but this could also be attributed to the long intake tract from carb inlet to valve face and the installation of a fairly wild cam. One turbo rat bike running around my area is a 1980 Shovel engine in a 1972 frame. It's been running on the street since 1986 without major trouble. The turbo was originally mounted on a Panhead for many thousands of miles and then hung on the Shovel. Other modifications include a 101ci kit, Crane cam, and trick suspension to handle the increase in power. The bike's double-ugly, but lord is it fast. The owner delights in showing rice rockets his rear fender at every opportunity.

Turbocharging

Turbocharging is a lot like getting something for nothing. A turbo makes use of the energy, in heat form, left in the exhaust gasses after combustion. A lot of energy is still contained in the exhaust flow, and power can be generated by tapping into the exhaust with some method of converting the heat energy back to work.

Aircraft engines have made use of turbocharging, or turbo-compounding, for years. Some World War II aircraft used turbochargers for additional power at high altitude. Boeing B-17 Fortress bombers had four 1,200hp Wright nine-cylinder radial engines with turbocharging, giving them a 323mph top speed and a cruising altitude of 35,000ft, carrying up to 12,800lbs in bombs over 1,100 miles.

The turbocharger is not a very complicated device, for all the power it is capable of producing. It consists of a single shaft fitted with two impellers: one driven by the exhaust and one that drives the intake charge. The exhaust impeller is driven by the exhaust gasses at speeds up to 120,000rpm. This in turn drives the intake impeller, compressing the incoming charge and packing the cylinder with a denser mixture.

The shaft rides on a center bearing, cooled and lubricated by engine oil. A line into the top of the bearing housing supplies cool oil, usually directly from the oil cooler or filter, at engine pressure. A larger-diameter line feeds off the bottom of the housing, allowing hot oil to run back to the oil tank. Some turbos are fitted with an additional set of taps to allow water to be piped through the bearing mount for even more cooling. If you ever get to see a turbo at high boost, you will understand the reason for so much cooling. The exhaust impeller is mounted in a cast-iron housing that gets redder than cheap lipstick after a very short operating time. The exhaust side can glow in the dark while the intake side stays relatively cool. I've measured over 600 degrees at the exhaust housing five minutes after shutting off the engine.

You can imagine how much heat is transferred to the intake charge by compressing the incoming charge and from heat bleeding through from the hot side. This is why you'll see intercoolers mounted downstream from the turbo in a lot of applications. An intercooler is nothing more than a air-to-air, or air-to-water, method of removing heat from the compressed inlet charge. Think of it as a radiator, taking heat out of the inlet air. A cooler incoming charge will be denser, packing more oxygen and producing more power.

As the throttle is opened, the exhaust gasses begin to pick up speed and temperature. This in turn causes the exhaust impeller to speed up, driving the intake turbine at the same time. The intake impeller compresses the incoming charge, packing more into the combustion chamber.

There is a noticeable amount of time between the twisting of the throttle and the increase of power, known as "turbo lag." This can be minimized by using a turbo with smaller wheels that spin up faster. Some systems have as much as 1–3 seconds of lag.

Newer installations, primarily on cars like the Porsche 930 Turbo, have eliminated most of the lag, but some still remains. If you've ridden turbocharged bikes, you have experienced lag when the throttle is cranked open. Some of us rather enjoy the feeling of the turbo's power inrush and are willing to endure the lag for the other benefits of turbocharging.

For off-the-line work, turbos don't work as well as mechanical drive superchargers where the engine speed directly controls the supercharger boost. A supercharger will build pressure as fast as the engine can rev, but it takes a lot of power to turn. A Top Fuel Dragster, mounting an 8–71 supercharger (8–71 refers to the GMC diesel engines from which the superchargers originated: eight cylinders; 71ci per cylinder. Also comes as a 6–71 and a 4–71) on a 500 cubic inch, V-8, nitro-burning engine, will eat up over 300hp just turning the blower. Your average street car couldn't put out enough horsepower just to turn a big blower at high boost. Superchargers won't necessarily make any more power than turbos, but they have the advantage of building power rapidly. Turbos use exhaust energy that would be otherwise pushed out the pipes and lost.

Not too many motorcycles have had turbos as stock equipment. Yamaha came out with a Turbo 650 built in the early eighties, but by the time all the additional plumbing, fuel pumps, and related equipment was hung on the bike, it weighed almost as much as an 1100cc bike. The additional complexity wasn't worth the extra power produced. I think Yamaha, and the other manufacturers of turbo bikes—Honda, Suzuki, and Kawasaki—built them just to show that it could be done.

Boost is measured in pounds per square inch in this country. Europe measures boost in bars, or millibars. Average boost on a car or bike is usually limited to 10–12lbs, or one to two bars. Any more than that, the dreaded detonation monster can chew up the pistons.

Boost is controlled by letting some of the exhaust bypass the exhaust impeller when the boost reaches a preset point. Bypass is controlled by a wastegate incorporating a diaphragm connected to the intake manifold. A calibrated spring holds the wastegate shut until manifold pressure exceeds the spring's set point. Once the limit is reached, the wastegate opens to bypass the gasses not needed for maintaining the set boost.

A computer-controlled or manually adjustable valve can be introduced in the line between the turbo diaphragm and intake manifold fitting, or tapped directly into the intake. Boost can then be set by dialing in the pressure at which the wastegate opens, thus controlling absolute pressure. Most turbos are

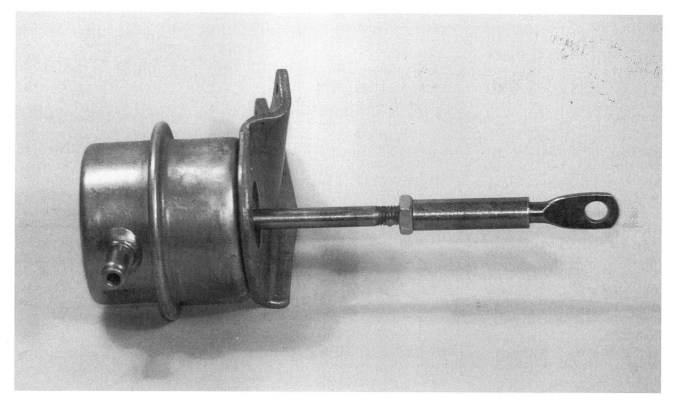

Same function as the Rajay wastegate, just a different design actuator. The manifold pressure is run to the inlet on the actuator cylinder. When the boost overcomes a preset spring tension, the actuator arm moves out and opens the wastegate, holding the boost set-point. *Turbo City*

capable of producing a great deal more boost than the engine can handle if the wastegate stays shut. This will make for some very expensive pieces of ex-racing parts bouncing off the asphalt if the turbo is allowed to run for any length of time in overboost conditions. What normally happens first is the engine detonates so badly that all the power disappears before much damage occurs. No matter how high the octane rating of the fuel, enough boost will eventually cause detonation.

Most new turbo engines use knock sensors and boost pressure regulators to back down the timing or open the wastegate if detonation is sensed. The timing can be electronically retarded at the onset of ping, but this will limit total power production. The best way to control detonation is to start with low boost and gradually increase it until the onset of detonation. Back down a pound, or two, and set the wastegate controller at that point. Every engine will be different, so I can't say how many pounds of boost your motor can handle. My last turbo motor ran high-octane fuel only, with a cam grind set up for forced induction and a manual boost controller.

Standard rate was twelve pounds of puff—twist the dial and seventeen psi appeared on the gauge. Needless to say, this did wonderful things for acceleration and top speed. With the turbo putting out 17lbs, top speed was mostly a factor of redline and gearing. The engine would pull so hard that every gear felt like first. Half the time, I wouldn't use the full boost in the lower gears because the revs jumped so fast that the rev limiter shut the motor down before I could shift into a higher gear. Then I had to wait around until the engine made up its mind to run some more, only to have the whole scenario repeated in the next gear.

By the time I was in third gear, everything slowed down enough to where I could keep up with the tach. Where the motor really shined was in roll-on in fourth or fifth. No more need to downshift; merely wind open the throttle, wait for the boost to go positive, and watch the scenery go by. Great fun!

A few things need to be watched when running a turbocharger. Killing the engine right after a hard run is a sure way to shorten turbo life. It depends on oil and/or water flow to carry the intense

Red Line offers a full series of synthetic oils. I currently run the 50-weight in my engine and the MTL in the trans. *Red Line*

cooking is to let the engine idle for one or two minutes prior to shutting down. This ensures enough oil flow during cool down to remove excess heat from the bearing area. Run a good oil, preferably synthetic, when turbocharging an engine. If you choose not to run a synthetic, then be sure to use a lubricant rated for turbo engines, and change it often.

When turbocharging an engine, care must be taken to ensure you have the correct fuel/air ratio, along with the proper timing under different boost conditions. Too much timing and the fuel will explode ahead of the flame front, causing detonation. Too little, and combustion temperature will soar, also causing detonation. Higher cylinder pressures will require an ignition system capable of delivering a hotter spark. The speed that a turbo motor accelerates will require the use of a good rev limiter. Numerous companies manufacture boost and rev control equipment for aftermarket turbo installations.

Nitrous oxide works well on an engine equipped with a turbocharger. The cooling effect of the N_2O helps lower the inlet temperature, raising the actual inlet charge density. Together, turbos and nitrous can increase horsepower over 50%. Unlike high compression and gynormous lift cams, N_2O and turbocharging can be dialed up or down as the need arises. The engine can wear its street clothes, running like the rest of the sheep, until you turn the boost up and hit the bottle—then instant turbo goat!

Synthetic Oils

Most oils work for their intended purpose, which is to transfer heat, carry particles in suspension until the oil is filtered or changed, resist molecule shear, and provide lubrication to moving parts under a wide range of temperatures. Today's new engines derive some of their fuel economy from using multi-viscosity oils in the 5- to 30-weight area, enabling friction and drag to be reduced. Less resistance in an engine's moving parts works out to less fuel needed to turn the engine against the drag.

Anyone who has built an engine has a good idea of how much drag oil can generate against bearings and rods. Most builders will turn an engine over manually to build up oil pressure and ensure that all the parts that rub on each other get oiled prior to firing the motor. When the engine is dry, it rotates easily. As oil is pumped through the passages and bearings, drag builds up and the crank turns a lot harder.

Well, when oil is circulating through the engine, even when hot, it has a certain amount of parasitic drag. In very simple terms, the lighter the oil, the lesser the drag. Multi-grade oils use viscosity index

heat produced during boost conditions away from the bearings. Once the engine quits turning, no more oil flows through the bearing. The oil that's left will soak up the heat from the hot exhaust side, causing coke deposits to form in the housing. Repeated buildup will cut down the oil flow to zero, with the usual results.

After running hard with a hair drier (race talk for turbo), the best way to keep the turbo bearing from improvers to make the oil function under various conditions and temperatures while still maintaining low-drag properties.

Viscosity is a measure of an oil's ability to flow through a given orifice. Natural mineral oils, without additives, have a very wide viscosity range. Low temperature can turn the best mineral oils solid enough to support your ex-wife. However, at elevated temperatures, untreated mineral oils will go out the pipe as a dense cloud of blue smoke.

Among the additives in oil are oxidation inhibitors, pour-point depressants, rust and corrosion inhibitors, detergents, foam suppressants, extreme pressure additives, and viscosity improvers. All of these contribute to the oil's ability to function over a wide range of conditions and in numerous engine types.

Oil works by preventing metal-to-metal contact. In a bearing journal, oil moves as if in layers. The bearing carries a layer of oil along with it. The next layer, in the middle, moves at varying velocities. The layer next to the crank pin has little motion relative to it. These layers prevent friction and wear-producing metal contact while providing a way to cool the journal and remove any particles that may be generated during startup or extreme operation.

Producing engine oil is a highly competitive business. Oil is formulated to adequately lube an engine under most street conditions but not much more than that. Probably the biggest improvement in petroleum-based oils in the last ten years is the square plastic bottle (more in a given space = more sales = more money). You won't find the world's finest oil being marketed through grocery stores for eighty-nine cents per quart, but you will get an oil that works in 95% of the situations encountered in real life. However, what about in air-cooled, V-twin racing engines?

Most oil engineers know that very few engines will be run hard enough on the street to break down the recommended oils used by the manufacturers. Usually, the Highway Patrol will break you down before the oil will.

The race track is a different story entirely. Most auto racers wouldn't use the "fuel economy" 5W30 oils in their tow vehicles, to say nothing of pouring them in a racing engine. When you start putting high-stress conditions on a racing engine, many conventionally formulated lubricants fail, with catastrophic results.

Synthetic lubricant producers, like Red Line (510-228-7576; 3450 Pacheco Blvd., Martinez, CA 94533) and Spectro Oils (203-775-1291; Route 7, PO Box 208, Brookfield, CT 06804), have evolved a line of lubricants to fill specific needs for the racer. Prior to synthetics, racing petroleum oils filled the

Spectro also carries all types of synthetic lubricant, including one made specifically for primary chains and transmissions. *Spectro*

need, but better living through modern chemistry has provided us with lubricants that far surpass any mineral-based oil.

Synthetics were first developed by the Germans and the Allies at about the same time during World War II. The U.S. had originally gone looking at synthetics for low-temperature use in aircraft bound for cold weather. The Germans had another reason completely for trying to produce a synthetic oil. Late in the war, they began to run out of mineral oil stocks, partially courtesy of the U.S. Eighth Air Force's urban renewal project held during 1942 to 1945 over the oil fields of Romania. The Germans had a serious motivation to try to develop a substitute for mineral-based oils.

The rubber discs in front of the flywheel are filled with a balancing liquid that flows to the light or out of balance side of the rotating mass. Since the fluid is free to travel all the way around the disc, rebalancing never becomes a problem. *Sun-Tech*

Many benefits then accrued from synthetic oil development. Aircraft engines ran cleaner, with fewer deposits. Cold-weather starting became easier, and synthetics operated in turbine engines at temperatures that mineral oils couldn't tolerate. Every ten degrees over 115°C cut mineral oil's life in half. An air-cooled racing engine, operating in ambient temperatures over 37°C (and many track surfaces easily exceed this figure), can see as much as 135°C. Mineral oil goes south real fast at that point. Mineral oil can allow pistons to start to scuff, causing power losses. Synthetic oils won't break down at that temperature; lubrication qualities will stay the same as at lower operating conditions, allowing the engine to still produce maximum power.

The superiority of synthetics lies in the fact that a 10W30 synthetic can provide the high-shear protection superior to a petroleum 10W40 in the bearings and cam, while providing a much lower viscosity on the cylinder walls and rings. This lower viscosity consumes less power and fuel.

Red Line considers that, in most cases, engines that currently run a 20W50 race oil are giving up 1–2% power to a 15W40 synthetic. Due to synthetic's higher vaporization temperature than petroleum oils, oil consumption can drop by as much as 40%. Under high-speed, hot-weather riding conditions, a synthetic will outshine a regular oil.

Dyno tests have shown that both Red Line and Spectro's Golden America oils will show a 1–3% power increase in racing engines. Ring wear drops off to virtually nil, and bearings that used to last three to five runs now go for an entire season. One area of an endurance racing motor that shows a lot of wear is the valve guides. Synthetic oils can keep guides from wearing for up to five times longer than petroleum oils.

People like Chicago Joe Scotella, Mike Hale, and Tim Kerrigan, all Harley drag racers, have switched to Red Line Oil and are more than happy with the results. Axtell sales, XRV Performance, and Victor Valley Harley all sell Red Line and run synthetics when they Dyno test their own engines.

With higher horsepower and raised redlines, Harley racing engines need a better oil than what's used on the street. Oils like Golden Spectro 4 and Red Line 40WT or 20W50 are the best way to protect your engine under high stress. Racing engines run very close to detonation conditions when pulling high revs under hot conditions. Synthetics, due to their composition, will form less deposits in the combustion chamber, helping to keep hot spots, which generate detonation, from forming. On the street, our "high octane" 92 gas will allow higher compression when run in conjunction with synthetics.

My brother, the hero bike racer, switched to pure synthetic oils in his bike over two years ago. He doesn't have any idea of what "take it easy for the first few miles" means and tends to think the red line on a tach is a nice place to start making power. He must have a fairly good idea of what he is doing, as he tends to run mostly in the top five and has learned not to fall off the bike more than once a year.

Last time we opened up his engine, the bearings looked like they had just been installed. Cylinder wear was so slight that a micrometer didn't show more than .001in deviation from new. Some of this can be attributed to his growing ability not to terrorize the equipment so badly, but a lot of it is due to the synthetic oil he runs. His parts bill has been cut way down, so there is more money to travel to more races (that is, unless he reverts to his former habits, and makes more expensive ashtrays out of forged pistons).

Synthetic oils, at eight dollars per quart, may seem like an expensive lubrication solution, but compared to the cost of just one run, they are a bargain hard to beat. Where money actually can be saved in oils is in not buying the "miracle" snake-oil products touted to run your engine for a half million miles, even if the oil gets accidentally dumped out. Most of these "wonder" products will make you wonder why you bought them.

Teflon seems to be the basis of a large number of these miracle oils. Dupont, the developer of Teflon, quit supplying oil companies with Teflon in 1980. Other suppliers, filling a perceived market, slid in to the gap. A lot of oil company engineers are not too sure that Teflon has a place any where near an engine's innards. They say stick to frying pans, not bearing surfaces. Think about how easy a Teflon-surfaced pan will scratch with metal contact. Think about those particles floating around in an engine's oil passages.

Above 400°C, Teflon can decompose into a particularly nasty type of acid, hydrofluoric. It's quite capable of eating any metal parts it touches, to say nothing of what it can do to human skin. Some anti-wear additive testing has shown that the product actually caused more wear than straight oil. If Teflon additives were found to help motor oil, manufacturers would find a way to incorporate it in their oils.

Some Formula One racing teams preheat racing oil prior to filling the sump. You don't have to go quite as far for your racing engine. Just stick with a good synthetic like Red Line or Golden America, let the engine warm the oil to a decent operating temperature prior to making a run, change it at recommended intervals, and be sure to use an oil specified for your engine situation.

As far as synthetics in the transmission, Spectro's SPL Transmission Fluid, a fully synthetic gear oil, has been used in world record-setting V-twin motorcycle racing. Red Line's Synthetic Gear Lubricant has tremendous thermal stability and provides the best load-carrying film strength available. Some synthetics have been found to lubricate transmissions so well that the syncros won't drag the gear speed down enough to allow gears to shift without grinding. In a constant mesh transmission, this isn't a problem. Efficiency improves by 1–5%. A side benefit in their 75W90S is quieter gear running. Synthetics will also do yeoman duty in your race bike transporter. Vans, or pickem-ups used for moving race bikes around the country, seem to suffer from a lack of maintenance at times. I know that my truck has gone over 20,000 miles between changes, and then only gets serviced when I feel guilty. All the time and money seems to go into the racer. The truck has to live as best it can; a full selection of synthetic lubricants might just save you a breakdown at five A.M., twenty-five miles from the track.

Active Engine Balancing

If you've ridden a Harley, you might have noticed a slight vibration coming from the engine area. Some have stated that this "light vibration" might have been a contributing factor to a part or two deciding to set out on its own, separate from the rest of the bike. Or, perhaps these gentle pulsings have made the rearview mirror totally useless while numbing your arms from the elbows down. Rigid-mount bikes seem to have a slightly larger problem with vibration than Rubber Glides—like severe-enough shaking to make keeping your feet on the pegs above 3500rpm a real problem.

I once owned a 1981 Sportster (Harley's dirt bike) that shook so badly that, at any speed above 55mph, my sun glasses would slowly bounce down my nose. Used to have to ride with one hand on the throttle and one hand holding my glasses—time for a different bike.

Well, now there's a company that claims it can cut up to 40% of vibration without spending hundreds of dollars in the process. Sun-Tech Innovations (PO Box 9154, Canoga Park, CA 91309; 800-786-8324) has come out with an active system of balancing the engine with a liquid (mercury, I would imagine) metal balancing agent that utilizes the centrifugal force of the rotating mass of the engine to flow to the optimum point. Engine changes, clutch wear, or other alterations won't affect its operation. Since the system is active, it always stays in balance.

Installation is simple. Sun-Tech takes your flywheel and machines a .438 x .380in groove so that the balance device can be mounted with a high-temp epoxy. If the motor is all together, a compensator can be fit on the compensating sprocket. On a racing engine the components should be rebalanced, but Sun-Tech says that a street bike doesn't need any further machining.

I don't have any first-hand experience with this product, but others who do include drag racer Don Prudhomme and racer Brad Lackey, a world-champ motocrosser of the late seventies and early eighties. Both men have the balancer installed on some fairly high-performance bikes. Brad's H-D is built by Jacques Ellis, a 200mph engine-tuner, and incorporates a balancer in the engine.

Sun-Tech asks only $49 retail and backs the balancer with a two-year warrantee against defects. If you're unhappy with the performance, you can send it back for a full refund. If this is all it takes to be able to see out of the mirrors with the motor running—I'm in.

Power Transmission

Now that you have figured out just how you're going to build that stage three engine and what frame to hang it in, you need to find the best way to get the power to the rear wheel. The stock transmission is nice and reliable for the street. The last California Highway Patrol Harley speedometer that I had the dubious privilege to observe while trying to be creative (me: "Honest, officer I really wasn't running at 75mph!" CHP: "Press hard—four copies"), indicated a little over 55,000 miles. Harley has had many years of experience making their clutches and trannies live forever under moderate use. Life span of a stock H-D engine and transmission should easily extend past 100,000 miles or twenty years. Life span of that same trans with 96 cubic inches hooked through it can be measured in hours.

The stock clutch's ability to absorb a major power increase is somewhat limited. It's quite possible to turn all that new-found horsepower into nothing but slip and stink without a clutch capable of standing up to increased usage.

Barnett Tool and Engineering (PO 2826, Santa Fe Springs, CA 90670; 310-941-1284) has been in the friction business for over forty years. Barnett clutches have been on more record-setters than any other brand. Whether you run a dry or wet clutch, pre-Evo or new bike, any time you modify your engine, the clutch needs to be updated to handle the power increase. Barnett clutches typically have 15–20% greater surface area than stock. Cost for a Big Twin clutch, including hub liner and rivets for pre-1984 bikes, is under $75. Their newer Kevlar clutch for Shovels runs $112. Newer 1984–89 Kevlar plates only are $72.

For out-and-out racers, Zipper's and Bandit Machine got together and engineered the fully automatic "Race Case" five-speed racing transmission. Engine development has evolved into a very sophisticated science, capable of producing 121+ cubic inch, 300hp ground rippers. The problem now is in getting all that power to the ground reliably and being able to shift gears in the shortest period of time.

Prior to the Race Case automatic, most racers were using aftermarket gears in a stock case, shifted with an air shifter. Every time the trans was shifted the ignition had to be cut long enough to take the load off the gears so that the next one could be engaged. All this took time that added to the ET. Plus, every so often the stock case would decide it had had enough and announce its displeasure by upchucking gears all over the track. A stronger gearbox was definitely needed.

Zipper's and Bandit produced a much stronger gearbox for racers only. This automatic eliminates the kill time between shifts. Its internals are all readily available gears and shafts, specially made for racing use. Nothing has to be custom-machined before installing. Zipper's can get replacement parts out within twenty-four hours, but you should still keep enough spares on hand to keep down-time to a minimum. The trans can run as either a four or five speed. It also can be set up to operate with as few as two gears, allowing use in every class from Pro-Stock to Top Fuel.

The engine drive's on the left, with output on the right—similar to a Sportster. This eliminates a lot of the custom fabricating required on the drive train as seen in other dragsters. The clutch can be either a Sportster or Bandit Machine, making installation and parts-availability much easier.

The Race Case uses a reversed-rotation drive gear that steps up the gear speed by 33%. This lets each gear tooth spend less time in contact, reducing wear and increasing reliability. Also, no outboard idler bearings need to be installed to help support the input or output shafts. There are enough different ratios available to suit any track situation or engine combination.

Aha, you say, this sounds like just what I need to make the old sled really shift, but there must be some sort of catch—how about cost? Wellll, now that you ask, the price is a tad above what a stock tranny runs. Zipper's lists it at a "Racer's Net" price of seven thousand, four hundred dollars. If I write it out, it doesn't look as expensive as $7,400. Then you can hang a Bandit Superclutch on the end for $500+. Throw in a couple of bucks for synthetic lube and nuts and bolts—you're pushing $8,000 pretty hard. Not only do you have to be fast to win, but also you need to be quick with a check.

Chapter 6

Suspension, Chassis, and Brakes

Unless you are building an out-and-out drag racer or Land Speed Record bike, the wheels have to be attached to the frame in some way other than metal struts. Most street/racing bikes need better suspension than that found on stock factory bikes. More horsepower will cause the frame and wheels to try to go in numerous new directions totally unanticipated by the rider. A big jump in torque will make a mild-mannered scooter turn into an almost unrideable bike if the suspension isn't capable of transmitting all the power to the ground. Sliding around on a spinning rear tire, or going through the gears with the front wheel above your head, is a good way to impress people (mostly yourself), but it has one drawback when it comes time to race: it's slow. Spending horsepower to hold a front wheel off the ground or using the throttle to turn the rear tire faster than the asphalt goes by is a sure way to waste power. If you think about it for a minute, spending large sums of hard-earned money on a big-horsepower motor only to put it into a frame with worn-out shocks, marginal brakes, or loose bearings is a major waste of money. All the modifications covered in this chapter apply to any stock or semi-stock frame regardless of the engine modifications.

Right about now I usually tell a story about how I learned the hard way about making a bike handle, but luckily I had a good teacher at an early age who taught me to put the money into making a bike stop and turn before buying horsepower. The only real incident showing my inability to learn from others that comes to mind occurred during the six-month period I owned a Vincent Rapide, set up with Black Shadow cams and heads.

For those of you who haven't reached my level of maturity or dignified old age (no, I'm not a licensed "dirty old man" yet, but I've got my learner's permit), a Vincent was an English 1000cc V-twin mo-

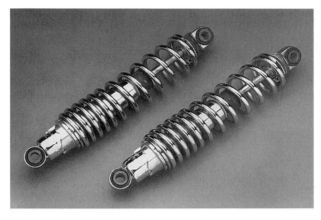

Koni shocks for the FXR are available through CCI in different lengths, ranging from 11.0in to 13.7in eye-to-eye. Spring rates are 100/140/185lbs/in except on the 11.0in size, which is rated slightly lower. Damping and preload are adjustable over a wide range. *Custom Chrome*

torcycle built by Philip Vincent in the 1950s from a design by H. R. Davies, founder of HRD Motorcycles. The peculiar part of the Vincent, other than being of English quirky engineering (old bumper sticker on my early British racers: "The Parts That Fall Off This Vehicle Are Of The Finest English Manufacture"), was that there was no frame to the bike. The girder fork-front suspension was bolted to the front of the engine. The rear end was hung off the back of the transmission with the springs going from a bar connected to the rear axle to the top of the rear cylinder head. The seat and tank were attached to the top of the motor. When it came to moving parts, whoever designed the bike evidently subscribed to the "Never use one when three will do the same job" philosophy. To say handling was interesting would be an understatement.

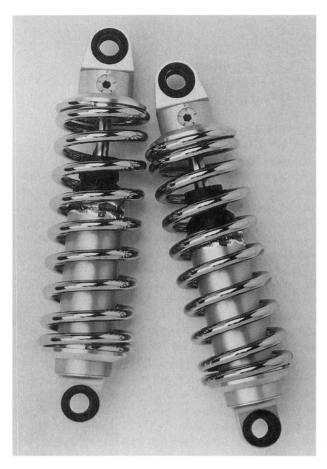

Progressive Suspension manufactures an aluminum-bodied series of shocks to fit all Big Twins from 1979–up. Springs are available either chrome or black. Damping can be set through five ranges by a dial just below the upper shock eye. The shock is completely rebuildable—it can be swapped from bike to bike. *Progressive Suspension*

After setting the choke, priming the carbs, lifting the compression release, sacrificing to the gods of kickback, and delivering a healthy stomp to the kick starter, I would sometimes get it to run. Proving that someone watches out for fools and small children, I didn't manage to start it by myself very often.

Right: Some of us like to go around corners rapidly, as well as go fast in a straight line. Getting a good set of shocks on the back is very important, but they have to be matched with a front end that works as well. Unless your idea of front forks involves tubes 12in over stock, Ceriani offers their 43mm cartridge-style forks to fit Big Twins. Offered in Wide Glide and Mid Glide widths, a set of Cerianis will wake up the front of your bike. For those of you concerned about weight, the 43mm forks weigh 6lbs less than the stockers, and give much better performance than can be had by modifying the factory forks. *Storz*

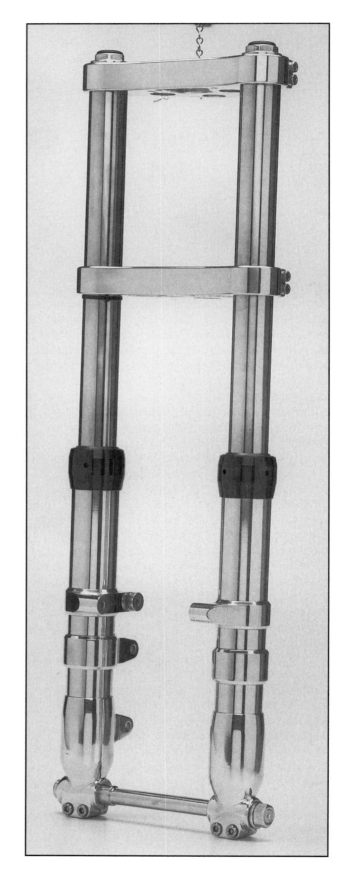

Cycle World Magazine stated that the bike reportedly handled like it had a hinge in the middle—they agreed partially, saying it felt more like a ball joint. Coupled with brakes that could only be charitably called "adequate," this made for a few interesting moments at speed.

One thing the Vincent did have was suds. My crazy buddy and I would go play "who's fastest in a straight line" games every so often. I always took the Vincent because when I ran with him I could usually get him to try to start it when my foot began to hurt.

We'd go find an open stretch of the road—usually early in the morning—ride up to 60mph, and then I'd wait for him to nail the throttle on his 1971 Sportster before I'd hammer the Rapide. It would pull up alongside him at 110mph, making chuff-chuff sounds like a slow-turning, stationary Diesel engine. After running beside him for a ways, I'd screw on the throttle and leave him for dead every time we played this game. I have no idea how fast this thing was, as my chicken factor took over when the bike started to wobble at 120, but it was a whole lot faster than me.

One memorable afternoon, the bike and I got into a contest to see who was stronger. It wanted to go into a high-speed wobble and I wanted to live. We didn't part company, but it wasn't from lack of trying on the bike's part. After describing large ellipses down the road, with black marks at the apex of each sweep, I finally coaxed the twin front drum brakes into slowly retarding progress to the point the

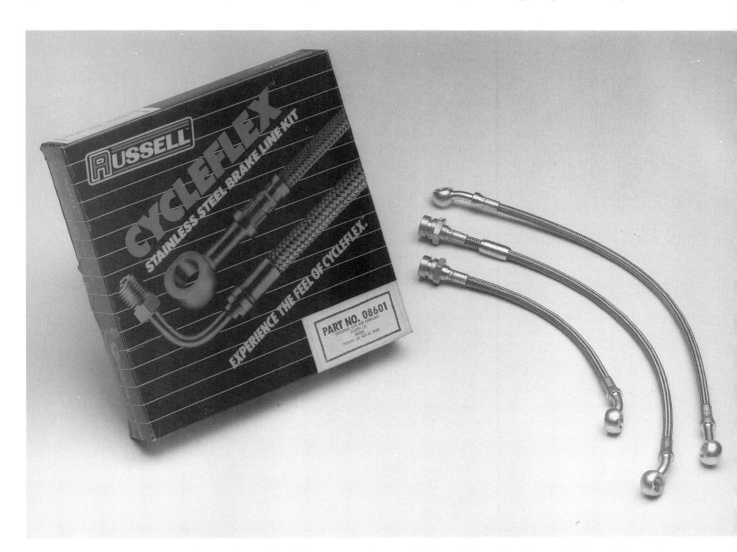

One problem encountered when trying to haul down from racing speeds is brake line swell. The factory rubber lines will expand when the fluid gets hot from hard braking. Stainless steel braided lines, like these from Russell, have a Teflon lining that has a high resistance to swelling. A set of these, with good brake pads from someone like EBC, and brake fade becomes only a faint memory. *Storz*

swoops desisted. I didn't need clean laundry, but it was a close call.

The Vincents are all high-dollar collectors' items now—but I sold this bike for $1,500 and considered myself fortunate. The next owner never did figure out the hard-starting problem, traced later to a misadjusted compression release, but he was able to destroy all the ligaments in his knee within two months of buying the bike.

Nowadays, handling is of much higher priority with me, partly from my youthful indiscretions, like the aforementioned, and partly from watching what the fast guys do.

How to Make it Go Up and Down

The first area to tackle on a bike's suspension is the shocks. Stock factory dampers do a fairly adequate job of keeping the wheels in contact with the ground but go all to pieces when asked to handle output from a 90hp + engine. Once the shock oil heats up only a Ouija board can predict where the rear wheel will go. One thing is for sure; it won't do what you want it to do. The springs on the back shocks will bottom on a stock H-D when dropping off a curb with two people aboard—imagine what they will do with lots of horsepower applied all at once.

As soon as the springs bottom you lose any and all suspension. For all intents, the rear end becomes rigid. This is fine if you are drag racing; however, it's not a quality to be sought in the real world of potholes and speed bumps. Hit a pothole with the wick turned up high, and the stock suspension will give you a ride to equal Universal Studios'. It will also give you a real honest set of white knuckles if it doesn't spit you off completely. High-performance engines need high-performance suspensions.

We'll start with the rear shocks, as they're the easiest to change. A bad set can create weird problems at both ends of the bike that are hard to trace. Front and rear suspension must be looked at as a package in order to set up a bike properly. It does no good to hang a set of Ceriani 43mm forks on the front of your scooter if the back end slides like a moose on marbles.

Progressive Suspension (11129 G Ave., Hesperia, CA 92345; 619-948-4012) carries a full line of replacement shocks for Harley-Davidson. Because each bike and rider weigh differently, fully adjustable shocks are the way to go. Aluminum or steel, the 4000 series of shocks comes with adjustable preload and five-position damper. The aluminum version is fully rebuildable; only one pair will ever have to be put on the bike. A pair will set you back $200, unless you are riding a Softail, which will take another $95 to fit.

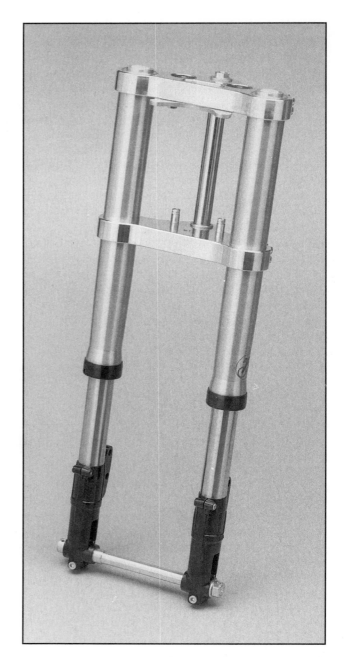

For a different way to take care of front end sags, check out the Forcelle Italia inverted forks for Big Twins. They have the lowest unsprung weight of any road-going fork. Damping can be set through air caps. Available in two lengths—30.5in or 31.5in—they will give your bike's front end a very different look. *Storz*

The 4000 series are available in various lengths, from 11.0in to 13.5in to fit 49–86 FL & FLH, 80–86 FXWG, and 73–86 FX. The later FLs and all in the FX series take an 11.5in to 14.25in shock, standard steel or adjustable steel and aluminum. If you

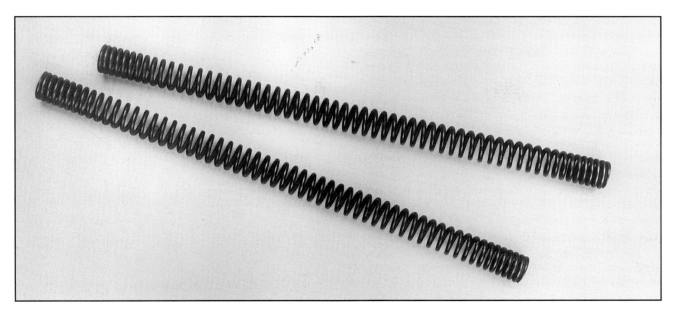

If you want a cheaper alternative to a complete fork change, Progressive Suspension offers progressive-wound springs to fit Big Twins. They start with a soft rate to soak up small bumps; then, as the suspension travel continues, the spring resists compression with an increased rate. These, the Cerianis, and the Forcelle Italia forks are available through Storz Performance. *Storz*

are fitting a shorter 11.5in shock in place of the standard 12.625in factory unit on a 93 FXDWG Wide Glide, the rear fender will have to be modified a bit to clear.

Big touring bikes and early FXRS and FXRT bikes can improve handling along with load-carrying capability by swapping the factory dampers for a set of air shocks. Progressive takes care of any spring problems by installing a set of dual-rate springs on their "Magnumatic" 1600 series air shock. Some air shocks don't have enough spring to handle a full touring load pulled by a 96ci motor. Adding air to overcome sag is one way to get around poor spring performance, but too much air pressure can cause stiction between the shock body and the shaft. By using a progressive-wound spring you will get the suspension to continue to work properly as increased loads are put on it. This way, the air pressure can be used just to trim-out the bike. Another advantage is that an air shock can be adjusted quickly as loads change. Most installations include an air gauge and Schrader fill valve that mounts up in the fairing. When air is added or removed, both shocks get the same pressure, eliminating the possibility of uneven operation caused by different pressures in each shock.

I've seen custom hookups where a small, onboard air compressor and release valve are tied into the gauge lines, allowing air pressure to be changed without resorting to a gas station's air line. I do advise making all pressure changes while the bike is stopped. Playing pogo stick while running down a freeway is a good way to create interesting handling problems.

Any changes at the rear end should be followed by improvements on the front forks. Progressive recommends changing both the damper rods and fork springs for better stability and improved rebound control. The springs are progressively wound so that the spring rate increases as the springs are compressed. Not quite as good as anti-dive; however, the springs do eliminate front-end sag and reduce hard-braking nose dives, along with giving much greater stability in corners. Hanging a lot of weight on the back of a bike can make the front end wander around under braking or during turn-in while entering a corner. Stiffer suspension will keep the bike from hobby-horsing or changing lines in the turn. If you've ever had the dubious privilege of having a heavily laden tourer bounce over two feet at the apex of a corner, then you know of what I speak. Sudden suspension shifts do wonders for your passenger's piece of mind. Too much power transmitted through poor suspension can put you up in the part of the performance envelope pilots call "the coffin corner." Too much aft center of gravity, coupled with a high corner-entry speed, and it's even money on which end comes around the turn first.

Steve Storz (239 S. Olive St.., Ventura, CA 93001; 805-641-9540) is an ex-HD factory tuner who started Storz Performance in 1979 to manufacture and distribute suspension products to professional racers. I've had the opportunity to use some of his products on my drag racer, with good results.

For the ultimate in front ends, he handles the 43mm Ceriani forks for Big Twins and Harley's little bike. A standard, late-model front fork is 39mm; the earlier ones are 35mm. A bike with a set of 43mm units hung on the front looks somewhat out of proportion because the tubes are so big, but I will guarantee that when you hang a set of these on your bike, front fork flex is a thing of the past.

They are available with either a "Wide Glide" or "Mid Glide" set of triple tees and will accept the H-D Wide Glide hub and wheel or the FXR hub. The Cerianis weigh six pounds less than the stock factory parts, while being over twice as strong in flex and torsion. If you want the best possible front-end control, these are the way to go. New for '94 is the Ceriani Wide Glide-style, inverted 43mm fork for Big Twins. These and the Forcelle Italia 40mm inverted forks have the fork outer tubes mounted above the fork legs. Lower unsprung weight and more controllable dampening are the chief advantages, other than a totally different look than the front ends of most Big Twins.

Cerianis run anywhere from $1,360 for the Mid Glide to $1,550 for the complete Wide Glide front end. Forcelle Italia inverted forks are another way to go at $1,650 per set. This may seem like a lot of money for a set of forks, but it's kinda like riding a Harley in the first place: once you've done it, you'll never go back.

For those of you who only need the forks to hold the front wheel on the track for a quarter mile at a time, a little under $1,000 will set you up with either 38mm or 42mm front forks and a billet triple clamp. These can be ordered with a variable length T-stem to accommodate most front steering head lengths to fit any frame. A collar must be heli-arced on and the excess stem trimmed to fit. This way, any custom frame can take a set of Forcelle Italia racing forks.

Steve also has had remanufactured the older-style 35mm forks, last produced in the 1970s. These aren't recommended for street usage on heavier bikes, but they work well on drag racers. They are fairly popular, due to their light—5lb, 4oz—weight. The 35mm forks and triple clamps list for $535 and $345, respectively. They can be ordered with handlebar mounts, for stock mounting, or without, for clip-ons.

My bike also has another Ceriani product on the front end that I swear by: an adjustable steering

Here's a set of Wide Glide Cerianis mounted on a Big Twin. The front fender has spacers between the mounts and the forks to fit. A spacer kit for the FXR narrow hub is also needed. *Storz*

damper. Once upon a time, my racer came down with a bad case of St. Vitus' dance in the front end, otherwise known as a steering wobble. One of these per lifetime is all you need. Installing a steering damper took care of the problem. Under $200, steering dampers are mostly found on road racers, but they do work well on all types of competition and street bikes as well. They are required on any bike that runs over 125mph at any SCTA event.

One way I have learned to use a steering damper on a street bike is on long rides. I can adjust it down to where the bike tracks almost like it's on autopilot. All the small bumps and twitches that affect a front end disappear. It makes long rides much more relaxing. Be sure to back it down before heading back to the surface streets, though, or the first time you take a tight turn, you're in

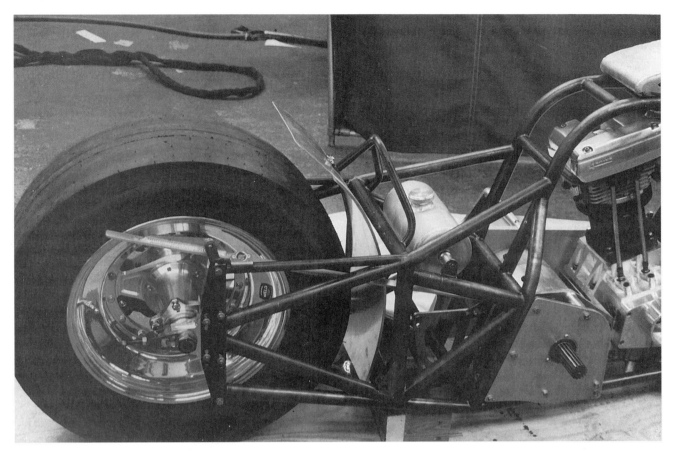

As you can see in the picture, Kosman has frame geometry pretty well dialed in. Check all the triangulation on the rear struts and transmission mount. Everything is built with the idea that it *won't* flex. *Kosman Specialties*

Kosman installs a steering damper on all the frames they produce. Most sanctioning bodies require one on any bike that runs over 125mph. It's fully adjustable for damping. It can be cranked down so tight that the bars take a definite effort to move. If you're the type who likes it tight, be sure to remember to loosen it at the end of the run, or you can be surprised when trying to turn the bike onto the return road. *Kosman Specialties*

for a surprise. Nothing serious, but the additional effort needed to turn the wheel might catch you off guard.

Storz is heavily into racing suspension products for Harleys and carries everything from Grimeca disc brakes to oil coolers. A catalog is four dollars and can be had with a phone call.

Frame

Now that you are surrounded by all these expensive parts, it probably wouldn't hurt to have a place to put them. A full drag racer uses a frame not found on street machines. Long and low gets the weight

down and improves handling. A long-wheelbase bike has a tendency to want to run straighter than a shorter setup. Other factors that you won't encounter on a

Left: This shot of the same frame shows the massive aluminum transmission support, and the small aluminum gas tank that fits under the fiberglass body. *Kosman Specialties*

street bike come into play when building a racer. Most drag racing frames, like a Kosman (available through Zipper's Performance or at 415-861-4262), have a large amount of adjustment built into them. Front and rear ride height, wheelbase, and engine placement can all be moved around. Some tweaks, like engine placement, are harder to change than others, but ride height and suspension adjustment are fairly easy to shift.

The Kosman Top Fuel chassis can be built around any engine/transmission combination. The wheelbase can be set anywhere from 84 to 86 inches. The rear section takes up to a 12in beadlock wheel on a hollow 1.25in rear axle.

Bottom: These are the external bearing supports for the engine output shaft and clutch hub. This engine has been turned 180 degrees to keep the proper rotation when driving a Kosman transmission without using an idler gear like Zipper's. *Kosman Specialties*

Kosman also can modify your existing stock frame with a new, raked Kosman head tube and chrome-moly top tube. This will increase cylinder head clearance. Other parts, such as wheelie bars, rear-frame sections, wheels, and tires are available through them.

Prices run:
Frame modification $1,250
Complete Pro Stock Harley Chassis .$12,500
Extended swing arm $450
Wheelie bars $325
Peg and pedal kit $112.50
Kosman Drag Forx . . . .$725 /$995 Pro
Modular front wheel $595
Modular rear wheel $960
Beadlock rear wheel . . . .$1,250 & up
Goodyear front tires $120
Goodyear rear tires . . . .$135 to $185
Labor to true tire $65
Battery box $50
Chain guard kit $57.50

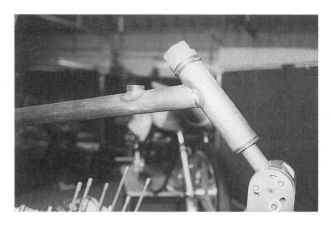

Kosman uses jigs to hold all the frame members in place while welding. Here, a front down-tube is welded to a horizontal frame piece. With Heli-arc welding, heat transfer and distortion are kept to a minimum.

Rear sprocket $65
Air tank option $50
Front 'glass fender $65

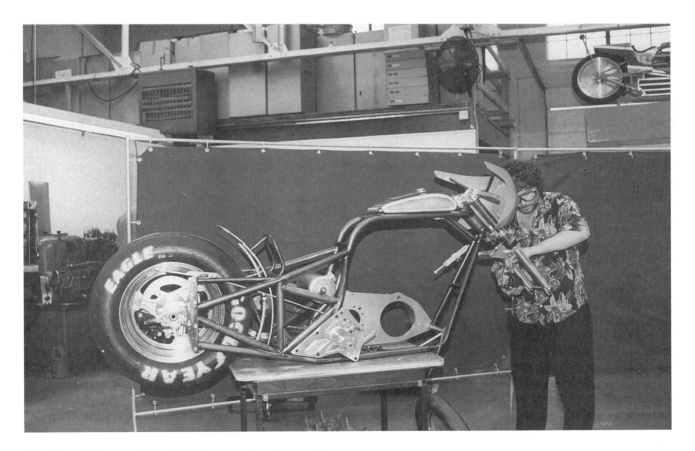

The front forks are being fitted to a racing frame. This gives you a good idea as to how much work goes into fabricating a Kosman frame.

Bandit Machine advertises their "Super Clutch" as totally bulletproof. It bolts right into a Big Twin case. Tied in with Zipper's Racecase, this makes for a just about inde-structible powertrain. Barnett also has a full line of clutches to fit every Big Twin. *Bandit*

Rear 'glass fender $120
Fuel tank $105
Pro seat/tail $120

For a price on their Top Fuel Harley chassis, give them a call. Current prices are in the $13,500 area—less engine and transmission.

All drag bikes are built with the engines placed under the rider. Whether there are two engines or one, layout is similar to stock. Not that we might not see a racer with the engine mounted behind the rider at some late date, but for now, all the scooters are set up rider-over-motor, with the seat set low behind the cylinders.

Engine placement in the frame is pretty much the same in all single-engine drag bikes. Transmission technology has changed a great deal in the last few years, and this will be covered in a later section. Belts may be the hot thing for the street; however, chain final drive still powers all racers. Engines and transmissions are tied together by way of an aluminum plate

on the clutch side of the engine. This plate, in some cases, is 3/8in thick, to prevent any flexing between the engine and trans. Nothing is mounted in rubber, for the same reason. Transmission of vibration to the rider is of no importance in a racing situation—retaining the engine/transmission alignment is much more critical than rider comfort. After all, how uncomfortable can you get in a ten-second or less run? Besides, your mind will probably be on things other than seating and vibration. The first couple of times you cut the lights at the starting line, adrenaline flow will probably keep you from feeling the ride at all.

To help keep the weight as low in the frame as possible, some frame manufacturers are building the oil tank into the area between the frame-front downtubes. A few years ago, there was a fad going to carry the oil in the frame of the bike. This was a real slick idea until someone blew the first motor. Trying to get all the metal particles out of the bottom of the tubes put a stop to that method of carrying oil. The entire bike had to be turned upside down to get all the gunk out. Even then, you weren't assured of completely cleaning the tank. Now, a streamlined aluminum tank, sitting right at engine height, carries all the oil needed for a run.

Wheelie bars bolt directly to the same vertical support that locates the rear wheel. Most bars are readily detachable, to make loading and unloading the racer much easier. Stock-framed bikes can substitute a strut bar for the rear shocks and bolt the wheelie bar to the shock mounting-tabs on the frame and swing arm.

Prices for racing frames are worked out between builder and owner. Many different points have to be considered when setting up a drag bike frame. Engine placement—normal or turned around, type of transmission, foot peg mounts, header pipe location, air shifter mounts, and oil and gas tank placement will all require individual treatment. Steering head angle and fuel tank mounts need to be determined for each frame.

You may have your own ideas about how you think a frame should work, but before you jump into rolling your own, spend some time learning how someone like Kosman does it. An acquaintance of mine (who shall remain nameless to protect his stupidity) built a frame with mild steel, a welding torch, and a prayer. He did manage to *braze* it all together—even got it to run, with a fairly modified Shovel engine providing motivation. Bad part was that he forgot to check the alignment before making a run.

He took this loosely connected group of spare parts out to an industrial complex with a long access road one sunny Sunday morning when all was quiet and peaceful. No one was about on this crisp morning, not even a security guard.

He started out with a few very mild runs up and down the long frontage road in front of the complex. Everything went real well right up to the time he tried to make the first full-power run.

Well, about the only thing he learned from that run was that, given the right amount of torque, mild steel tubing will flex in new and strange directions. He semi-underrated the ability of the frame to accept torsional loads, too. By the

As you can see, a lot of work goes into manufacturing a clutch. Linings used on a Bandit are Kevlar, supplied by Barnett. Different springs can be ordered to provide different pressures. The street setup has light spring pressure for light lever pressure. *Bandit*

Zipper and Bandit developed the Racecase as a stronger replacement for the stock trans. In order to use the necessary parts to eliminate kill time between shifts, the Racecase uses a drive gear system that reverses the rotation of the gears and steps up the transmission speed 33%. The entire transmission case is machined out of one billet, giving light weight along with being hell for strong. *Zipper's*

time he got the high-speed wobble stopped and the bike shut down, the front wheel was so far out of true, the bike made two distinct tracks. Afterwards, it made right turns real easy, but it wasn't much for going left. I think the frame ended up with push pedals and bicycle wheels for his four-year-old son. Even then, it was still a little shaky during full pedal-power runs.

The pros have all the frame jigs to build a racing frame and keep everything straight during the welding process. They also have the knowledge as to how to build one that will run straight. A lot of things, like tube wall thickness and frame gusseting, need to be more than guesses. The old "see what breaks and weld three more pounds of metal on it until it stops breaking" method doesn't work on bikes making sub-nine-second runs in the quarter mile. This is one area where I would stick with what the professionals build.

Stopping Power

All good things must come to an end sometime, and in racing that happens when the checkered flag falls—hopefully, with you being the first bike across the line. So far we've spent most of our time talking about making your bike go quicker or faster; now it's time to bring things to a halt.

Brakes on any motor vehicle use the friction generated between two dissimilar surfaces to convert forward motion into heat. This heat is then transferred to the air and dissipated. The efficiency of the friction material in disc brake pads, or linings in a drum brake, determines how fast the mechanical energy of the rotating disc can be converted into heat. Most street usage only requires that brakes work at around 35% of their capability. The actual chances of incurring repeated panic stops from 60mph are so slim that most road tests are of academic discussion only. If you find that you are

This shows the drive from the engine entering on the left and the final drive on the right, as in a Sportster. The engine and transmission are tied together by one solid piece of aluminum plate on the drive side. *Zipper's*

using 100% of your bike's braking ability on a regular basis, you either belong on a racetrack or in a nice secure place where someone will watch over you before you get killed.

Racing is another story entirely. The front wheel on a race bike is required to do 95% of all the braking on a race track. Rear brakes don't get much use in competition. It's much too easy to tap the rear just hard enough to make the wheel stop turning. If the brakes aren't immediately released, the bike will immediately separate thee from it, with the usual consequences when you fetch up against a solid object. At times, this ignominy is compounded by the bike following you to the solid object to deliver another thump from the other side. My semi-crazy road racing brother has bent the rear brake pedal so far into the frame that he has to lift his foot off the peg to apply it. He says he only uses the rear stopper for slowing down in the pits anyway, so why have it out there where he might be tempted to use it. Pro road racers do use the rear

brake sometimes but only to help set the bike in a turn; not for serious braking.

Some race bikes' front brakes are so strong that the riders can literally rotate the bike around the front axle under hard braking. My brother thinks these "brakies" or "stoppies" are great fun. My opinion wasn't requested.

With the massive horsepower injections possible on a Big Twin, the factory brakes can be easily overloaded. This is usually announced by the front brake lever pulling all the way to the throttle while the bike sails merrily on. Anyone who has been introduced to brake fade at a very inopportune moment will carry the memory forever. The rest of us who narrowly miss becoming part of a motorhome will just be scared stupid.

Tell me, those of you who have found yourself in the situation where the road turns before the bike wants to, and you have to keep telling your body to release the brakes so the wheels will start turning again while your body keeps trying to put them on harder, is there any worse sensation than the sinking feeling of

The top of a Harley transmission, with the cover plate pulled, shows the shifter drum with detents. As the drum is turned by the ratchet on the left, it causes the shift forks to select another gear. If the transmission has a lot of load against it when it is shifted, the shift forks (at the rear, or left, of the case) can bend or break. Then you end up with a box full of neutrals at the best; a case full of broken parts at the worst.

dread right about where your lunch sits? I know I've been so close a few times that the engine died when I stopped because I was shaking so badly I couldn't pull in the clutch—not fun.

My early Panhead came with a front brake that could only charitably be called a speed reducer. This was long before the advent of disc brakes; drums were the norm. Whatever was passing itself off as linings inside the front drum had the life span and stopping qualities of a post-it note. It did make a good hill holder, though. The rear brake worked much better. It had no problem stopping the wheel from turning. Unfortunately, this did little to retard forward motion of the bike, causing a certain amount of anxiety at times.

When I first started playing fast and loose with Harleys (no, I won't say how long ago), some of my cohorts actually removed the front brake from the bike, preferring to run a spool wheel carrying a

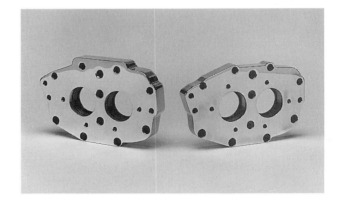

The transmission doors on Big Twin five-speeds are somewhat of a weak link when subjected to the strains of racing. Sputhe manufacturers aluminum billet doors, machined out of 6061-T6 and show-polished. The doors come in both early and late ball & ramp style. The door resists flex and will take much more horsepower without distortion. *Sputhe*

3.00x21 tire. They were of the mind that hitting the front brake was a good way to have the bike flip over their head. They preferred to take their chances by locking up the rear brake and laying the bike down. If you think I speak in jest, go talk to some old bike riders of the 1950s and 60s.

Things sure are different today. Now, companies like EBC (from England; see your retailer. Tech support, 206-485-7610) manufacture brake pads with a high Kevlar content that are just about fade-proof. Eighty percent of the Harley Supersport racers use EBC pads on their race bikes. The fibers in the pads are made out of DuPont Kevlar, the same material as in bulletproof vests. By eliminating asbestos from brake pads, engineers had to find another material capable of being temperature-resistant up to 1,000 degrees while keeping their resiliency and not eating up the rotors like older compounds would. Early metallic compounds would guarantee to keep your rotors clean from rust. They were so hard that they didn't work until hot, then proceeded to turn the rotors as efficiently as a lathe. They would stop a racer, but when cold had the friction coefficient of a Teflon frying pan.

The newer materials, like Kevlar, don't need to get hot to work. They are almost the best of both worlds. Kevlar pads will out-stop the old semi-metallic pads and last over twice as long in the process.

One area of the brakes seldom thought about is the lines running from the calipers to the levers. The stock rubber lines do a great job of keeping the brake fluid from leaking on the floor but blow up like a balloon when asked to work hard. Hot brake fluid will cause the stock lines to expand enough to run you completely out of braking power.

A stainless steel braided line set will improve braking significantly. Storz and Zipper's retail Russell and Cycleflex lines to fit all Big Twins and tourers. Just replacing the stock lines and changing to a set of EBC pads will improve braking up to 50%. A good hose kit (there are poor ones—don't try to economize here) retails for under $100, front and rear. Pads are $30 per set. On the street, the rear brake never gets hot enough to worry about, but I found that new pads and braided lines gave me much better control in traffic.

My old Shovel really perked up when I changed brakes. The original pads took so much force to operate that I thought the lever was hooked directly to the frame. The bike would stop quickly, just not easily. New lines and pads didn't turn stopping into a one-finger exercise; however, my right hand doesn't feel like it's been unscrewing mayon-

On a Kosman frame, the output shaft drives from the right side of the trans. The drive sprocket is shown sitting in its outboard bearing support. Without a method of holding the end of the shaft in place, the sprocket could move enough to spit off the drive chain or bend the output shaft when the hammer's dropped.

naise jars all day, either. Not all of us make a living cracking walnuts with our bare hands, so any help relieving brake lever pressure is welcome.

Performance Machine (PM—PO Box 1739, Paramount, CA 90723; 310-634-6532) carries a full line of calipers and brackets. They offer a four-piston caliper available with an 11.5in cast disc or with a bracket set up for stock H-D 10.5in disc. Their top line rotor has 30% better friction qualities than stock. Best part—it's guaranteed not to squeal. The system can be retrofitted to older drum brakes by using the stock drum hub. The caliper bracket is chrome steel and self-centering. If the forks have had their fender tabs removed, a weld-on anchor is available.

The master cylinder is the primary component in a brake system. It must be the proper size to provide the right volume of fluid at the right pressure to

EBC, out of England, makes brake pads for almost all types of bikes. These Kevlar pads provide better stopping power than earlier, semi-metallic pads; work fairly well in the rain; and don't have any of that ol' nasty asbestos in them. *EBC*

work the calipers properly. PM recommends using a 5/8in master cylinder on single caliper applications and a 3/4in on dual assemblies. The larger master moves more volume with less lever travel and less line pressure than the 5/8in master, so it requires more pressure to get the same stopping power.

For drag racers, there's a left-hand master for rear calipers. This gives added stability during burn-

outs and controls wheel spin during a pass. It lets you keep both feet on the ground while staging, making the initial few seconds of drag racing much easier.

On Harleys intended for high-performance applications, where braking will be of paramount importance, full floating discs should be used. When a disc is used under extreme conditions, it can get so hot that it distorts. A floater allows the disc to expand

When building a bike from scratch, finding good brakes and rotors is a necessity. Performance Machine's (PM) four-piston caliper can be ordered for almost any year or model rear-frame and wheel setup. *Performance Machine*

with the heat, eliminating most distortion. The floating elements allow radial expansion while limiting side movement. PM recommends the "silent" version for Harleys where rattle might be a problem at low speeds. All the PM discs are made from high-

Should your braking needs be extremely high, PM offers a six-piston caliper designed mostly for intensive use on race tracks, but it will provide the ultimate in stopping power for any bike in any situation. I've got a thing about having more brake than I can possibly use, so this setup is real appealing to me. *Performance Machine*

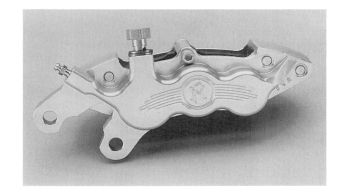

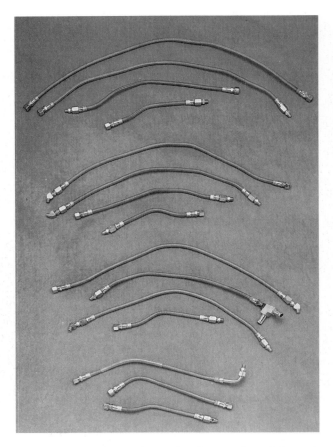

All fluids on a motorcycle need to be transferred through braided Teflon lines. Brake fluid gets hot and will blow up a stock set of lines like penny balloons. Gasoline has a rather nasty habit of burning if leaked onto a hot pipe. Either problem will cause a lapse in concentration if allowed to happen. Most lines can be ordered as a set: fuel, oil, or brakes. Use the good lines that thread onto A&N fittings, not the type that have screw clamps at the end. These are for Softail oil lines. *Custom Chrome*

grade cast-iron, formulated to produce a high coefficient of friction and excellent heat dissipation. The discs are drilled both for lighter weight and to help provide a wiper action on the pad surface for self-cleaning and anti-glaze.

All discs are zinc-plated or flash-chromed for appearance, so don't go using them in anger prior to breaking them in and bedding in the pads. Pads and discs have to be worn-in to each other before maximum braking can occur. Any coating, grease, or oil must be cooked off before they will work. Pads should be handled carefully during installation to

Right: The same goes for new brake fluid—change it whenever lines are replaced, or every two seasons. *Custom Chrome*

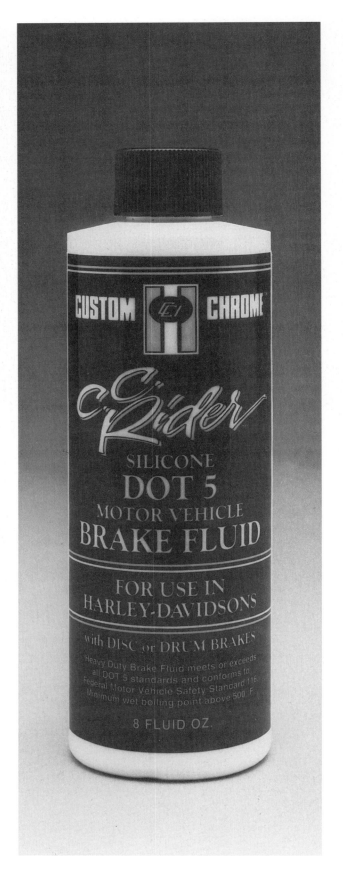

I know you don't need to be told, but other guys might—use a new chain on your bike when you build a new motor or first go racing. I have an O-ring chain on my FXRS and have only had to adjust it twice in 10,000 miles. *Custom Chrome*

prevent any lubricants from coating their surfaces. Short-term oil spills can be removed by using a good spray brake cleaner with lint-free rags.

Use only the type of brake fluid recommended by the manufacturer. Take time to bleed the lines properly. A pressure-bleeder that pushes fluid from the caliper into the master cylinder is the best way to ensure all air is removed. Motorcycle brake systems hold such a small volume of fluid that any amount of air, no matter how small, can cause spongy brakes. A big bubble trapped in the caliper on a dual-caliper set will keep the brakes from working at all while driving you crazy trying to remove it.

Any time brakes are worked on, the master cylinder O-rings and piston should be replaced, or at least checked for wear. O-rings are relatively cheap so I make a habit of replacing them every season. One case of sinking brake lever due to a worn master cylinder was enough for me. Saturday, the brakes worked perfectly. Sunday, I bled them: zilch—no brakes. Turns out the piston in the master was moved just enough to push the O-rings past their normal travel, and that alone put enough wear on them to let fluid slip by. I discovered this as we were loading the bike in the trailer the day before the race. The brakes had worked OK after bleeding, but, after sitting for a while, they went away. I thought the loss was due to air and about went crazy trying to bleed them. In sheer desperation, I pulled the master apart and replaced the seals: presto—brakes were back. I do learn things the hard way at times.

Wheels and Tires

Drag racing puts much higher loads on all parts. Wheels are no exception. Top Fuel and Funny Car racers only use their wheels for a limited number of runs before turning them into coffee tables. Bike racers should operate the same way. If your front wheel gets

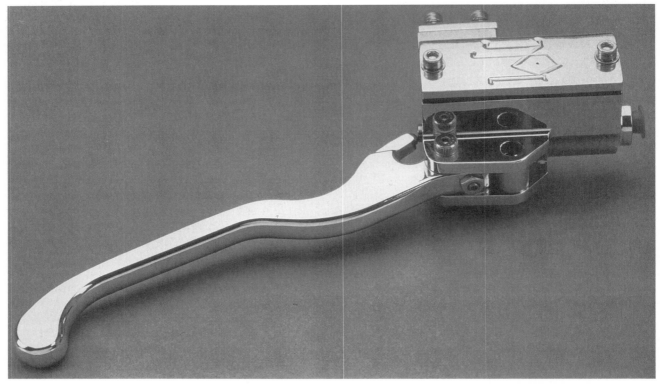

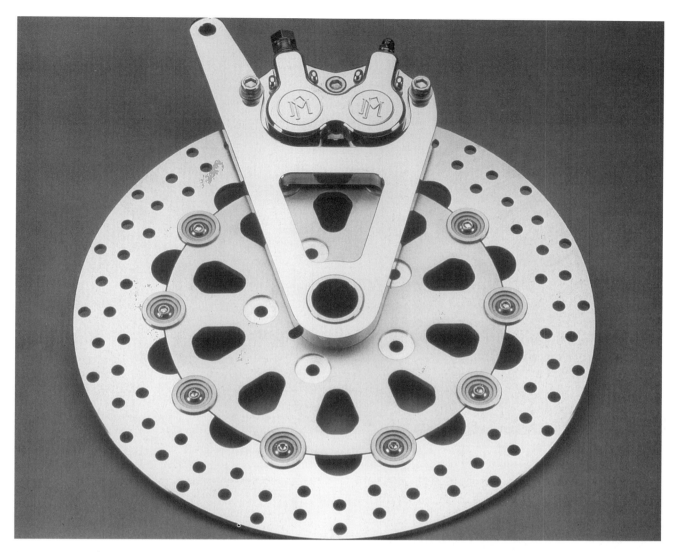

Most street applications, rear or front, can be handled by a four-piston caliper. Even Springers (shown) can benefit from full-floating discs and four-piston calipers. You may not need good brakes very often, but when you need them, you need them worse than Maalox after cheap Mexican food. *Performance Machine*

Left top: Full-floating disc brakes are used mostly on the racetrack, or when maximum braking effort is needed from a street setup. Under extreme conditions, discs can cook so hot they warp. Floating discs expand with the heat, eliminating almost all distortion. When using my favorite six-piston caliper, I find floaters are a necessity to maintain 100% braking ability. *Performance Machine*

Left bottom: Master cylinders are available from PM with either 5/8in or 3/4in bore. This one comes with a dog-leg lever that should bend, not break, if struck with a blunt object, like the pavement. *Performance Machine*

banged off the track all the time, consider changing it every other season and watch for cracks after every event. Needless to say, any crack, no matter how small, the wheel is junk. Make sure it's altered in some way so no one can use it after it's discarded.

Elmer Trett and Jim McClure use PM 6061 T4 aluminum wheels on all their record-setters. Wheels are available in many styles, and anodized in red, blue, and black. Various patterns are available, including solid. PM recommends solid wheels on the back of race bikes only, as a solid front wheel can cause lane changes under high wind conditions.

For drag racing only, 15in spun aluminum wheels are available in widths from 7in to 10in for

Kosman uses the lightest front forks, wheel and disc brake system possible while still providing excellent strength and stopping power. "Drag Forx" are light while still being able to handle wheelies and 200mph runs without flexing. They are not intended for the street, however.

the rear wheel. The 15x7 wheel, including bearings and spacer, weighs 11lbs, 8oz; the 15x9 is 12lb, 15oz.

Superlite front wheels (18x1.850, or 18x2.125), are intended for drag racing only, and have been used by Elmer Trett to go 213.98mph. All wheels, front or rear, will accept PM's universal brake systems.

Tires are pretty much a matter of personal choice. Leo Hess' A/Fuel drag bike runs a Goodyear Eagle 11x29in slick on the back with an 18in Goodyear on the front. His Bonneville tires are either Mickey Thompson 300mph tires or Goodyears.

Stock-frame street/race bikes have the option of selecting from numerous V-rated (over 155mph) tires. Avon builds their AM 22 and AM 23 GP tires for custom and drag race purposes. Fronts are available in sizes 110/80 VB 18 and lower-profile 110/70 VB 18. Rears are 140/80 VB 16, wider 160/80 VB 16, and 130/70 VB 18 to 180/55 VB 18. All tires are legal for any sanctioning body. Two compounds are available: GP Track Formula, for fast abrasive track conditions; and GP Sprint Com-

pound, for Sprint (Limey for Drag) Racing. Built in England, where I hear it rains from time to time, Avons are especially good in the wet slimy stuff. They won't last as long as their H-rated Roadrunner AM 20 and AM 21 tires, but they will stick like bill collectors. Other manufacturers such as Goodyear, Pirelli, Dunlop, and Metzeler manufacture equivalent tires. My Land Speed Record bike carries a set of Metzeler V-rated tires on it while my street bike rides on Dunlops. Motorcycle tires bear speed and size ratings on their sidewalls. Different letters signify rated speeds:

H=130mph
V=149mph
Z=149mph and up (some manufacturers have tested Z-rated tires at over 200mph).

Right: ...and it all comes out here. This is what you buy when you get someone like Kosman to build a custom frame. The quality of all Kosman's work is the best to be seen. Aluminum work is up to aircraft standards, and I wish I could run a Heli-arc as well as their craftsmen.

Performance Machine's aluminum wheels held up both ends of *Easyrider's* Bonneville Streamliner when it went 322mph, so they ought to be able to keep the front end of your bike from dragging the ground up to any speeds you can hit. *Performance Machine*

Most street bikes will perform just fine on V-rated tires. The main criteria is to choose a compound sticky enough to give good traction. Most Harley shops will have someone behind the counter who can give you the hot set-up.

What's super-sticky when this was written might be obsolete by the time you read this. Racing tire technology changes so fast that any information on compounds and models probably won't apply six months later.

Custom Chrome offers a whole group of different wheel sets for Harley-Davidsons. Pentastar, cheese slicer, or solid—it's your choice. *Custom Chrome*

Avon's Super Venom tires are V-rated to sustained speeds up to 149 mph. Possibly your Softail spends little time at these speeds; however, it's nice to have the best in tires keeping your rims off the ground. *Avon*

For those who wish to roll their own, custom-polished spoke rims are available in many widths, for front or rear wheels.

Pro Stock or Fuel bikes require all the rubber possible on the back end. Goodyear's ET Drag is pretty much the standard when laying down mega-horsepower. I've seen it run on a few bikes at EL Mirage for top speed record runs but without an excess of power; the wide casing actually can hurt performance at the high end. *Kosman*

Chapter 7

Going Racing

Most motorcycle owners think about getting on a race track at least once in their lives. Usually the desire to go fast and do it under sanctioned conditions comes about after selling a smaller bike and buying a new one that's a lot faster than the national speed limit. Or, perhaps you're at the point where one more ticket and your license turns into a pumpkin, so it's time to go run legal. How do you get started?

Well, just about any bike can be drag raced, but lets pick a specific bike and walk through the necessary steps to get from the street to the track. We'll take a Harley FXDL Dyna Low Rider with 3500 street miles on it, a modified induction system, a hotter cam, and a set of good aftermarket pipes to the race track.

First, join a racing organization like AHDRA or IDBA (addresses in the appendix). All of them will send you a one-year list of events where races will be held. Figure out how many races you'd like to hit—be it only once for the thrill or a full season's compe-

Kelly Kerigan, of Red Line Oil, on board a 105 cu. in. drag-ster, owned by George Matthews, built by Dorn Benson in Petaluma, CA. You want one just like this? Give Dorn a call at Westside Motorcycles (707) 778-8856. The engine has Del-cron cases with Axtell 3-13/16" bore cylinders driving through a Bandit clutch into a 5-speed full of Andrews gears. Cam is from Zipper's. Lift is .710 - definitely not a street cam. The smoke you can see, the sound can only be imagined.

tition for points. Plan in advance and go to an event for two before actually putting your bike on the track. Walk the pits, see how others with similar bikes are setting up their bikes—what kind of fuel are they running, how much air pressure in the tires, and a lot of other things you'll want to find out. You'll probably have to affix a number plate and a tether cord kill switch to your bike in order to compete. Check out how racers are doing these things—you can usually get by for one race with a box of shoe polish and some creative work with your stock kill switch. If you race more, spend the money for a aftermarket tether cord and mount number plates to the bike.

Talk to the builders and racers. I've never met a racer who doesn't like to talk about his or her bike. Most racers have no problem with enlightening you with everything from speed secrets to burnout tips.

Next, are you going to ride to the event, race the wheels off it, and then drive it home? Or, will you transport the bike with a truck or trailer? I lean heavily towards transporting the bike to the track. If something goes "blooie," you have a way to get home. Also, a support vehicle can carry tools, air tanks (you'll need one eventually), spare parts, and another person to held you load and unload.

The bike will have to be gone over thoroughly prior to racing. Change the oil. Buy some fresh gas. Check *every* nut and bolt twice. The most important item to check is yourself. The first time out on a race track is primarily a learning experience. There is no comparison between blasting through the gears from a stoplight and cutting the lights at a track. You will have to learn to leave the line with enough wheelspin to keep the engine from bogging without sending the rear tire up in smoke. Staging and launching properly is at least fifty percent of racing. Most people can at least get down the track with the engine at redline in every gear—getting off the line the first time will be an experience you will remember.

Leaving the starting line improperly can result in high elapsed time (ET). You can ride the bike off the line, using the clutch to keep the engine revs up until speed is high enough to let it all the way out, but this method has drawbacks. It's hard on clutches, and it's the hard way down the track—my grandmother could beat you on a tricycle. To lay down decent times, you gotta' come off the line hard with the rear wheel turning, stay in your own lane, and shift at the engine's peak. Your times and the time the guys in the magazines run will be significantly different. They do it for a living; you are just out for fun. Concentrate on learning how to make a good run rather than setting the top time of the event.

The single-trailer can easily support any size Harley up to the largest tourer, or a fuel bike, with all its spares and tools. *VM Trailers*

I'll repeat—there are no similarities between running the street and racing. The first time you go racing, bring a net and a jar. You'll find enough butterflies to start a collection.

Time to quit telling stories—throw a leg over the seat and go run a sanctioned meet. Don't worry, the butterflies will go away before the run (usually). Warm the bike up and get in line. When you get four or five bikes from the burnout box, put on your helmet, zip up your leathers, and pull your gloves on. If you've been in line for a long time, make sure your bike is still warm. Watch the guy in front of you as he does a burnout and moves to the starting line. The track officials will motion you forward before the bike on the starting line gets the green. Watch the starter, not the bike in front of you. When motioned forward, move into the burnout area and warm your tire. The first time you wind up the motor and drop the clutch will be interesting, to say the least.

I had a real hard time teaching myself how to spin the rear tire. I made about a dozen runs just driving off the line, slipping the clutch—that's why I know it's the slow way to launch. I finally got so desperate, I put the front wheel against a telephone pole and dropped the hammer at 6000rpm. That broke the rear tire loose, you bet. Dumped about a gallon of adrenaline into my system, too! I don't advocate learning how to do a burnout this way, but it worked for me. Practicing burn-outs on the street, by the way, is a good way to get acquainted with your local law enforcement officials or maybe even spend a

A travel trailer makes rainy days at the races a piece of cake. Everyone else is huddled under an umbrella or stuffed into the cab of a pickup while we put on another CD and argue over who has dinner duty. Meanwhile, the bike sits in the back of the trailer waiting out the storm. *Weekend Warrior*

night courtesy of the county. Learn to run on private property, not on the street.

After the burnout the starter will motion you up to the line. Usually the butterflies disappear about this time—too many things to concentrate on. Ease the bike forward until first one and then the second small yellow staging light comes on. Be ready—the lights will flash at any moment after the yellows are lit. Get the revs up and watch the starting lights (otherwise known as the "Christmas tree). Usually, three or four yellows will flash before the light turns green. The fastest way is to anticipate the green light and drop the clutch on or just after the last yellow. If you drop the clutch when you see the green light turn on, you'll be left in the dust. Getting a good hole shot takes some talent and a lot of practice. If you leave too soon, you red light and lose. Leave to late, and you'll be all alone.

The tree is lit—drop the clutch and pin the throttle. Spin the wheel just a bit—too much and all your forward motion will go up in tire smoke—and keep the bike in a straight line. Shift three more times and the finish lights flash by. Be sure to keep the

This is why we all work so many hours. He's just about at the mile-marker finish at El Mirage. The plastic barrel slightly in front of him is over a quarter mile from the front tire. He's running right about 200mph. If you're the type who thinks bungee jumping is rather tame, and the thought of one more football game on TV bores you beyond belief, a 200+ run on two wheels might be just what the old adrenaline pump needs. Picture running full-out over a timed course. The bike's traveling a little over three miles a minute. While a massive V-Twin thunders below. While the front end dances from side to side as it crosses the ripples on the salt. While you have time to think—really think—"here I sit over 200 with just a few square inches of rubber between me and all that salt." There's sometimes actually enough time to take a look at your surroundings. 'Course they're going by sorta' fast, but if you wanted pictures, you could have bought 'em at the airport.

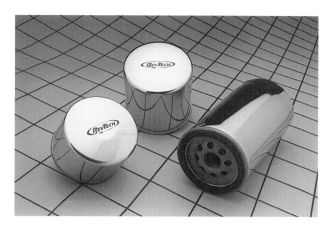

Do remember to take good care of your oil. Filters are cheap. Hang a new one on every time the oil gets dumped. *Custom Chrome*

power on beyond the finish line because there is another set of lights 66ft past the line. These, and a set mounted a similar distance in front of the finish line, give top speed. Chop the throttle too soon and your top speed will be down.

Slow down and head back on the return road. Zip down your jacket for a little fresh air—you'll need it. Drive over to the timing box and pick up your ET slip. Ride back into the pits and park the bike. Once you calm down, take a closer look at the timing slip. You should get several numbers on it—your elapsed time in the quarter and your reaction time. In bracket racing, elapsed time (ET) is just for bragging rights—good reaction times and consistent ETs take home the hardware. A perfect reaction time is 0.500. Top drag racers are consistently under 0.550. If you're under 0.700, you're doing pretty well. If you're time is less than 0.500, you left before the light turned green and "red lighted"—you were instantly disqualified.

Going Whole Hog

After a few years of racing, you might want to get serious and build an all-out drag bike. Watching the pros run over 150mph in less than ten seconds makes you want a faster bike. Plus, your street scooter is starting to show a lot of wear and you want to ride it for a few more years before it needs a rebuild. Time to pull the plates off and park it.

Now you're serious about racing with a bike built for a specific class. Let's say Pro Stock appeals to you; exactly how would you go about building one? First place to start is with a healthy checkbook. Not that putting together a race bike will cost as much as building a car but expect to lay out something near $25,000 to get on the track.

Almost all components will be from aftermarket suppliers, so it's best to start from plans and build a bike from scratch. Begin with a list of all the parts you will need to build an engine. Because of the necessary machine work involved in building a motor, there will be a certain amount of dead time while parts are out being worked on. This is the time to start work on the chassis and suspension. What frame to use, what size rear slick, what type of front suspension, brakes, fuel tank, etc.? Will you use an air shift transmission? Body work or not?

While the heads are being flowed or cases machined for breathers or cam clearance, will you be able to dummy up another engine to start building motor and transmission mounts? Pipes have to be fabricated for your particular engine/frame combination.

The frame will have to be set on a level surface to set up alignment and locate parts relative to each other. If you run an air-shifter, or N_2O, mounting points will have to be fabricated for the air tank or nitrous bottle. There is a school of thought called "milk carton engineering" that uses upended crates as frame jigs. This works for bolt-together bikes, but if you are going to fabricate frame parts, wheelie bars, and the like you will definitely need more than plastic crates to set up the bike.

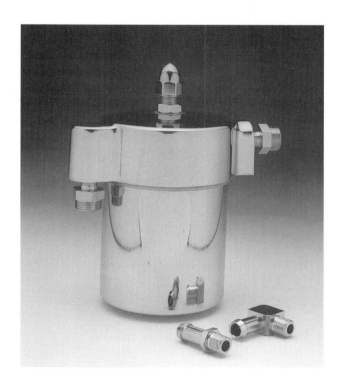

Here's a way to do a remote oil filter if your bike doesn't have one installed. This can be mounted almost anywhere it's out of the way. *Custom Chrome*

Left: Some Big Twins don't come equipped with tachometers. Trying to figure shift points or any type of power curve without one is impossible. Also, you want it right in front of you where your eyes don't have to move very far to read it. Actually, you don't so much read a tach when drag racing as watch the needle sweep. After a while, you know exactly where that needle should be when it's time to dial in the next gear. This mounting panel comes with four holes for warning lights, like oil pressure lights. Some tachs can be wired so that a light turns on when the engine reaches a preset shift point. *Custom Chrome*

garage, the man realized that the market might be a little soft for baskets, so he advertised the welder to help offset his losses.

I had spent many years making a mess with an arc welder, but had never played with a MIG unit. I can't call myself much of a welder; however, the MIG unit makes anybody look good. I would advise taking a few classes, or practicing on scrap, prior to sticking foot pegs or wheelie bars on a racer. Making a pass, only to have a foot peg break off as you shift into top

Over in Watsonville, CA, Mike Corbin makes high-quality seats that give you a secure anchorage while getting on with the business of racing. Along with providing a good place to sit, they remain comfortable enough to spend a full day making the scenery go by. *Corbin*

Find someone who has a metal inert gas (MIG) wire welder and make fast friends. Or go down to your local welding supply store and invest in a Miller or Lincoln 220-volt MIG welder. I own a fifteen-year-old Millermatic 35 wire welder that I purchased as a lease return. Actual cost was less than 45% of new. It had been used by a one-man shop to build wire flower baskets. After about 30,000 baskets filled his

gear, can provide no end of embarrassment—to say nothing of grinding valuable body parts off on the asphalt. MIG welding isn't hard; it just takes practice and a little knowledge.

Your first project can be a roll-around cart to mount the frame on while building the bike. Some angle iron, four wheels, and a piece of 1/4in plate is all it takes. Plus any mistakes can be easily rectified in the privacy of your own garage. Build it high enough to where you don't have to bend over to wrench on the bike. Your back will thank you profusely. Wheels let the cart be spun to any position. Build some clamps to hold the frame (if you're good, you won't build them right in the way of the motor mounts, like yours truly did). Now all the work can be done with the bike set upright, as it will be on the track, allowing all components to be easily set up as they will be when the bike is finished. When utter frustration or exhaustion causes you to head for some liquid refreshment, the whole thing can be rolled back into a corner until next time.

My first racer had everything painted before it was put on the frame for a trial fit. I got to repaint a lot of parts. Now I would make sure everything works together; then disassemble the racer and paint it. That way, the seat bracket that was forgotten won't ruin the frame's finish when it gets welded on. As many times as the seat/fender assembly and the fuel tank will go off and on the bike, wait to paint them until after the engine has run. A trick paint job isn't cheap. Repairing a scratched trick paint job not only isn't cheap, but doesn't do much for the blood pressure either.

Getting There

While working out a parts list, you might want to give some consideration as to how the racer will be transported to the track. This isn't something that can be rolled in the back of a pickup bed, strapped down, and the tailgate slammed. Not unless your bike is a lot shorter than most racers—like four feet shorter.

I pull a trailer built strictly for a drag racer. It solves a lot of problems not found on a regular bike trailer, like how to fit a Goodyear racing tire into a set of four-inch-wide frame rails without permanently cutting two groves in the slick. A sixteen-inch-wide aluminum rail lets the rear tire sit centered on the trailer with plenty of clearance to the sides. The wheelie bars have to be removed before loading, but this is a simple affair and makes the racer much easier to handle. I spent my share of time lifting a 350lb bike in and out of a van because it scraped when run down the loading ramp before I went to a trailer. Do this for a few years and a low-mount trailer begins to make much sense.

V/M Boat Trailers (5200 S. Peach Ave., Fresno, CA 93725; 209-486-0427) has a custom trailer built strictly for heavy bikes, or they can build a trailer to any specification you want. This way, you can carry a camper on the pickup or outfit the van for comfort. The first time you spend a weekend in 100-degree

heat and try to race, you'll learn to appreciate the benefits of a self-contained, air-conditioned camper. Let's face it, leathers are hot. Sitting under a sunshade or tent doesn't come even remotely close to relaxing in a controlled environment away from the noise. Listening to one Top Fuel bike is real neat. Listening to 100 Top Fuel bikes is real tiring. Being able to get away from the heat and noise while staying cool and relaxed is worth another 25hp. After all, if the Indy drivers have motor homes to hide in, why can't you—the up and coming Top Fuel World Champion—have a place to go?

V/M Trailers builds a very pretty trailer. They use polished aluminum tread plate on the main and side ramps, with polished stainless steel fenders. The

For a slightly different look, Dakota Digital can provide a digital readout speedometer to replace the stock analog unit.

wheels are chrome-modular thirteen-inchers, with chrome center caps. The trailer has a built-in loading ramp mounted under the main plate. It can be color-keyed to the bike or painted in black, white, or blue urethane paint.

Weekend Warrior Trailers (at your nearby RV sales outlet) are fully enclosed pull- or fifth-wheel trailers built for the racer who wants to take it with him. They are built along a plan that allows almost any self-contained configuration to be tailored to your needs. The "Classic" has full-sized bathrooms and bedrooms, lots of closet space, and full kitchen. They come in lengths from 24ft to 32ft in the pull-trailer; fifth-wheels are available up to ten feet longer.

The list of accessories would make a book in itself. Suffice it to say that anything you can envision, they can build. Air conditioning, outside showers, multiple-sized fuel tanks (handy way to transport racing gas), overhead storage cabinets and intercom—anything your checkbook can stand.

The main point that sets them apart from other trailers is the open rear area with drop-down loading ramp. The back fifteen feet of floor space can be easily set up to carry any size racing bike. Tables, dinettes, and carpet can easily (emphasis on easily) be removed. A street bike and a drag bike will fit side by side, leaving the front of the trailer free for living space. Even two street bikes will slide in with room to spare.

trailer, I could wash the dust off of me and the bike. Made working on the bike much easier—to say nothing of more comfortable. Try spending ten hours on the salt, only to have to spend another five replacing a cooked piston. Your body is so liberally coated with white granules that every time you bend over or move, something goes *crunch*. Add a little oil for that total scuzzy feeling and you begin to appreciate the ability to wash everything before getting in the trailer. 100 gallons of fresh water will last a long time; twenty gallons per day will cover longer than you want to be in an aluminum box on the salt—but if necessary, long periods can be endured in some comfort.

Another advantage to an enclosed trailer is it gives you a place to keep your electronics without

Above and next page: There are many different ways to make your bike stop and go; here are just two of them. The throttle is one-piece of aluminum running a single

cable. The rear swing arm is a full triple-chrome-plated show piece. There's enough polishing on this bike for a full time job.

The loading ramp is 3/4in by 1-1/2in tubing supporting a 3/4in deck rated at 2000lbs. A/C, microwave, refrigerator, and receptacles are wired for 110v. Long weekends are readily accommodated by twin fifty-gallon freshwater tanks. Fire extinguisher, smoke alarm, and escape windows are standard. One feature I found handy at Bonneville was the external shower receptacle mounted behind the right axles. 105 degrees radiating off of fine, powdery, blowing salt gets in everything. Before tracking all the powder into the

them filling with salt or dust. With the advent of computers in tuning and timing positions, a clean environment becomes necessary. Pretty soon bike racers will begin to use the onboard computer technology currently favored by Indy and Formula One racing teams. New programs let you analyze different parameters of the racing vehicle in real time. Rpm, shift points, distance covered, time between points, engine operation, suspension feedback, and wheel slippage can all be relayed to a central com-

The truck just left a package from Bonnie Truitt. Now it's time to see what we all bought. Packed along side were engine plates, bearing supports, rear fender, oil and fuel tanks, battery box, foot pegs and wheelie bars. A Red Wing front end was used.

puter for instant analysis or later consultation. All the data acquisition equipment will have to be mounted in an area free from airborne contaminants and wide temperature swings. A trailer setup where the bike's relay equipment and transducers can be accessed for calibration, with the computer at hand to check as you go, would work out best.

Building the Racer

Don Rich and his sons, owners of Rich Performance Products, built an out-of-the-box Pro Fuel drag bike last year. The frame, seat/rear fender, motor plate, transmission, and hardware all showed up in one crate; the rest, including motor, came from numerous suppliers. Don's idea was to see if he could build a drag bike simply by ordering parts and doing some in-house engine work himself. He told me he wanted to show that there was no magic or mystery involved in building a racer, just hard work. Also, he hoped it could be built for a reasonable sum of money, proving it affordable to many racers who want to move up from street bikes to pure racers.

STD partially machined heads: $1,000;
Porting and valve job, roller rockers: $2,200.
Total cost in parts: $16,500
Other parts (cam, breather, pushrod tubes, valve covers, crank pins, ignition, carb, and pipes): approx. $3,000.

Rich could do all his own machining, but you might have to add another $2,000 for your shop work. Tires and chain add another $450. Add 10% of total as a fudge figure and you end up with $24,150 for a bike ready to race. Rich's bike first ran with son Jim Rich aboard in November 1993. The bike turned a 8.34 and 163mph performance on the first weekend. Not bad for a first-time-out-of-the-box racer.

Starting with $24,000 in the checkbook, you should be able to assemble a similar racer in two and a half months from receipt of parts, depending on your skill level and outside help. After racing bikes for a few years, you should have a good collection of extra parts already in the garage, including nuts, bolts, and washers of Grade 5 quality or better. Don't use any fastener of lesser quality on any part of the bike. Most sanctioning bodies require at least Grade 5 for attaching frame or suspension parts, and it's a good idea to use them throughout the bike.

Go to a few races and take lots of pictures of drag bikes. This will help you figure out things like control positions and which bolts need to be safety-

The truck's just left. Drag the crate into the shop and open it up—Christmas in October. He's a little dangerous with a crowbar, so we stuck to taking pictures and letting him make wood chips. *Rich Products*

The frame and related parts came from Bonnie Truett Frames (1314 E. 31st St. South, Wichita, KS 67216); cost, with front end: $3,200.
Transmission is a B&J three-Speed—$4,500.
Clutch is a Master Performance Slipper (93707 Rochambeau Dr., Williamsburg, VA 23185)—$2,100.
Wheels from Performance Machine—$1,400.

Engine parts are as follows:
STD cases, bored for 3-13/16 cylinders: $1,000;
S&S 5-1/4 stroke flywheels: $300;
Axtell Cylinders with JE pistons: $800;

Most of what was in the crate plus a tranny and rear wheel are mocked up to see how things fit. So far, about $9500 is sitting there.

175

The rear view shows the chain and air tank for the shifter. Everything was mounted and checked for interference before any painting. Actually, the bike was run at Sacramento before any paint hit the aluminum. *Rich Products*

wired. Ask around—everybody started the same as you at one time. The racing fraternity is a close-knit group of friendly people who are more than willing to help a newcomer in the sport.

Above all, remember it *is* a sport, and sports are meant to be enjoyed. Go race and have a good time doing it. Good luck!

It may be on milk crates, but they are on a lift, so access is real good. Check the aluminum plate connecting the engine and trans. *Rich Products*

Building an engine only takes a few simple hand tools found in an average garage. *Rich Products*

The first engine is running finless cast-iron Axtell cylinders with J.E. pistons. They sit on STD cases bored for 3-13/16 cylinders. Next step is to dyno the motor. In this case, the sparks run through a set of points, and the pushrods operate exposed. *Rich Products*

We decided there was a need for more cubic inches. Here, the cylinder meets the boring bar. *Rich Products*

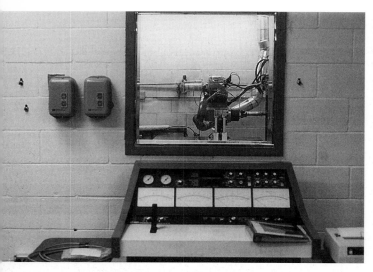

Almost ready to fire it up. All the tuning will be done here. When the engine hits the frame, it'll be ready to run—no break-in needed. *Rich Products*

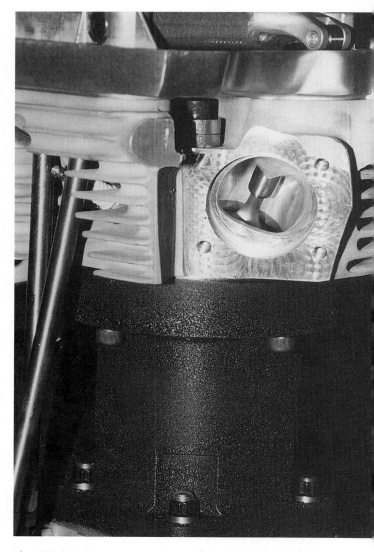

The STD heads were ported by Baisly. Here, the relationship between roller rockers and the valve is clearly shown. *Rich Products*

At the same time, a magneto-fired Shovel was built for a backup. *Rich Products*

Looking straight down on the heads, you can see the roller rockers and open pushrods. At this point, about all the engine needs is a fuel mixer, plugs, and pipes to run. *Rich Products*

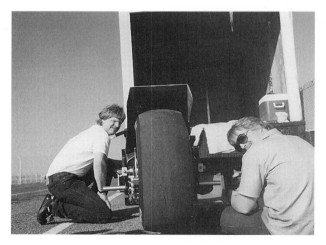

Donny and Jim Rich look like they're having a good time getting ready to run for the first time, but Jim's trying to cope with a set of butterflies making carrier landings in his stomach. He gets to make the first run in a few minutes. *Rich Products*

The butterflies must have flown away: Jim went 8.34 and 163mph first time out. You can't see it from here, but he's grinning in this picture. *Rich Products*

Leo Hess—
The Fastest Harley in South Dakota

Leo started out racing cars on the Sioux Falls streets for money. Later, he moved into a Harley Panhead and continued to lighten slower rider's wallets until a rather large ticket taught him the error of his ways. In 1977, he built a gas-powered 1961 Sportster strictly for the track. As time progressed, he went to alcohol-powered engines; then, at a Louisville, Kentucky, race, he tipped the nitro can for the first time—coming within four one-hundredths MPH of setting the national record. At the next race, he was first to run an eighth-mile in less than six seconds and in excess of 133mph.

Today, Leo operates out of his Harley high-performance shop in Sioux Falls—Full Blast Engineering (605—332-2659), specializing in motors, transmissions, valve work, and other aspects of building fast Harleys. His prior experience includes eight years as a mechanic and service manager for a Harley dealer in South Dakota. Full Blast Engineering has been in existence for the last seven years, helping to pay for his racing.

Hess built a fuel-injected, fuel-burning, 350hp drag bike in 1986 that is currently carrying him to 180+ in the quarter mile. Harry Bunker, Mike Colchin, and Randy Ofstad are the guys who keep the bike running and ensure that all the parts point in the same direction.

In 1992, Leo set a national MPH record of 181.34. The bike ran its fastest quarter mile at 7.358 seconds, along with winning two races and finishing second in three others during the year.

The Kansas City Invitational provided Hess with his only win in 1993, but he picked up two second-place finishes: Firebird Raceway, AZ and Truett-Osborn Bike Nationals in Kansas City. He hopes to continue winning in 1994 and beyond.

Leo has another bike that I met at El Mirage Dry Lakes in November 1993. This is his twin Shovelhead-engined U/SPFM salt racer, running anywhere from 70% to 100% nitro through 184 cubic inches. The chassis is two rigid frames welded together, with a custom-fiberglass body. Right now, two S&S carbs mix the fuel, but soon fuel injection will take their place. A five-gallon tank holds just enough ethanol/nitro mix to make one run on the salt flats.

The cylinders are a little different from what is normally seen on an air-cooled engine. They are R-R Cycle water jackets, helping to remove the large amount of

continued on next page

Leo's A/Fuel Bike comes off the line smokin'. Burnouts lay down a fresh patch of rubber for the rear tire to bite. The run for the money won't be anywhere as smoky—making smoke is just wasting horsepower. It's what the paying customers and your competition want to see, 'cause it's the slow way to get down a track. Full Blast Engineering heat generated during a run on the dry lakes or Bonneville salt. Quarter-mile bikes don't usually run long enough to need to shed the same number of BTUs of a Land Speed Record machine, so water-cooled cylinders are still rare—though probably not for long. Porsche found out a few years ago that their air-cooled, turbo, endurance racing engines needed to have additional water cooling to keep the pistons from melting into the crankcase during long races; as V-Twin power grows, water cooling will become a necessity.

Leo's twin has run 236 in a single pass at Bonneville; however, a melted piston kept him from backing up the run. He went 187.236 at El Mirage on the drag bike when I was there in November. The big double has to be heard to be believed: you think one engine on fuel is loud—try two! Sunday morning, he became the first Harley to go over 200mph at El Mirage—207.261. To really put this into perspective, consider that this was done on a dirt racetrack just a little over one mile in length from start to finish line. To say traction was a sometimes thing would be a major understatement.

As you can see in the pictures, the A/Fuel drag bike carries a rear Goodyear eleven inches in width, and will almost stand up by itself. The twin-engined ni-tro bike's rear 19–15 Mickey Thompson tire is a lot narrower and has to transmit a lot more torque to the ground. Shifting the Andrews-modified transmission into top gear while running on the dirt surface of El Mirage gives a whole new meaning to the term "wheelspin." I could hear the engines running up and down the rev range as Leo tried to hook the bike up all the way down the track. I think I'll stick to writing—takes a braver man than me to handle spinning tires at close to 200mph.

Leo's records set in 1993 include the World Land Speed Authority record, set at Bonneville, of 200.638mph over a measured mile; a world record SCTA class U/SPFM 3000 of 207.261 on the double; and 187.235, also set at El Mirage, on the drag bike.

Leo plans on breaking more Land Speed Records in the future. He would like to go for the current two-wheeled record of 321mph if sponsorship can be found to build an unlimited class H-D streamliner. Leo Hess is one very fast man on a Harley.

The helmet shield's down, just a smidge of wheelspin; this run's for serious. Leo took the twin-engined machine down the track at El Mirage at 207.261—the first Harley-Davidson to break 200 at the Lake. All this on distilled corn—a somewhat different use for "white lightning." Full Blast Engineering

Early morning on the salt, and the crew pushes the high-geared twin off to a 192mph run. The sound of the twin echoing across the salt on a still morning was worth the price of admission. Barnett/Full Blast Engineering

Sometimes catching Leo and the bike standing still is a challenge. You can be sure this is the last time today he'll be standing around—there's speed to do!

Racing Organizations

All Harley Drag Racing Association (AHDRA)
PO Box 1429
Elon College, NC 27244
(919) 229-4877

American Motorcycle Racing Association (AMRA)
PO Box 50
Itasca, IL 60143
(708) 250-0838

Bonneville Nationals, Inc.
22048 Vivienda
Grand Terrace, CA 92324
(714) 783-8293

East Coast Racing Association (ECRA)
219 East White Horse Pike
Galloway Township, NJ 08201
(609) 652-1159

International Drag Bike Association (IDBA)
3936 Raceway Park Road
Mount Olive, AL 35117
(205) 841-0553

PROSTAR
PO Box 182
Atco, NJ 08004
(609) 768-4624

Southern California Timing Association (SCTA)
12534 Cypress Ave
Chino, CA 91710
(714) 627-9260

Appendix B

Performance Parts and Services

ACCEL Products
PO Box 142
Branford, CT 06405
(203) 481-5771

Air Flow Research, Inc.
10490 Ilex Ave
Pacoima, CA 91331
(818) 834-9010

Andrews Products, Inc.
5212 Shapland Ave
Rosemont, IL 60018
(312) 992-4014

Avon Tire
Hoppe & Associates
PO Box 336
Edmonds, WA 98020
(800) 624-7470

Axtell Sales, Inc.
1424 S.E. Maury
Des Moines, IA 50317
(515) 243-2518

Bandit Machine Works
222 Millwood Rd.
Lancaster, PA 17602
(717) 464-2800

Barnett Engineering
PO Box 2826
Santa Fe Springs, CA 90670
(310) 941-1284

Branch Flowmetrics
556 Corporate Dr.
Cypress, CA 90630
(714) 827-1463

Bub Enterprises
22573 Meyer Ravine Rd.
Grass Valley, CA 95949
(916) 268-0449

Carl's Speed Shop
9339 Santa Fe Springs Rd.
Santa Fe Springs, CA 90670
(310) 941-9385

Carrillo Industries
990 Calle Amanecer
San Clemente, CA 92672
(714) 498-1800

Champion Spark Plug
900 Upton Ave.
Toledo, OH 43607
(800) 537-8964

Corbin Pacific
11445 Commercial Parkway
Castroville, CA 95012
(800) 538-7035

Crane Cams
530 Fentress Blvd.
Daytona Beach, FL 32114
(904) 258-6174

Custom Chrome, Inc.
One Jacqueline Ct.
Morgan Hill, CA 95037
(800) 729-3332

Delkron Manufacturing
2430 Manning St.
Sacramento, CA 95815
(916) 921-9703

Drag Specialties
PO Box 9336
Minneapolis, MN 55440
(800) 222-3400

Dunlop Tires
PO Box 1109
Buffalo, NY 14240
(800) 548-4714

Earl's Performance Products
189 W. Victoria
Long Beach, CA 90805
(800) 533-1320

EBC Brakes
12860 Bradley Ave.
Sylmar, CA 91342
(818) 362-5534

Feuling R&D
2521 Palma Dr.
Ventura, CA 93003
(805) 650-2598

Gerolamy Co.
3250 Monier Circle
Rancho Cordova, CA 95742
(916) 638-9008

Harley-Davidson Motor Co.
3700 West Juneau Ave.
Milwaukee, WI 53208
(414) 342-4680

Jacobs Electronics
500 N. Baird St.
Midland, TX 79701
(800) 627-8800

K&N Engineering
561 Iowa Ave.
Riverside, CA 92507
(800) 858-3333

Kal-Guard
16616 Schoenborn St.
Sepulveda, CA 91343
(818) 894-3615

Kerker/SuperTrapp
3910 Seaport Blvd.
West Sacramento, CA 95691
(916) 372-5000

Klotz
PO Box 11343
Fort Wayne, IN 46857
(800) 242-0489

Kosman Racing
55 Oak St.
San Francisco, CA 94102
(415) 861-4262

Loctite Corp.
4450 Cranwood Parkway
Cleveland, OH 44128
(800) 321-9188

Mac Tools, Inc.
S. Fayette Street
Washington Court House, OH 43160
(614) 335-4412

Manley Performance Products
1960 Swarthmore Ave.
Lakewood, NJ 08701
(800) 526-1362

MC Advantages
PO Box 22225
Des Moines, IA 50325
(800) 726-9620

Metzeler Tires
4520 107th St. S.W.
Mukilteo, WA 98275
(206) 348-4000

Michelin Tires
PO Box 19001
Greenville, SC 29602
(803) 458-5000

Mikuni American
8910 Mikuni Ave.
Northridge, CA 91324
(818) 885-1242

Moroso
80 Carter Dr.
Guilford, CT 06437
(203) 453-6571

Morris Magnetos, Inc.
103 Washington Street
Morristown, NJ 07960
(201) 540-9171

MSD Ignition
1490 Henry Brennan Dr.
El Paso, TX 79936
(915) 857-5200

Nitrous Oxide Systems
5930 Lakeshore Dr.
Cypress, CA 90630
(714) 821-0580

Performance Machine
PO Box 1739
15535 Garfield Ave.
Paramount, CA 90723
(310) 634-6532

Pingel Enterprise
2076 C 11th Ave.
Adams, WI 53910
(608) 339-7999

Progressive Suspension
11129 G. Ave.
Hesperia, CA 92345
(619) 948-4012

Red Line Synthetic Oil Corporation
3450 Pacheco Blvd.
Martinez, CA 94553
(800) 624-7958

Red Shift Cams
8040 Washington Blvd.
Jessup, MD 20794
(301) 799-9451

Rich Products Co.
12420 San Pablo Ave.
Richmond, CA 94805
(510) 234-7547

Rivera Engineering
6416 S. Western Ave.
Whittier, CA 90606
(800) 872-1515

Russell Performance Products
2645 Gundry Ave.
Signal Hill, CA 90806
(800) 394-1120

S&S Cycle, Inc.
Rt. 2, County G
Box 215
Viola, WI 54664
(608) 627-1497

Sifton Motorcycle Products
943 Bransten Rd.
San Carlos, CA 94070
(415) 592-2203

Snap-On Tools
2801 80th St.
Kenosha, WI 53141
(414) 656-5372

Spectro Oils
PO Box 208
Route 7
Brookfield, CT 06804
(800) 243-8645

Sputhe Engineering, Inc.
11185 Lime Kiln Rd.
Grass Valley, CA 95949
(916) 268-0887

S.T.D. Development Co., Inc.
PO Box 3583
Chatsworth, CA 91313
(818) 998-8226

Storz Performance
239 Olive St.
Ventura, CA 93001
(805) 641-9540

Supertrapp Industries
3910 Seaport Blvd.
West Sacramento, CA 95691
(916) 372-5000

Torco International
9916 Pioneer Blvd.
Santa Fe Springs, CA 90670
(310) 942-8480

Trett's Speed & Custom
Rt. 1, Box 1715
Demorest, GA 30535
(404) 754-3784

Trick Racing Fuel
1189 Morena Blvd
San Diego, CA 92110
(800) 444-1449

Truett & Osborn
3345 E. 31st St.
Wichita, KS 67216
(316) 682-4781

V-Thunder by Competition Cams
3406 Democrat Rd.
Memphis, TN 38118
(901) 794-2833

White Brothers
14241 Commerce Dr.
Garden Grove, CA 92643
(714) 554-9442

Wisesco Pistons, Inc.
7201 Industrial Park Blvd.
Mentor, OH 44060
(800) 321-1364

Works Performance
8730 Shirley Ave.
Northridge, CA 91324
(818) 701-1010

XRV Performance Products
10428 Burbank Blvd.
N. Hollywood, CA 91601
(818) 762-5407

Zipper's Cycle
8040 Washington Blvd.
Jessup, MD 20794
(410) 799-8989

Index